Praise for

Running with the Bulls

"In *Running with the Bulls*, Valerie Hemingway, an honest and graceful writer, takes us inside Papa Hemingway's complicated psyche, inner circle, and family in a fresh and instructive fashion. It's a stunner."

—Tom Brokaw

"[Valerie Hemingway] writes lucidly and without affectation."

—*The Washington Post*

"This is the best, and best written, of all the reminiscences of Ernest Hemingway, in part because its adventurous author, Valerie Hemingway, is such an absorbing character herself. There is far more here than the looming Papa, but what there is of him is at uncommonly close range and changes our picture of him substantially. For once, the great artist, the hero, and the fool seem to be the same person; and the long list of fascinating people in his train are seen with rare frankness."

—Thomas McGuane

"Fascinating."   —National Geographic *Adventure*

"Valerie's tender account has its share of sunny locales (Pamplona, Provence, Paris) and glitterati (Lauren Bacall, Cyril Connolly, bullfighter Antonio Ordonez), but its undertone is deep sadness."   —*Booklist*

"*Running with the Bulls* is hot to the touch. I was not a little dumbfounded that Valerie Hemingway endured and survived the events of her life to write this improbably skillful memoir that frequently made me wish to climb a mountain and sit on a friendly glacier. The author's life with the Hemingways is utterly compelling, and we must praise her for her gifts in giving us the most lucid look yet at this haunted family."

—JIM HARRISON

"Vividly written and rich in atmosphere and anecdote."

—*Publishers Weekly*

"This is a startling complicated book. As a memoir of the great writer, it's graceful and fresh, trenchant and intimate and revealing, yet sweet spirited. But it's more than that—a story of several lives and one tangled family, told by a woman with a wonderful voice of her own."

—DAVID QUAMMEN

"Up close, personal and well-written."   —*Deseret News*

"A life of adventure and excitement, heartbreak and tragedy."

—*The Missoulian*

"By far the most reliably intimate, compassionate, but unsparingly straightforward portrait of the aging lion, author, husband, and father that I've read. And if that weren't enough, Valerie's bizarre and moving marriage to his son and its dramatic conclusion reads like a—well—like a Hemingway novel."   —BARNABY CONRAD

"An invaluable record."   —*Kirkus Reviews*

RUNNING WITH THE BULLS

Running *with the* Bulls

MY YEARS WITH THE HEMINGWAYS

Valerie Hemingway

BALLANTINE BOOKS | NEW YORK

2005 Ballantine Books Trade Paperback Edition

Published in the United States by Ballantine Books, an imprint of The Random House
Publishing Group, a division of Random House, Inc., New York.

BALLANTINE and colophon are registered trademarks of Random House, Inc.
READER'S CIRCLE and colophon are trademarks of Random House, Inc.

Originally published in hardcover in the United States by Ballantine Books, an imprint of
The Random House Publishing Group, a division of Random House, Inc., in 2004.

Grateful acknowledgment is made to the following for permission to reprint
previously published and unpublished material:

The Ernest Hemingway Foundation: Unpublished letter of October 30, 1959, from Ernest Hemingway to Valerie
Danby-Smith. Copyright © 2004 by The Ernest Hemingway Foundation. Excerpt from "The Garden of Eden
Revisited" by Valerie Hemingway (originally published in *The Hemingway Review*, Vol. 18, No. 2). Copyright © 1999
by The Ernest Hemingway Foundation. Excerpt from "A Tribute to G. Hemingway" by Valerie Hemingway
(originally published in *The Hemingway Review*, Vol. 22, No. 2). Copyright © 2003 by The Ernest Hemingway
Foundation. All rights reserved. Reprinted by permission of The Ernest Hemingway Foundation.

Faber and Faber Ltd.: Excerpt from "Little Gidding" from "Four Quartets" from
Collected Poems 1909–1962 by T. S. Eliot. Reprinted by permission of Faber and Faber Ltd., London.

The World & I: Excerpt from "The Author as Character" by Valerie Hemingway
(originally published in *The World & I,* April 2000). Copyright © 2000
by *The World & I.* Reprinted by permission of *The World & I,*
a publicaton of *The Washington Times Corporation.*

For this book the author has also drawn upon portions of articles previously
published in *North Dakota Quarterly,* Vol. 68, Nos. 2 and 3.

Library of Congress Cataloging-in-Publication Data

Hemingway, Valerie.
Running with the bulls : my years with the Hemingways /
Valerie Hemingway.
p. cm.
Includes bibliographical references and index.
ISBN 0-345-46734-5
1. Hemingway, Ernest, 1899–1961—Homes and haunts—Spain.   2. Authors,
American—20th century—Family relationships.   3. Authors, American—
20th century—Biography.   4. Americans—Spain—History—20th century.
5. Hemingway, Ernest, 1899–1961—Family.   6. Hemingway,
Mary Welsh, 1908–   7. Hemingway, Valerie, 1940–   I. Title.

PS3515.E37Z54 2004
813'.52—dc22   2004047071

Printed in the United States of America

www.thereaderscircle.com

2   4   6   8   9   7   5   3   1

Frontispiece: Cano. Collection of V. Hemingway.

Book design by Barbara M. Bachman

For Brendan, Seán, Edward, and Vanessa

APR 2006

Remember rather the essential moments
    That were the times of birth and death and change
    The agony and the solitary vigil.

                                        —*T. S. Eliot*

ACKNOWLEDGMENTS

I COULD NOT HAVE WRITTEN this book without the encouragement of friends and family. First of all, my thanks go to my agents, Dan Green and Simon Green of POM, Inc. Over a twenty-year period Dan urged me to put pen to paper. I am grateful for his persistence, patience, and guidance. I owe a special debt to my good friend Jeffrey Meyers for his careful reading of the manuscript and for his invaluable comments. I am equally fortunate that Valerie Meyers offered her expert opinion on the early chapters. Michele Zackheim gave me excellent technical advice and assistance.

For their steadfast trust in the value of this work, I would like to thank Barnaby Conrad, Michelle Flenniken, Brian Gaisford, Samuel Hazo, Lorian Hemingway, Mary O'Donnell, Pamela Olyphant, Mollie Rogan, Robert Vavra, and Margaret Woods. I am also indebted to David Quammen and Betsy Gaines Quammen.

I am grateful to Linda Wagner Martin, president of the Ernest Hemingway Foundation and Society, for allowing me to quote in its entirety a letter from Ernest Hemingway. James Hill, of the John F. Kennedy Library and Museum Audiovisual Archives, was most gracious and helpful in providing photographs.

I would like to thank my editor, Nancy Miller of Ballantine Books, for her sound advice and good humor.

Finally, my gratitude goes to my four children, who have not only endured but excelled. I especially acknowledge my son Edward, who has been a constant support in this endeavor.

CONTENTS

RUNNING WITH THE BULLS

CHAPTER ONE

Endings and Beginnings

"THE DECEASED REQUESTED no speech or prayers are to mark her passing," the severe-looking young man in the black suit with sleeked-back hair declared without fanfare or emotion. It was a bleak November day in 1986, and I was standing on familiar ground, the little cemetery in Sun Valley, Idaho. I watched the poker-faced funeral director place a small pine-colored plastic box on an oblong piece of emerald Astroturf that covered the freshly dug grave. It could have been a cheap toolbox purchased at Kmart. The brief ceremony was over. The two small scatterings of people standing by solemnly started to disperse in opposite directions. An elderly man, tall and graying, tapped my shoulder. "Do you remember me? I'm George Saviers," he said.

I had driven from Montana to Ketchum to attend the funeral for my step-mother-in-law, Mary Hemingway. No one else present had crossed a state line to be at Ernest's last wife's burial. The only family members I could see were Jack "Bumby" Hemingway, his wife, Puck, and their daughter, Muffet, who lived close by. Jack had waved as I approached, and motioned to me to stand with his family. At the other side of the grave I recognized a few long-time friends, all locals, led by Clara Spiegel. Dr. George Saviers was among them. I had not laid eyes on George, Ernest's physician, close friend, and confidant, in almost a quarter of a century. I learned before setting out that Mary's administrator had asked Clara to take care of the funeral arrangements, snubbing Jack, the eldest of the three Hemingway sons and heir apparent. How predictable that another family encounter should be marred by friction and controversy!

I joined Jack, Puck, and Muffet at a local café afterward. The meeting was surprisingly congenial. Absolutely no mention was made of Mary. How odd, I thought. In Ireland, where I come from, a funeral is a time of celebration. The departed guest of honor, present yet not present, is feted with stories, music, toasts—a proper send-off for friend or foe alike. A funeral is a time to remember, to put aside grievances, reevaluate lives and friendships, a catharsis, an awakening. What we had just witnessed, I mused, was a nonevent. No wake, no ceremony, no tears, no celebration afterward. Despite this, I felt immensely liberated. A new chapter in my life could now begin.

History repeats itself, it is said. A previous chapter in my life had ended and another one had begun twenty-four years earlier as I stood in that same graveyard on that very spot witnessing Ernest Hemingway's funeral. George Saviers was present then too. At the end, he had been the Hemingways' closest friend. It was under George's name that Ernest had entered the Mayo Clinic to combat his terrible depression. And Mary was there, in the spotlight: the grieving widow, reeling from shock. She did not have to imagine the gruesome self-inflicted shot that sent her husband into blood-splattered oblivion. She had been a witness, she and George Brown.

Hemingway's funeral had been a private affair, admission by invitation only. Most especially no journalists were permitted, though the entire world was eager to learn the details. Every newspaper, radio station, and television station reported the event. After all, one of the greatest literary figures of the twentieth century had died by his own hand. Mary vehemently denied that suicide was the cause, claiming her husband's death resulted from a gun-cleaning accident. She was not so much trying to hide the facts from the world as from herself. The cruel, unbearable truth would only add to her tragic loss. Mary was in a state of denial.

Endings and beginnings punctuated by funerals. Ernest's funeral ended an intense period of my own life. Just two years before, during Madrid's San Isidro festival of 1959, I had first met the Hemingways. In July 1961, as he was laid to rest, I observed some of the characters who had influenced Ernest's life. Marcelline, the barely older sister who was paired as his twin in their infant years and a constant rival throughout their childhood. Within my hearing he had never spoken of her with affection. Younger brother Leicester—sixteen years junior, nicknamed the Baron—received more scorn than esteem from the writer whom he physically resembled. Leicester had inherited bluster, bumble, and congeniality rather than genius. His antics were a constant source of embarrassment to his exacting, exasperated brother. There was the octogenarian, Charlie Sweeny, a retired colonel, whose association with Hemingway had spanned two wars and many decades; George Brown, who had driven Mary and Ernest back from the Mayo Clinic three days before Ernest's death and who was the only other person present in the Ketchum house when the fatal "accident" occurred. Notably absent was friend and collaborator A. E. "Hotch" Hotchner, soon to be the renowned author of *Papa Hemingway*. Hotch had been a key player in the final year of Ernest's life and a close confidant of Mary during the months preceding his death. Mary would try unsuccessfully to suppress publication of Hotch's memoir, which she considered an unthinkable breach of friendship.

Measuring up, not measuring up. These people had been put to the test, and many of them had been found wanting. Although I had met only a few before, I knew something about each one—what they had meant to the person whose memory they now honored by their presence.

On that day too I had felt a hand on my shoulder as soon as the priest concluded the prayers for the dead. I turned to see a replica of Hemingway as he would have looked fifteen years before—this was Leicester. He urgently whispered to me, "Your Ladyship" (his standard respectful address for women), "do you know where my manuscript is?" He was referring to the autobiography he had mailed to Ernest at the Finca Vigía in the spring of 1960. The day of its arrival, Ernest took no pains to hide his rage. "If the Baron wants money, why doesn't he ask me for money?" he fumed as he brought the package outside through the library door and deposited it in the burn barrel. He poured on lighter fluid and struck a match. The flames curled upward to the sullen sky. Smoke trailed into the warm air, obscuring the view of Havana and the harbor beyond. It took hours before Ernest's equilibrium was restored. Not then, nor ever, did I reveal to Leicester the fate of his labor.

By the time I arrived in Sun Valley two days before Ernest's funeral, Mary had remembered I was working for *Newsweek*. She then regretted inviting me. In her grief-filled state, she imagined I would use my invitation to further my career (as she herself most certainly would have done). Indeed, in giving me the time off, *Newsweek* welcomed the opportunity to secure this scoop, making offers that I declined. For my pains, I now found myself an outsider, ostracized from the family gatherings and outings. I felt chagrined and annoyed that I had bothered to come. However, destiny, as always, played its part. My presence at Ernest's funeral changed the course of my life. Within a month I would give up my magazine job and escort Mary back to Cuba to sort out all of Ernest's belongings. Together, with great ingenuity, we managed to bring back to the United States a million dollars' worth of paintings, priceless manuscripts, letters, and memorabilia from the Finca Vigía at a time when nothing was allowed to leave that country. I spent the next four years reading and sorting every piece of paper, manuscript, and letter pertaining to Hemingway's life in a little office given to me by Charlie Scribner on the tenth floor of his Fifth Avenue building.

There was an even more significant outcome to my attendance at Ernest's funeral. His youngest son, Gregory, had long been estranged from his father. Mention of his name was forbidden in the Hemingway household during my stay there. Since he was not spoken of, I had no idea what had caused this fall from grace. Gigi, as he was called, fit no more easily into this funereal family gathering than I. He too was at loose ends. As outsiders, we found ourselves pairing off as we encountered each other sitting alone in the lounge of the Christiania Lodge or roaming this one-street cowboy town. A bond was formed then that led to marriage sometime later. For nearly twenty years Gregory and I lived a turbulent, wonderful, dreadful, exciting life. At the time of Mary's funeral, this too was coming to an end. We were in the midst of divorce proceedings. Beginnings and endings, endings and beginnings.

CHAPTER TWO

Dublin's Fair City: A Family Album

EVERYTHING AND NOTHING IN my origins hinted at the adventures that lay ahead. My family and childhood were a mass of contradictions and inconsistencies, a paradox from beginning to end.

I was born in Dublin in 1940 of Anglo-Irish parents, a Protestant father who grew up in Ireland, a Roman Catholic mother who called London her home. The small provincial town that Dublin was then lingered still in the laced girdle of the Victorian Age. John Huston's film *The Dead* could easily have taken place in the house of my Dublin relations on any Epiphany or at an Easter meal. Almost fifty years after James Joyce described his native city, the scenes continued to be replicated in the damp and stuffy sitting rooms of middle-class Dublin. The parlor with the upright piano, the aspidistra, the antimacassars on the stuffed chairs, the overt politeness in the conversation with its undercurrent of dissention and prejudice—these were the trappings and essence of my childhood.

In our family, rows were more likely to erupt over religion than politics. Joking, recitation of poetry, discussion of literature, singing, and the enactment of skits my aunt Constance wrote filled the festive evenings. "An old maid," my mother called Constance, my father's younger sister, with disdain. Con was registrar at the Royal Hospital for Incurables in Donnybrook, diminutive with a deep voice ("mannish," my mother said) and a talent for quick-witted dialogue. Sharper than a serpent's tooth, Con's barbs were, while my aunt Eileen, my father's older sister, was sweet and charming. "Wolf in lamb's clothing," warned my mother, who was excluded from these gatherings. Eileen was always in good humor, in contrast to her Scottish husband, gruff Uncle Alec, whose military bearing and sharp tongue made us feel ill at ease in his presence. Punctuality was a pet peeve of his, and his pocket watch, appended to a silver fob, was consulted at every turn to make sure that life was running according to the clock—an instrument that had yet to be invented in Ireland; leastwise, it was never heeded. Due to being gassed in the Great War, Alec wheezed and coughed with ferocity, his rasping sounds disturbing to healthy, young children.

I remember the house where I was born, the terraced garden laced with flowers in front of the detached stone building in Stillorgan with its slate roof and large bay windows. I became aware of the world in that garden, where I played with my older brother, Peter, who was deeply irritated at having to share his parents and possessions with a newcomer.

My parents were an ill-matched couple. Fair-haired, blue-eyed, and of medium height, my father, Tom, was a handsome, articulate, athletic man in his mid-thirties when he married my mother, Millicent, whose jet-black curly hair, hazel eyes, and winning smile belied her fierce pride and unrealistic expectations. She was twenty-nine, haughty, chic, and a talented musician and dancer. She had tarried in finding a suitor because no man had come close to fulfilling her requirements, and now she grew eager to wed before her dreaded thirtieth birthday. That landmark could easily confer spinsterhood—a fate she considered far worse than marrying a less than ideal man.

My mother wore her mother's wedding gown. The wedding photos suggest a handsome, smiling couple with a world of possibilities ahead. After the honeymoon they settled in Dublin in a comfortable, upscale area with the requisite cook and parlor maid, as well as a brand-new double-barreled name, Danby-Smith, suited to their social life of tennis, sailing, parties, and of course prospects. My father had prospects.

The Second World War, which began in 1939, changed the texture of Irish life. Although the island remained politically neutral, it sat too close to England to be unaffected by the trauma. Rationing became the norm. Bombs threatened to damage Dublin, the capital city, which lay only fifty-six sea miles from the Welsh coastline. Gas masks and air-raid shelters are among my earliest memories. Ireland was emotionally torn about which side to support. England was the traditional oppressor, yet it was there that the breadwinners of numerous families worked. The English pound sustained many an Irish family when employment could not be found at home.

By 1943, unsuccessful in business, without any regular employment or occupation, with his weakness for drink and fondness for gambling, my father seized upon the opportunity to leave Ireland. Although in his forties, he joined the British army to serve for the remaining war years. He left behind a distraught wife, three children, and massive debts.

When I was two years and three months, my brother Robin was born. Unlike the sunny May Sunday afternoon when I arrived, bringing a renewal of hope and joy to both my parents and sweet promises for the future, Robin's entrance into this world augured disaster. Her marriage failing, disintegration of the family imminent, my mother hit rock bottom physically and emotionally. She was unable to care for another child. Peter and I would not know our brother until our adult years.

Oblivious to the unfolding tragedy, my older brother and I played in the garden of our beautiful home, our needs taken care of by nanny, cook, and housemaid. Our parents might come and go, but the schedule of meals, baths, and bedtime was immutable. If I noticed changes, I do not recall them, until that midwinter day when I was three that brought the ominous presence of my father's sister, Aunt Constance. My father's family never visited us. There was a mutual dislike, even contempt between my mother and my paternal aunts. Without explanation, Peter and I were whisked away by Aunt Constance in a small black car.

Our destination was Dublin's north side, grim and gray, already showing signs of shabbiness. Ignoring the rows of county council houses, the car pulled up before the imposing entrance to a large estate protected by a high stone wall, stretching on either side as far as the eye could see. An odd-looking figure with black headdress and white robes emerged from the gate lodge with a large iron key to open the lock and wave us through. The gates were shut firmly behind us. We drove up an avenue lined with beech trees, cutting through a sculpted lawn adorned with flower beds, crunching to a stop on the graveled circle leading to the wide front portico. Without a hint of warning, Peter and I were handed over to the nun in charge, and the little black car disappeared in a cloud of dust. We were at St. Mary's Dominican Convent, Cabra, a boarding school and the motherhouse of the Dominican Order in Ireland. This was to be my main home for the next fourteen years. I had the distinction of being the youngest pupil ever to enter the boarding school as well as the student who spent the longest time there.

The penguin-looking creatures gathered around, smiling down at us, full of good humor and anxious to please. Had I come to a zoo, a pantomime, or a circus performance? I wondered, completely unaware of the permanence of my situation. As Sister Mary Cecilia, head of the girls' Junior School, took us around the many buildings, she made the mistake of telling me I could choose to live in whichever section of the school I wanted. I followed her, keeping close to Peter, with little real interest in my surroundings. I knew where I wanted to stay. First we toured the Junior School, with its dormitory lined with neat rows of beds and washstands. On one particular bed there was a green felt teddy bear with a red stitched nose and mouth and brown glass eyes. Downstairs, past a row of classrooms, was the play hall with a grand stage hidden by heavy red velvet curtains. There were highly polished wooden floors, tall windows looking out on buildings all around, and Indian clubs hanging on the walls. We genuflected as we entered the Gothic church: candlelit, reverent, smelling deeply of incense.

Our next stop was the school for deaf girls, which had started as a foundling home. As recently as the 1940s a baby girl diagnosed as deaf could be deposited on the steps of the convent without a clue as to her parentage or family circumstances. In the previous generation, these deserted children had received minimal education, were trained in domestic tasks, and were given a lifetime job as servants to the nuns and the schoolchildren. They knew no other home or family. They lived and died within the convent walls, taking care of all the menial chores. This slavelike labor allowed the nunnery to function economically and at a reasonable level of efficiency. Before I graduated in 1957, however, tremendous strides were made in the education of deaf children. Cabra was placed firmly on the European map as a pioneer in the field.

We toured the extensive grounds, a veritable medieval village, utterly self-contained and self-sufficient. There were playing fields for the younger children, with a half-mile jogging path and many horse chestnut trees providing conkers in summer term and in the fall houses mapped out by walls constructed of fallen leaves. There was a Senior School park with hockey fields, tennis courts doubling as net ball courts in season, jogging paths, and a pavilion. There was a beautifully laid out rose garden where each Sunday in May the entire school walked in procession, chanting the fifteen mysteries of the Rosary. The girls who received their First Communion that month wore their white dresses and veils and carried baskets filled with rose petals. They closely followed the statue of the Virgin Mary held under a canopy by four senior prefects, scattering the fragrant petals along the paths.

Our final stop was the boys' school, equivalent of grades one to six. It was made clear to us that Peter would reside here. He was given no choice. Sister Mary Cecilia peered at me through her rimless glasses: "Shall we go back and see the nice teddy bear?" She smiled condescendingly. "Then you can decide where you want to stay."

"I already know," I replied. "I'm going to stay here with Peter." I was adamant. No reasoning was necessary. I knew what I wanted.

Sister Cecilia's smile froze as she attempted to dissuade me, foolishly imagining that the lure of a stuffed animal would sway my decision. She was flat out of luck. Dragged back to the Junior School building yelling and screaming, I felt angry and dreadfully betrayed. All attempts at conciliation on both sides soon disappeared. "You *will* do as you're told," the petulant penguin screamed. I was undressed roughly, my face and hands washed in icy water with a cloth of sandpaper consistency, then tucked tightly into bed. I didn't meet any other children that day. I went to sleep mad at the world.

Gradually I became accustomed to the rhythm of life in the convent. The seven o'clock bell abruptly summoned us from bed. It was always cold in the large room, and speaking was strictly forbidden. Because of our close association with the deaf-mutes who cared for us, we learned a rudimentary sign language that made a subtle form of communication possible. Windows were flung open first thing, no matter what the temperature, to flush us out of the warmth of our beds and force a hurried exodus. Within twenty minutes of the first bell we were lined up outside the dormitory, two by two, and marched to the chapel for Mass.

Breakfast followed: a somber repast of tepid, lumpy porridge with milk, slices of buttered white bread, and a form of tea, the leaves, milk, sugar, and water all placed in a giant aluminum pot and brewed together. The long wooden refectory tables—each seating a biblical twelve—were sheathed in starched white linen cloths. As we ate, a senior prefect read from Thomas à Kempis's *Imitation of Christ,* followed by a chapter from Butler's *Lives of the Saints.* Only the sound of cutlery could be heard along with an occasional stifled cough. Every convent meal commenced and ended with grace. We marched back to the dormitory to make our beds and brush our teeth. This was one of the few times of the day we were allowed to visit the toilets.

The large tiled room comprised six stalls side by side, each divided by a wooden partition and with its own door. Six washbasins lined the wall. Nowhere in the school was there a mirror. Self-reflection was discouraged as an exterior preoccupation, a first step on the road to perdition. As soon as I learned to read, this dank lavatory held a particular fascination for me. Inside each stall was a small box filled with squares of newspaper. It was the only opportunity we had to learn anything of the world outside. A complete newspaper was forbidden even to the seventeen- and eighteen-year-old graduating senior girls. In our caregivers' opinion, a newspaper, lacking literary style or uplifting content, was an unfit instrument for the cultivation of delicate minds. How, then, could there be enough paper to clean the behinds daily of a community exceeding four hundred people?

THE FIRST SPRING holiday of 1944 was spent at the home of my parents' friend, the eminent geographer Eleanor Butler. Summertime brought difficulties, with three months' vacation and nowhere for Peter and me to go. Our parents were in England, our home sold, and apparently no one was responsible for us. Aunt Constance came to the rescue. There was a boardinghouse called Summerhill above the village of Enniskerry in County Wicklow. It was run by a family named Dunne who were taking in "war orphans." Peter and I found a spot where we fit in. Our circumstances were not considered unusual, nor did we elicit any particular sympathy. Life was expected to have its ups and downs. These good country folk stepped in to fill the parental gap, and at first a little money changed hands to sweeten the deal.

In June 1944 my mother returned to Ireland alone, nine months pregnant with my youngest brother, Michael. She and my father would never live together again. The lives of her first three children were set upon a course in which she would play only a peripheral part. Her father had given her a little money to set up on her own in Ireland. Michael became the focal point of her life, her raison d'être.

From our early teens onward, Peter and I would set out once a week during the summer holidays to visit our mother and brother in Dublin. The journey took more than an hour each way, and if we stopped to do some exploring, which we usually did, it took a great deal longer. Mother was agitated when we were late. Upon our arrival, we were expected to wash and change into clean outfits that she kept for us. We would put our grubby Enniskerry clothes back on again before we left. Life was a study in contrasts. My English mother with her fastidiousness and faux aristocratic facade, living in poverty yet with an aura of wealth, introduced us to the finer things in life. Underneath all the pretentiousness she had a serious interest in music, art, and literature. My mother deceived herself that our sojourn with the Dunnes was a temporary measure. One day, she dreamed, we would live in a fine mansion and hobnob with lords and ladies, as was our birthright. When I was with her, I had a sense of being a completely different person. She bought us books, introduced us to the theater, and told us of the glories of her youth, of her aspirations and hopes, which now she placed in us. Back at Summerhill that night, sitting around the turf fire, we would regale the Dunnes with tales of the city, Peter mimicking my mother's prim English accent to great guffaws.

When the war ended the other children were reclaimed, but Peter and I remained at Summerhill. In 1946 the boardinghouse was transformed into a small country hotel with fifteen bedrooms, bar, lounge, and ballroom. Summerhill soon became a popular destination for artists, writers, and theatrical people of all sorts. The hotel was run by forty-year-old Mary Ellen Dunne, whom we called Auntie Ciss. A wisp of a woman, Ciss had entered the convent as a teenager but was soon discharged on account of her delicate health. She returned to her parents and lived with them for the rest of her life. Ciss was devout. She had a childlike simplicity tinged with a keen sense of humor and an air of martyrdom. She worked incessantly, a slave to her parents, her six brothers, and later the hotel guests. She was the kindest, dearest, most unselfish person I have ever known.

The Dunnes' charity to us was greatly motivated by the threat that if we left Summerhill, we would go to live with our father in England and be brought up Protestant, as our brother Robin eventually did. Book reading (as opposed to spiritual reading or saying prayers) was discouraged. Reading was an idle occupation. It turned the mind and would bring no happiness. But my mother always gave us books for Christmas and birthdays: for me *Alice in Wonderland* (my favorite for many years), *The Secret Garden,* Louisa May Alcott's books, classics of all sorts. Peter received the Captain Marryat books, *Treasure Island,* and other boys' adventure stories. I accumulated stubs of candles and matches, later saving up to buy a flashlight with batteries. In the cupboard under the stairs, I hid with my clandestine book, lost in a make-believe world, until jerked out of my reverie by the high-pitched "Va-ler-ie, Va-ler-ie" from Ciss, who had suddenly realized I was missing. Peter, on the other hand, was a free spirit. Boys were supposed to be outside, gaining strength from the fresh air and learning the ways of the world.

My father returned to Ireland briefly in 1948. I had not seen him in five years. "Poor soul," the Dunnes said. "Your father's not at all well. He suffers from the weakness." As we grew older it became apparent that "the weakness" was an overindulgence in whiskey or Guinness—in short, alcoholism. This affliction in a man was a cause for pity and understanding. In a woman, it was considered disgraceful.

Visits with my father were magical interruptions to life at the hotel. Each outing brought a new experience. It was the only time we were treated like children. We might swing on the merry-go-round in the little park by the sea or watch the uniformed members of a brass band playing at the trellised octagonal stand on the promenade. We visited the carnival, where we drove bumper cars, ate candy floss, and aimed rubber rings at a bottle in an attempt to win a stuffed animal. As I grew older I became more aware of the whiskey breath and unsteadiness my father displayed as these days of pleasure wore on. I also noticed that he would disappear, especially when we went to the pictures or were concentrating on some activity. He was always jollier when he returned. My father spoke softly, inquiring how we were doing at school and what our interests were. I don't recall thinking of the visits as more than a passing moment or ever wishing that my father lived with us. The only real kinship we felt was for the Dunnes. They were our family, and Summerhill was home.

My brother Michael was a good scholar. He and my mother had moved to a flat in Monkstown overlooking the Irish Sea. A keen swimmer, Michael whiled away the summer afternoons fishing from the gray stone pier at Dun Laoghaire harbor. He had a crisp English accent and was accident-prone. We rarely heard of our other brother, Robin, and had never seen him.

While Cabra stimulated young minds and provided a secure and sheltered haven, it gave us few tools for tackling a secular life. The highest we girls could aspire to, we were told, was to join the order, to become a nun.

Being a wife and mother rated a poor second. No other alternatives were considered. The nuns never befriended the children, although some had favorites. Snobbery was prevalent, sarcasm and irony the teacher's preferred weapons. As a scholarship student, I received my share of disdain and belittlement. "How could anyone with a name like Danby-Smith expect to learn the Irish language?" Sister Mary Irenaeus scoffed at me if I made an error in Irish class. She was a tiny, ill-tempered woman we nicknamed "Irri Fly," short for "irritating fly." In 1956 I played Portia in *The Merchant of Venice.* The production was so successful that we put on the school's first public performance to benefit the orphans of the Hungarian revolution. When I won first prize that year for drama, I received a one-shilling pamphlet on the Abbey Theatre, which I still have. The second prize, a finely bound copy of Shakespeare's works, was awarded to one of the wealthier children. Such slights were considered character builders and a boost to one's humility, for we were told pride was the greatest deadly sin. After all, pride was what had brought us to the sorry state we were in. Was it not pride itself that caused us to be banished from Eden?

Every Friday after tea we lined up in the corridor class by class and marched to the church for confession. Hats donned, knees pressing against the hard wood, heads bowed reverently, we preceded the act with an acute examination of conscience. As a seven-year-old, I had found it a terrifying ordeal to enter the small dark box and utter aloud all my despicable faults and failings, but over the years, with frequency, it became a habit. It was often hard to conjure up venial transgressions: "I was lazy, I was mean, I told lies, I didn't share my sweets." When I was older, "I had unpure thoughts" was a daring and not completely comprehended declaration. "Bless me, Father, for I have sinned." It was a natural cleansing, as natural as the bath we took every other Friday. "Go, my child, and sin no more." The ritual taught us to acknowledge our faults and endeavor to overcome them. That done, the slate was cleaned and our lives as pristine as the pressed laundry we found lying on our dormitory beds that Friday night after our baths.

In the early 1950s the Irish government was dominated by the teachings of the Catholic Church. Every area of life and Catholic morality was synchronized. There was a stern censorship system. To an inquisitive teenager, there seemed hardly a book worth reading that had not been banned. For years my mother took us to the Globe Theatre in Dun Laoghaire when we visited her. On grander occasions we went into town to see an Edwards-MacLiammoir production at the Gate, and at Christmas-time Ciss Dunne would take us to the pantomimes at the Gaiety with Jimmy O'Dea and Maureen Potter. Soon Peter and I took part in the annual pantos Mrs. MacNeice produced in Bray. I found acting and the theater greatly stimulating, saving every shilling I could to buy a ticket to the Abbey or to attend a foreign production that came to the Theatre Royal for a limited run, such as Lorca's *The House of Bernarda Alba.*

My best school friend, Delphine, invited me to spend a fortnight each summer at The Garland, her home in Mallow, County Cork. Delphine's uncle Andy was on the censorship board. She whispered this to me in the strictest confidence. Del was always in the know. She absorbed information like a sponge and dispensed it with such aplomb that her precociousness largely escaped notice. Uncle Andy kept a stack of banned books on his bedside table, she confided, and if I could keep a secret, I would get to see them. On my next trip to The Garland she would arrange an invitation for us to visit her cousins for an afternoon's ride. At some point we would find a pretext to go into the house while the young cousins were still busy with the horses, and she would show me the books. They were well worth screening, she said. And so it happened the next summer. Everything went exactly as planned. We had to be quick. I rifled through the books. One caught my attention. I was attracted by the flashy cover showing a torero wielding the muleta in front of an angry bull, with the hint of frenzied onlookers in the background, a sight quite distinct from anything I had yet encountered. It was the first time I set eyes on *Fiesta,* as the English edition of Ernest Hemingway's *The Sun Also Rises* was called—a fairly grubby paperback copy, well scrutinized by the censors. I slipped the book into my pocket, determined to read it as soon as I could.

CHAPTER THREE

New Horizons: London and the Continent

JUST BEFORE MY SIXTEENTH birthday my mother made a surprise announcement. As soon as school finished in June I was to accompany my uncle Patrick from London on a two-week tour of the Continent, driving through France, with stops in Portugal and Spain, followed by two weeks back in London. Uncle Patrick was the parish priest of Bethnal Green, a dreary section of London's unfashionable East End. The focus of the Continental trip was a pilgrimage to Fatima, during which Uncle Pat would shepherd some elderly and devout members of his flock.

My uncle Patrick terrified me. A large man, wide and round with curly black hair and dark piercing eyes, his bulk, voice, and demeanor reminded me of Orson Welles—a plus in my opinion, but not enough to establish a rapport between us or to put me at ease. Disdainful and sarcastic, the burly priest was always at a loss as to why I was not brimming with affection and gratitude toward him for the great kindness he was showing me.

One of the joys of my uncle's life in those days was his newly acquired motorcycle, which he was still learning to ride. It was no secret, since the lightweight vehicle had a large red *L* on white cardboard attached above the back license plate. This made for a comical sight: his oversize figure in black suit, Roman collar, and broad-brimmed, flat-topped hat astride the motorized two-wheeler speeding along the London streets. I had no wish to share the experience, nor did the opportunity arise. When we went out together we took a sedate black London cab. Uncle Patrick was intent upon improving my education, hoping to fill the gaps my unfortunate Irish upbringing had created. Eating and drinking were at the top of the list. To this end we dined at a fashionable West End establishment, where I was introduced to the finest of wines and victuals and learned all the niceties, snobberies, and eccentricities of gourmet pleasures. I willingly complied. My one lapse occurred when his repeated criticism so greatly irked me that I declined wine. Summoning the waiter, I said, "Double vodka, please." A daring move, because the intentional social gaffe of choosing spirits over wine was underscored by my ordering a "communist" drink.

Life eased a little as we set out for the Continent on a plush tourist bus. The good pastor was preoccupied with dates and schedules, keeping count of his charges, and entertaining them with his knowledge or quips. He was like a jolly shepherd herding his flock into and out of buses, hotels, restaurants, cathedrals, museums, and gardens. There was a display of good humor that heretofore had escaped my notice. I had a chance to observe an entirely different side to my protector, a man who reveled in being the center of attention, in displaying his savoir faire, his considerable knowledge of foreign parts and languages, and a complete "You can rely on me" attitude, which was welcomed by the mostly elderly and pious citizens in his charge. So much in demand were his attentions that he had little time for criticism or to notice my failings. Relieved, I felt free to enjoy the strange delights of foreign travel.

We arrived at Le Havre on June 9 and headed directly south, entering Spain the next day and Portugal the day after in order to arrive at Fatima in time for the celebrations on the thirteenth. France had been a part of my consciousness from an early age. Studying the French language, literature, and poetry was part of an Irish convent education from the first form up. My knowledge of Spain and Portugal was negligible. We drove leisurely through Spain, visiting the many cathedrals and towns before arriving at Avignon in France, where the feast of John the Baptist was celebrated with great festivities; eating, drinking, singing, and dancing around briskly burn-ing bonfires. France had a charm of its own, but the people appeared dour compared to my Irish compatriots. Spain instantly won my heart. The sun-shine and the happy faces full of fun and curiosity made me feel certain I would return.

My final year at Cabra was anticlimatic. For the first time Spanish was offered, and I took the class dreaming of Iberia. I had no idea what I would do when I graduated. The Dunnes hoped I would work full time at the hotel and eventually manage it. My mother expected me to get a suitable job and move in with her; we would make up for the lost years. Neither prospect appealed to me. I could not stay in Dublin. I had to get away.

My one love was literature and writing. I longed to go to the university, like all of my circle of friends, but I knew there was no money for that. If I couldn't go to the university, I thought, maybe I'd try journalism. My men-tor was Terry Cronin, a New York woman who successfully launched the first Irish glossy magazine, *Creation*. Terry was dynamic. She also led a double life. On one hand she was a high-profile celebrity among celebrities; on the other she was the wife of the hunted chief of the IRA, Seán Cronin, who had escaped from the Curragh and was on the run. I had met Terry when she stayed at Summerhill a few summers before to effect a clandestine rendezvous with the escaped Seán. During my teen years at Summerhill, I had met some of Ireland's most interesting people.

Aunt Constance said she would pay for me to go to secretarial school for a year and then I could take the Guinness exam. She had connections. I was sure to be hired. Guinness was the highest-paying and most beneficial company to work for in Ireland at the time—a job so highly prized that once accepted, there would be no escape. The entire family would depend on my check and the benefits that went with it. The prospect was even less at-tractive to me than my other options. I could see myself sitting at the same desk year in and year out. On the other hand, I reasoned, a free ride through secretarial school would give me some journalistic skills.

I moved into a flat with my Cabra chum Delphine and two other girls at 13 Hume Street and settled into a lovely bohemian Dublin existence. Between classes (and often instead of them) I spent my time with artists and writers, actors and singers in Neary's Pub, the Pearl Bar on Fleet Street, or the Players Club after the theater. Terry Cronin reserved a table daily at a popular restaurant to meet with her writer and journalist friends. Through Terry I ran a number of errands for *The United Irishman,* the newspaper of the Sinn Féin party. Terry was tailed everywhere she went in the hope that she would lead the police to Seán. I remember our having coffee in Bewley's on Grafton Street one afternoon when she said, "Don't turn around. There are two B. Specials right behind us. We'll shake them off as soon as we get out of here." B. Specials were secret agents. It didn't seem odd to me that we were being shadowed. There was an edge of excitement and adventure to Dublin life in the 1950s.

CHAPTER FOUR

Spain

ONE DAY I RAN into my old school friend Honor Chance. To our mutual surprise, we found we were both attending the same secretarial school. Neither of us had ever been there on the same day.

"What are you going to do after Miss Meredith's?" Honor asked. "I'm off to Madrid to teach the March children English."

The banker Juan March, a friend of her father's, was one of the richest men in Spain. The family had castles, palaces, and a private plane. Honor's job sounded very attractive, and she was keen that I should find a similar position, saying that we could have a high old time together.

With no employment in sight, the prospect was tempting. I had inquired if they were hiring at the *Irish Times* and was told that if I was patient, a job might be available in the newsroom as a copy girl at two pounds ten a week. The main duties would consist of making tea and shuffling papers. I made up my mind. At lunch one day with Terry Cronin and company, my announcement that I was going to Spain was met with encouragement. Garry McElligot approved. The recently appointed editor of the new *Irish Times* Sunday magazine said I would have a much better chance at a journalistic career after a stint abroad.

"I would be willing to look at any articles you write, and if they suit, I would publish them," he told me. That settled it.

I lined myself up with a family in the Chamartin area of Madrid. The Apontes were a humble family in comparison with the Marches, but when I told them of my interest in writing, I learned that my *señora*'s sister was married to the brother of the famous José Camilo Cela, whose work later gained him the Nobel Prize for literature. The two Cela girls were often in my care those first months, and I met their uncle the writer himself on a couple of occasions: a serious man, slightly balding, introspective yet not unfriendly. My duties at the Aponte household multiplied weekly, often with as many as eleven cousins from one to fourteen years left in my care. Honor was living the high life, she reported: servants tending her right and left and airlifts from palace to castle during weekends and holidays. She urged me to find another family where I would have fewer duties and more free time. She knew of a Brazilian diplomat named Paranagua with three boys, no relatives close by, and a household of servants, where I would spend four hours daily after school with the children and occasional weekends when I took the boys riding in the Casa del Campo or on educational outings to Toledo or Segovia with the chauffeur and sometimes a maid in attendance.

A chance encounter with an Australian girl on a train in England the year before had supplied me with an address of friends in Madrid who lived close to the Apontes. This was a fortuitous contact for me. José Maria (Joe) Ochoa was a jolly Basque from Pamplona, his wife, Nancy, a reserved Englishwoman, and their three boys a delightful mixture of Latin and Anglo-Saxon. Joe worked in the movies. The big film studios were on Madrid's north side. At the time I met him, Joe was production manager for *Solomon and Sheba,* originally starring Tyrone Power. Power had died of a heart attack, and Yul Brunner replaced him as Solomon. Every Friday and Saturday night there were lively parties at the Ochoas'—music, dancing, singing, wine and fruit, cheeses and bread, young men with dark curly hair and wide grins strumming guitars or tapping flamenco rhythms on tiles in the courtyard, laughing women whose bright skirts whirred around to the rhythm of the music when they danced. There were painters, writers, and journalists.

Nancy loved having someone of her ilk to talk to. She and Joe were both welcoming, so I began spending all my spare time there.

Joe had once lived in Dublin, where he worked at the Gate Theatre with Michael MacLiammoir. We knew many of the same people. One night a couple came to the party. Joe called me over.

"I want you to meet the Holsteins, Geneviève and Axel. They're from Alsace. They run a news service here," he said. "Maybe they would have some work for you." He knew of my aspirations to be a journalist.

That evening it was agreed that I would be available to conduct interviews in English when needed. Marianne Tenaille, a young Parisian scarcely older than myself, was their French interviewer. This was the break I had been waiting for. I left the Apontes and moved in with the Brazilian family, where the days—and often the weekends—were my own. I was now able to attend several Irish functions and sent back dispatches to McElligot at the *Irish Times*. I later learned that a lot of what I sent was published as "our friend in Madrid writes." An occasional note from Terry or Pan Collins told me they were delighted with my long, newsy letters, the contents of which were promptly incorporated into their own columns. My only recompense was a hearty toast in Neary's Pub or the Fleet Bar to my good health and further adventures.

On Easter Sunday 1959 I attended my first bullfight. The Paranagua boys were in my care, so our seats in the Madrid ring were far better than I could have afforded. I was enthralled by the spectacle. In an effort to recapture the Dublin stage, I had spent many evenings at the theater watching seventeenth- and eighteenth-century plays that were dry, didactic, and frankly disappointing. Here in the bullring was the drama I sought, the parallel to my beloved Dublin theater. I determined that whenever possible the corrida would be my entertainment.

In May the Holsteins sent me to interview Ernest Hemingway. Geneviève gave me an outline with sample questions. She told me I could find the author at the Hotel Suecia. It was San Isidro week, and her source said he lunched at the hotel each day before the bullfight. Hemingway was visiting Spain for the first time since the Spanish Civil War, she said, and I was to find out what had prompted him to return as well as his present feelings toward Spain and the Franco regime. That was to be the thrust of the piece. I welcomed the assignment because of its literary bent. Previous interviews I'd done concerned business interests, oil in the Sahara, and other mundane matters. Although I had read *The Sun Also Rises, Men Without Women, To Have and Have Not,* and *For Whom the Bell Tolls,* Hemingway was not my favorite author, lagging far behind Evelyn Waugh, Graham Greene, James Joyce, G. K. Chesterton, and a host of other English and Irish writers.

I made my way to the Suecia, where I reserved a table for lunch. I placed myself strategically so that I could view those entering and leaving. I planned a long meal. Once I had ordered I looked around. The tables were full. The only photograph I had was the small head shot on the back of the well-worn Penguin edition of *Men Without Women.* It had been taken some fifteen years before, but I did not know that. At last I saw someone who vaguely resembled my photo. I called the waiter.

"Is it possible that could be the great *norteamericano* writer Ernest Hemingway?" I asked, feigning surprise.

"Oh no, *señorita,*" he replied. "That's not Hemingway. Don Ernesto is sitting over there."

He pointed to a white-haired man at the head of a table of some eight or nine people. I would never have recognized him. As Hemingway made his way out of the room I was waiting in the lobby. I approached politely and stated my business, and he asked me to come back the next morning at eleven. He gave me his room number.

The next day I knocked on the door of suite 809. Ernest introduced me to his wife, Mary, and friends Bill and Annie Davis. He motioned me to sit on the sofa.

"We'll be about half an hour," he told Mary as she and her companions left. He sat down in the adjacent armchair.

He asked me to tell him about Dublin. Although he had some good Irish friends, he had never been there. He mentioned Chink Dorman-Smith first of all, and then James Joyce and his wife, Nora. Joyce he called "Jim." Then he said that Dublin was one city he'd like to see.

I later wondered if it was because my surname, Danby-Smith, was reminiscent of his friend Chink's that Hemingway so readily granted the interview. We chatted about Dublin, and he was delighted to hear the literary gossip. He had read *Borstal Boy* when it came out in 1958, and his eyes sparkled when I told him that I knew Brendan Behan, whom I had seen just before leaving Ireland. Brendan had been one of many writers and artists who frequented Summerhill during my teenage years. As I set out for Spain he had grudgingly given me his blessing.

"Why would you waste yer time in a country governed by a horse's ass?" Behan had asked me. Then he went on to tell me of his only visit to the country. At the height of his fame Behan had landed on Mallorca and was met by a bevy of reporters.

"What would you like to see most on your first visit to our country, Mr. Behan?"

Without missing a beat, Brendan had replied, "Franco's funeral." Before he knew what hit him, Behan had found himself yet again behind bars. He had been returned to Ireland, his wish of seeing a funeral or any other Spanish sight unfulfilled. Ernest relished the story.

I started my interview.

"What brings you back to Spain after an absence of more than twenty years, especially since the political climate has not changed here?"

Not twenty years, less than five, was his response. He had been in Spain in 1956 and before that in '53 on his way to Africa.

My premise was incorrect, my story line fallen apart. All my subsequent questions related to the first one, so I had to wing it. I told him of stealing *Fiesta* from the banned-book stack at Delphine's uncle Andy's, and of smuggling a copy of *Ulysses* into Ireland from London two years before. It cost ten shillings and sixpence, a large investment for me. He seemed to overlook my poor research and instead asked me about my journalistic career and what I was writing. I told him of covering the Irish embassy and local Irish news.

I was going about my work the wrong way, he said. I should forget Ireland and see and learn as much about Spain as I could. He asked me where I'd been since I arrived.

"Nowhere, really, except a few day trips outside Madrid." I was again redeemed by my description of the Easter corrida and my reaction to it.

That was more like it, Ernest thought. I should learn and experience everything I could about this new country I was living in, the people, customs, history, current affairs. Then he rattled off a dozen or more places I must see, books I should read, people I should look up. He waited until I had written it all down. He became quite enthusiastic as he explored the possibilities for furthering my career.

He asked me if I was going to Pamplona for San Fermín, which started July 7.

"I haven't planned on it."

He said I must. It was almost too late to get accommodations, but Juanito would find me a place.

Our half hour was up. Mary had returned with a small florid-faced Spaniard, Juanito Quintana, a Pamplona native who was the model for the innkeeper Montoya in *The Sun Also Rises*. Down on his luck, he was serving as general factotum for Ernest and Mary and what came to be known as the Hemingway cuadrilla.

Ernest told Juanito to take down my address and phone number. I needed a room for San Fermín. And he asked him to add another corrida ticket to the list. It was settled, then, he said, offering me a firm handshake. They would see me in July, and should there be any change I was to let Juanito know.

I found my way out, amazed at how well things had turned out. I chided myself for relying on the Holstein questions without checking them. It would have been easy enough to do my own research. But all in all, it had been a good interview. I had plenty of material, and the discussion of Dublin would be of interest to the *Irish Times*. I went home and typed out my copy.

May ended, and so did my job with the Paranaguas. I was ready to get my own place and try to live on my earnings from doing interviews, supplemented by giving English lessons. I was caught up in my new routine, and in trying to make ends meet, memory of my promise to go to Pamplona faded. I was living in a German household and had added rudimentary German to my language skills.

One day as I walked past my former residence, the concierge shouted to me, "Hey, there's some mail here for you. Wait a minute." He disappeared into the building and returned with a package and a letter. I did not recognize the writing. Both had Málaga postmarks. The letter was from Juanito.

"I have made reservations for you," he wrote. "We hope you will be able to come to Pamplona. If you can't, I must hear from you no later than June 15."

The package contained a copy of *Guerre à la Tristesse,* a book on bullfighting with wonderful photos by Inge Morath, who would later marry Arthur Miller. Juanito's note enclosed was dated June 16. "We are very pleased you are coming to Pamplona. Don Ernesto asked me to send you this book so that you can learn a little bit about the fiesta before you arrive. See you July 6. Cordially, Juanito Quintana."

June 15 had come and gone. Fate decided for me. I could not back out now. I telephoned Joe Ochoa. He attended his hometown *feria* every year. He had just returned from Málaga, where they were filming *Scent of Mystery,* Mike Todd Jr.'s experimental Smell-O-Vision movie with Peter Lorre and a new young star, Beverly Bentley.

"Pamplona?" Joe said. "That's great. We met the Hemingways in the bar of the Miramar hotel. It will be fun to see them again. I'm taking the train on Sunday. Some of the cast will be along too. Why don't you join us? We are in for a very jolly week."

I found my pension in Pamplona and was greeted warmly by a buxom Basque woman as she wiped her wet hands on her apron. A head scarf framed her round weather-worn face, and her wide grin showed gaps where teeth were missing.

"Welcome, *señorita,*" she said as she shook my hand. "Your corrida tickets are here. The Hemingways are expecting you at El Choko bar for drinks at eight. Make yourself at home."

I had planned to catch up with Joe and his friends later but thought it only right that I should greet the Hemingways beforehand.

El Choko looked out on the main square. A noisy group sat around a long table—ten, maybe twelve people all drinking and laughing loudly. This time I had no trouble spotting the writer with his distinctive white hair and beard. As soon as I sat down a drink was placed before me.

After asking if I had received my corrida tickets, Ernest said I should meet them for dinner at ten. The meal would be followed by dancing in the square. It became clear that I was part of the cuadrilla, expected to join in the drinking, eating, watching the corridas, and the daily excursions.

I was introduced all around the table. Besides Ernest and his fourth wife, Mary, Hotch, Juanito, Bill and Annie Davis, and George and Pat Saviers (George was Ernest's doctor from Sun Valley), there were several others whose names I did not catch immediately. Beside me sat Scott Brown, a young journalist who wrote for the *Christian Science Monitor*. He had an anxious expression, was neatly dressed with a crew cut, and was quite unfriendly. I paid him little attention. At the evening's end I learned that he was to be my escort for the week. Ernest had paired us off, placing us side by side at meals and the corridas. I could tell Scott was not keen on the arrangement. The next day we went to the corrida together, but that was the last any of us saw of him. A couple of years later, when I had come to the United States, I inquired at the *Monitor* if he was still there, and learned, sadly, that he had hanged himself a few months before.

Ernest was furious at Scott's disloyalty and withdrawal from the group. He felt bad for me, thinking I was insulted. From then on, he went out of his way to make it up to me, often asking me to sit next to him at Choko's or at meals. That first night of the feria we joined the dancing in the square to the rhythmic beat of the *riau-riau,* local Basque folk music, loudly adding our voices to the singing and laughter. I had never before encountered such unrestrained merriment.

Antonio Ordóñez arrived. The leading bullfighter of the day, he was the son of the model for Romero in *The Sun Also Rises.* At twenty-eight, he was at the height of his power and fame: dark, handsome, and full of fun. He was Ernest's protégé. His wife, Carmen, was a favorite "daughter" of Hemingway, who said there was a physical resemblance between Carmen and myself. During this week, Carmen stayed at home with their daughters. She would join the Hemingways in Málaga for Ernest's sixtieth and her thirtieth birthday one week after the fiesta ended. Antonio, recovering from a *cornada* (goring) and unable to fight, intended to enjoy his leisure time to the full. There was a lightheartedness and gaiety in our group, in fact throughout the town. We saw little of Joe Ochoa and his companions, but Beverly Bentley, the young blond actress, soon deserted them to join the Hemingway cuadrilla, which seemed bent upon collecting as many pretty young girls as possible.

Late on the second night Ernest, Antonio, and friends "captured and took prisoner" two young ladies from the Midwest who were celebrating their graduation from Northwestern University. Their plans for the remainder of the journey were diverted, and they stayed with the cuadrilla until their return to the States some weeks later. A young English couple, Hugh and Suzie Millais, were also included in the company. He was tall and lanky, played the guitar, and sang troubadour songs. Ernest named him Boxman. Suzie had short dark curly hair, freckled pink cheeks, and a sweet voice.

On four successive afternoons before the corridas we took a picnic lunch to a stretch of the Irati River that Ernest had discovered when he first came to Spain in the 1920s. Having written about it in *The Sun Also Rises*, he had not returned there since. The clear, cold river ran through a forest that was tall, dark, and primeval. We settled by some trees, leaving the picnic basket in the shade. Ernest lodged the wine in the river to keep it cool. The girls stripped to their bikinis, tested the water with loud splashes and laughter, and then lay in the sun to dry. They were closely watched and attended to by Antonio, Hotchner, and the other men. On that first trip Mary slipped on a stone in the stream and broke her toe. A moment's solicitude was quickly succeeded by annoyance on the part of her husband, who disliked it when attention was diverted from him for any length of time. He quickly calculated what an inconvenience it was to have a crippled mate demanding his attention and devotion. I observed a darker, meaner side of the writer. We saw less of Mary for the rest of the week. She attended the corridas and appeared for a drink at Choko's but often excused herself early. For the most part she stayed close to their lodging, nursing her injured toe. She put on a brave face at first, but by week's end her temper was on a short fuse.

Mary had reason to be edgy. Limping around, she calculated she had only seven days left until Ernest's sixtieth birthday. In that time she had to put together all the preparations for the great party she planned to give at the Davises' house, La Consula, in Málaga. Friends from all over the world were expected: Ambassador David Bruce and his wife, Evangeline, from England; the maharajah of Jaipur and his brother-in-law, the maharajah of Cooch Behar, from India; the Ivanciches, from Italy; and General Buck Lanham from Washington, D.C., were just a few who accepted. And now Ernest was expansively inviting all those around him in Pamplona to join the fun. The midwestern girls and Beverly Bentley agreed to be there.

A couple of days before we were to leave, Ernest wanted to know if I would come to his birthday party.

"Sorry, I can't," I replied breezily. "I must get back to Madrid, back to work." Though I was glad he had asked me and I had enjoyed the week, I was ready to return to a life of my own.

I noted a shadow of disappointment on his face, hurt in those brown eyes.

"You have plenty of friends to make a jolly party. They have all the time in the world. I'm different. I earn my living."

Ernest was silent for a moment. He said that if it was a matter of money, he could fix it.

"You've been too generous already. I'm grateful, but I need to be independent. I prefer to pay my own way."

Next day when the three of us were together Ernest asked Bill Davis offhandedly if he thought the cuadrilla needed a secretary, and would he agree to hiring "Miss Val" to be his assistant for the summer?

"It's a fine idea," said Bill.

Ernest turned to me and asked if $250 a month salary would suit. I could work three months, until early October, and then return to Madrid. I would see Spain, meet people, learn about the corridas. It would be a good experience for my career. And besides that, he could do with my help. Mary was hurting. I could be useful to both of them.

"I shall have to think about it," I said as I recalculated the dollar amount in pesetas and Irish pounds. It was far more than I could earn in Madrid, and it might be fun too. "I'll let you know tomorrow."

Parting was easier when we knew we would all meet up again in a few days. It had been a crazy week. In spite of the fun and hilarity there was an undercurrent of true madness and destruction. Bullfighter Antonio, already recovering from a *cornada,* had been gored again during the running of the bulls. It had occurred when the matador distracted a bull's attention after the galloping animal had tossed a man and was about to attack him on the ground. Using a newspaper for a muleta, Antonio deftly made a few passes. On the last pass the paper curled up, leaving his left flank open. Due to the ignominious nature of the incident, Antonio delayed treatment for days until Ernest finally persuaded him to let George Saviers clean and dress the wound. Also, Mary's toe continued to be a source of pain and irritation for her and for Ernest, whose temper flared in earnest when he learned that David O. Selznick was in San Sebastian for the summer film festival. Hemingway had recently received a telegram from Selznick, who had completed yet another remake of *A Farewell to Arms* with his wife, Jennifer Jones, as the heroine, Catherine Barkley. A total mismatch, fumed the author. It always irked Ernest that shortly after the book had come out, thirty years before, he had sold it outright to the movies with no provision for remakes. Up to that point, he said, there had been nine versions, and he had not benefited from any of them. He vented his rage on the absent but not too distant Selznick.

The drinking escalated, as did the frenzy of the throngs and the singing and dancing to the throbbing of the *riau-riau* music in the streets. The town was teeming with tourists, almost to a man lured there by the romance of Hemingway's *The Sun Also Rises.* The locals stood out in their white shirts and chinos with blood-red kerchiefs around their necks and their black or red berets. Our nerves were tense from the excitement and strung out from lack of sleep. Ernest, never given a moment's peace when in public, was besieged with requests to sign autographs and pose for photos. For the most part he maintained an equilibrium of patience and good humor, playing the impeccable host. He drank, sang, told stories, ate, and danced. He carefully studied each bull and torero before the daily fights and afterward analyzed the corrida moment by moment. That is, he did so before Selznick's telegram arrived—after, he unleashed all the anger his raw nerves could summon on the absent movie mogul. I can see Ernest now, his bulky, energetic figure walking briskly from the square brandishing a pocketknife, threatening castration to the producer if he dared to show his face in Pamplona. It was not especially alarming; instead it all seemed quite natural, a momentary flare. Then Lauren Bacall turned up, and Ernest's temper as quickly abated. A sweet calm was restored. Seeing Bacall in Pamplona drew Ernest from his black mood. I have a photo of the two of them happily sipping drinks together at a side-street café, recalling Humphrey Bogart and the times their paths had crossed. This was a serene moment in Ernest's madcap world.

More disturbing to me than the Selznick flare-up was a small incident in which Ernest and I were walking away from the square one late afternoon, linked arm in arm, quietly reminiscing on life in Spain and sharing our delight in things Hispanic. Quite suddenly we were interrupted by the flash of a camera. Cuevas, a short, round-faced Basque photographer, grinned at us—quite innocently, I thought—nodding to acknowledge that he was satisfied with his shot. Ernest turned on him in a rage. To the astonishment of the little man, the irate author threatened to smash the camera if he was not immediately given the film. Cuevas profusely apologized for intruding. He said the other photos on the roll were important to him because that was his livelihood, but he would cut the negative and not print it but send it to Ernest as soon as the roll was finished. Ernest relented, but not without threatening him and his family and all his descendants if he did not keep his word. I still have that negative with Cuevas's letter of apology in my files.

The incident took me by surprise, but I did not pay much heed to it. During the week—from the time that my assigned escort vanished and

Mary absented herself to nurse her painful toe—Ernest had insisted on my staying by his side. I was the only one there who was not an old friend or an avid fan, and perhaps he found my neutral stance refreshing. I was not in awe of him. I enjoyed all Pamplona had to offer, his insight into bullfighting gripped me, and my Irish background gave me great stamina for enduring the long hours of drinking, storytelling, and merrymaking. My only agenda was to enjoy the moment. That I did to the fullest.

Upon my return to Madrid I walked along the Paseo, finally finding a pretty dress to wear at Ernest's birthday party. In Lederer I chose his birthday gift, a bell with bull brands engraved on it. I had often lingered at the window of that fine leather goods store wishing for a reason to go inside. Nothing in Dublin could match its chic and pomp. Mary and Annie Davis had set out straight from Pamplona to Málaga in Annie's little Volkswagen Bug to prepare for Ernest's birthday celebration, while he and Bill loitered on the way down so that I could accompany them for the long drive southward in the Hemingways' rented pink Ford, dubbed the Pembroke Coral after its designated color on the car rental slip. I remember that route well, traveling it again and again over the next few months. That was to be the first of many trips the three of us would take on the highways of Spain and France. That crazy roller coaster of a summer felt as if it could never end.

CHAPTER FIVE

Birthdays, Bull Fever, and a New Title,
La Secretaria

*L*A CONSULA WAS A LARGE, cheerful two-story house, beautifully symmetrical, with wide verandas upstairs and down, whitewashed inside and out. The house was snugly set in a forested garden and protected by a pair of manned wrought-iron gates. Tall, dark cypresses stood sentinel on each side of the long driveway. A pair of handsome, amiable hound dogs ambled the grounds. White marble floors met white walls hung with Jackson Pollocks, Goya prints, and old maps. Books abounded. White linen covered the furniture, a striking yet oddly effective contrast with the tones and themes of the Pollocks' brightly painted splashes. I was given a spacious bedroom on the ground floor. Ernest and Mary had adjoining rooms on the upper level. Every evening at poolside where the guests gathered before dinner, drinks and tapas were served. The air was warm and fragrant, and Fats Waller's voice crackled from the speakers above: "Don't love you 'cos your feets too big," he crooned as we sipped, splashed, and rehashed the day's events. "I'm goin' to sit right down and write myself a letter and make believe it came from you" always made Ernest smile and hum along. At other times Frank Sinatra sang to us. I kept my distance from the water, finally admitting that I didn't swim. Hotch was assigned to instruct me, a task he carried out with good humor and considerable success.

Bill Davis had once been a taxi driver in San Francisco, or so he said. That was all I knew about him. Clearly it was not his vocation or how he came by his apparently abundant wealth. I also heard that he had moved to Spain after his divorce from his first wife, taking the Pollocks with him. It was said he could not return to the United States or his ex-wife would claim her share of his property. He and Annie were devoted to each other and had two young children, Teo (Timothy), and Nena (Jean), who mingled with the guests inconspicuous and contented. Annie's older sister, Jeannie, had been Cyril Connolly's first wife, his great love. She later married Peggy Guggenheim's sometime husband, Lawrence Vail. Her life had been a turbulent one, and she died young. Her niece was named for her. In his fifties, Bill was a large, awkward man, with a Dickensian face and a tangle of hair around his balding pate. Because of his wide nose and thick lips, Ernest called him "El Negro." El Negro was quiet and acquiescent with Ernest, his demeanor more that of a chauffeur or paid servant than lord of the manor, but I detected a cynicism and cruel streak in him as I observed his behavior with the lesser beings in the entourage. Annie had a sweet face and an entirely agreeable personality. She quite accepted Bill calling her his "squaw." She and Mary became close and were constant companions on the road. It was extraordinary how those two people, the Davises, shelved their own lives for a summer to entertain the writer and his wife.

Bill Davis had bought La Consula in the summer of 1953. From the outset this huge, comfortable house was a lure for the intellectual, the artistic, and the well connected—particularly the English, who eagerly sought an escape from their damp and dreary island following the restrictions of the war years. Wonderful hosts, Bill and Annie entertained with generosity and good taste but always remained conscious of their guests' pedigree and celebrity. Until 1959, Cyril Connolly, brother-in-law emeritus, Britain's hyperintellectual, was foremost among the guests. Gerald Brenan referred to Cyril as La Consula's "presiding genius, even in his absence," and British theater critic Kenneth Tynan called him "the house writer and master of ceremonies." Tynan said that La Consula provided Connolly with "a momentary glimpse of Eden from the wastelands of middle age."

The Hemingways' tenancy that dangerous summer trumped all La Consula's previous houseguest records. Ernest's sixtieth-birthday party was the focal point, the centerpiece. Gradually friends arrived. Gianfranco Ivancich and his wife, Cristina, drove over from Venice in a brand-new cream-colored Lancia purchased with Ernest's Italian royalties. Gianfranco's sister Adriana had become Ernest's idol when he'd met her ten years before. At the time she'd been nineteen, the same age I was then. He had written *Across the River and into the Trees* about her and *The Old Man and the Sea* with her in mind. She had painted the jacket illustration of the old man and his boat. Ernest told me he had fallen in love every decade of his life. About every ten years, his creative juices were revived and started to flow again better than before.

He was as excited as a child at the prospect of seeing his old friends and of showing off Antonio Ordóñez, whom he hailed as the greatest living matador. Antonio was fearless in the ring and unbending in adhering to the classical movements that Ernest so admired. Antonio's brother-in-law Luis Miguel Dominguín was thirty-four, six years his senior, and nearing the end of his career. Once Spain's supreme bullfighter, Luis Miguel had come out of retirement the year before. Still a formidable fighter with great presence and a wide following, he had once been Ernest's favorite. Luis Miguel had visited Cuba and spent time at the Finca Vigía, the Hemingways' home there. As the years took their toll, Luis Miguel compensated by resorting to crowd-pleasing passes, which Ernest deemed cheap tricks. The older bullfighter had a beautiful wife, the Italian actress Lucia Bosé. He was poised and socially skillful. Cool, intelligent, suave, self-confident, Carmen Ordóñez's older brother did not need to rely on the patronage of the great American author to bolster his considerable ego. Rarely joining us socially, he was the star of his own entourage. Though not as sharp and savvy as Luis Miguel, the good-natured and amiable Antonio was in awe of the writer. Compliant and respectful, he enjoyed being the protégé, the center of Ernest's attention.

Ernest's original intention that year was to update *Death in the Afternoon* with an appendix. That summer the rivalry of the two matadors came to a head, with a series of mano-a-mano's scheduled. It was for the express purpose of following this professional rivalry between the brothers-in-law that Hemingway was in Spain. *Life* magazine had contacted him, sending Will Lang as emissary to negotiate an exclusive account of the duel for them. In a mano-a-mano, two matadors are slated on the cartel instead of three, dividing the six bulls between them. It is a clear contest to see who has greater skills, endurance, and luck. The Hemingways' schedule specifically followed the course of Antonio Ordóñez and Luis Miguel Dominguín in the ring. Already at this time, July 21, both had received *cornadas* and had been out of action, upsetting the competition's pace. Fortunately, Ernest's birthday party became the main distraction.

In the days leading up to the big event I heard countless stories about the friends who were coming. Some of the best stories featured General Charles T. "Buck" Lanham. He had headed Ernest's favorite U.S. Army regiment, the 22nd Regiment in the 4th Infantry Division, during the Second World War. Courting Mary at the time, Ernest had written to her, "Buck Lanham is the finest and bravest and most intelligent and able Regimental Commander I have ever known." He and Ernest knew each other then and had continued their friendship with a vast correspondence supplemented by meetings whenever possible. They had a mutual respect. Ernest had an acute knowledge of the strategy of war and a feel for the complicated and contradictory forces behind it. He loved the drama war entailed and the courage it brought out in heroes as well as its treachery and wickedness—the fabric of great literature. When Ernest described his friends and their exploits, they took on epic proportions. I could barely wait to meet them. I imagined Lanham as a tall, imposing figure with a booming voice whose presence commanded the attention of all. When a group of newcomers arrived no one matched that description.

I asked Bill Davis, "Has General Lanham arrived yet?"

"He's over there." Bill pointed to a short, balding man. "Let me introduce you."

Buck was mild-mannered and diminutive, with a soft, husky voice. He treated Ernest with a deference that amounted to awe. Far from boasting of military exploits, he voiced many misgivings and fears regarding his present position and his future economic prospects. I was disappointed. Over the next couple of weeks we traveled together for many hours in the Pembroke Coral. Nothing in his demeanor came close to the lively description Ernest had given of him. That was often the way. Ernest, ever the novelist, embellished for better or worse the personae of his friends and enemies. In real life, they little resembled his description.

On the other hand, Gianfranco Ivancich was intriguing. He too was short, with murky blond hair and a lined and leathery narrow face. He spoke a smattering of languages and was quite voluble if not entirely incomprehensible. I took to him immediately.

Rupert Belville, who had flown his own plane on the Nationalist side in the Spanish Civil War, was both a wartime friend of Ernest's from London and an old friend of Bill Davis. He had stayed at La Consula in May and followed the fights with the Hemingways. Now returned to England, he sent his son, Hercules, who turned up with two companions. We were of a similar age, so we had some fun together. Perhaps the most distant travelers to the party were Bhaiya, the maharajah of Cooch Behar, with his English lady friend, later his wife, Gina, and his brother-in-law, the maharajah of Jaipur, with his wife, Ayesha, and their son. The Hemingways had met Bhaiya in October 1956 at the feria of Zaragoza. He was an aficionado and a follower of Ordóñez. He had sparked Ernest's imagination at that time by inviting him to a tiger shoot in India. The hunt never took place, but the two kept in touch.

The birthday party was as sparkling as any, with music and entertainments. Mary rented a shooting gallery from a traveling carnival, and it became the main attraction when Ernest, to the horror and fascination of the onlookers, blasted the ash from Antonio's lighted cigarette with a .22 rifle as the matador held the butt between his lips. A flamenco troupe performed. Following dinner were dancing and a fireworks display, the fireworks imported from Valencia, the home of pyrotechnics. Champagne flowed unceasingly. No one noticed that an errant firework sparked the top of a royal palm tree close to the house until it was too late. Feeble attempts failed to extinguish the fire, so the local fire department was summoned. The *bomberos* promptly arrived and quelled the flames. Their work completed, they cheerfully posed for photos, lent their hats to the pretty girls, and drank a toast to the birthday honorees, Carmen and Ernest, before departing. Breakfast was served at six-thirty, and the remnants of the party disbanded after nine when David and Evangeline Bruce left to fly back to London.

Three days later we were on the road to Valencia. The beautiful new Lancia, bought with Ernest's Italian royalties and brought to Málaga by Gianfranco, had replaced the Pembroke Coral. We drove in a caravan along the wild coastal road north and east. I sat between Bill and Ernest in front; Hotch and Buck were in the back, conversing all the way until we reached our destination, a seaside town with a fine feria, an excellent cartel of bullfights, some of the best food in Spain, and the very best fireworks of all. Beverly Bentley was still with us. When she could not get a reservation anywhere, I offered to share my quarters at the Victoria Hotel with her. We became friends, and remain so to this day. We dined late after the bullfights at a beachside restaurant called Pepico's, which had indescribably delicious fresh seafood and paellas. A long table seating up to twenty people was reserved for us each night. My designated seat was at Ernest's left; Antonio sat at his right. As the week wore on Beverly and I became restless, irked by the incessant praise of Antonio and the nonstop regimen of eating and drinking that required our constant presence and attention. We decided to use a little initiative.

Curro Girón, the middle of three torero brothers, was on the cartel the second day of the bullfights. He had a charismatic charm and used all the petty tricks Ernest abhorred in the ring. Somehow this endeared him to us, and the next day Beverly bought a bouquet of flowers, which she threw to him in the ring. Emboldened by this gesture of independence, we planned to take the evening off. We put out the word that we both had a touch of stomach flu and would not join the group for dinner. We thought we might take a look around the town.

We were in our room sorting out what we would wear and where we would go when there was a knock on the door. It was Dr. George Saviers. Ernest had sent him to see if we needed medical attention. George was instructed to have room service bring us a suitably bland and boring dinner. We decided to wait until after dinner before leaving. We were again preparing our escape when we heard another rapping on the door. This time it was Hotch. He had been sent to report on our progress. We chatted awhile, Hotch questioning us closely on our opinions of the rest of the group, especially what we thought of Mary. He seemed disappointed when we voiced our admiration and declared we both liked and thought highly of her.

When he left, we looked at each other. We rehashed the conversation. There had been something sinister about it. Then it dawned on us at exactly the same time. Hotch must have brought his "devil box" with him and taped the entire conversation. We went over the dialogue again. His questions had been provocative, clearly intending us to bad-mouth our companions in the group. However, we had both been careful to give neutral, noncommittal answers. Hotch's toy, which Ernest had named, was no secret. He brought it out and played with it on several occasions. It afforded some lighthearted fun. But I had observed Hotch taping Ernest's conversations surreptitiously on occasions when I know he was clearly trespassing and overstepping the bounds of friendship. I did not doubt that Hotch was equally capable of using his "devil box" on any of the rest of us when he felt so inclined. Bev and I were so shaken by our two unexpected visitors that we canceled our evening out. Instead, Beverly had a copy of *The Old Man and the Sea,* which we read aloud amid giggles and saucy comments. It was my first reading of that book, and a very irreverent one.

Antonio and Luis Miguel both fought during the feria on the first and second days, Luis Miguel and then Antonio. It was my first time seeing each of them fight. Ernest took great delight in instructing me and analyzing pass by pass each matador's performance. It became clear that Antonio had the edge with his style and grace. Luis Miguel was recovering from a *cornada,* and his left leg was stiffening. He was having trouble killing. Unashamedly rooting for Antonio, Ernest was pleased to see his protégé take the lead even if he felt kindly toward Luis Miguel, now the underdog. It was no surprise when the two met in a mano-a-mano on the fifth day that Antonio dominated the ring. Luis Miguel grew less confident until, during the faena with his last bull, the wind lifted his muleta as the bull was charging. A horn went straight into the groin and penetrated upward, just missing his intestines. Luis Miguel was rushed to the hospital and later flown to Madrid. Antonio had won the first round.

At the end of the week, we said goodbye to the birthday party guests who had followed us on to Valencia and to the two beautiful midwestern prisoners, released on their own recognizance. Beverly now headed for Paris to purchase a purple Citroën with the proceeds from her Smell-O-Vision movie. She shipped her trophy to the United States. Forty years later, no longer roadworthy, the remains of her 1959 Purple Turtle have become an objet d'art on display in her Provincetown dwelling.

The dwindling cuadrilla headed south through Alicante, Murcia, and Granada. In teacher mode, Ernest enjoyed showing me each new place and pointing out its strength. Murcia was the home of knives and pickpockets. Alicante boasted great melons. I had learned earlier on the first trip to Málaga from Madrid that Aranjuez grew the finest asparagus in the world. C. Z. Guest, socialite wife of Winston Guest, grandnephew of Winston Churchill, was affectionately called the Asparagus of Aranjuez, though sometimes this was said with a little irony and even a tinge of malice. Winston was a great pal of Ernest's, a frequent visitor to the Finca Vigía, and a comrade in many escapades—most notably submarine hunting off Havana in Hemingway's fishing boat, *Pilar,* during the Second World War.

Granada needed no epithets. I had visited three summers before and had been charmed by the mystical Alhambra with its Moorish brilliance calling out through the ages. Tales of the caliphs had nowhere been found in our Dublin curriculum, where pagans were given little credit for cultural enhancement of the universe. Built on three hills at the center of a wide plain, Granada looks out to the snowcapped Sierra Nevada on the horizon. From each of the hills, the Albaicín, Sacromonte, and Alhambra, there are infinitely varied views of the red-walled Alhambra palace. Granada was our last stop on the way back from Valencia. We planned to return to Málaga the next day in time for the first fight of the feria.

Next morning we visited the Alhambra. On the way out of town, I listened avidly to Bill and Ernest discussing Lorca. I had seen a production of *The House of Bernada Alba* in Dublin a couple of years before, and it had prompted me to read everything I could by and about the Spanish poet. *Alba* had been his last play, completed only two months before he was killed. Now we mourned Lorca and his fate as we departed his hometown. Born twelve miles from Granada in Fuente Vaqueros in 1898, he had moved into the city when he was eleven. He died about the same distance outside the city of his birth in 1936, murdered by the Fascists in the civil war. It was on that road driving out of Granada that I first heard of Ignacio Sánchez Mejías, the bullfighter who lost his life in the bullring of Manzanares on that fateful August 11, 1934, his life and death made famous by the elegy his friend wrote for him. Ernest could recite the lines by heart, and before long I found myself chanting the refrain, "*A las cinco a las cinco a las cinco en punto de la tarde.*"

The Málaga festival took place the first week in August. The town overflowed with people, from princes to pickpockets, and the mayhem and madness lasted nine days. We watched the first fight in the arena with Diego Puerta, Manolo Segura, and Gregorio Sánchez and took a horse-drawn carriage to the Miramar Hotel afterward, where we found a spot in the crowded bar. Serious discussions of the corrida took place in several languages. To my surprise, we found the British theater critic Kenneth Tynan there with his American wife, Elaine Dundy. Tynan was one of my all-time heroes. I had been reading his criticism for years and had gone to a lecture he had given in London the previous summer. If anyone had asked me three months before whom I would prefer to meet, Hemingway or Tynan, I would have not hesitated to name the latter. Up close he was just as I might have expected: a quiet presence, slightly supercilious, with his cigarette lodged between his third and fourth fingers, seated on the bar stool holding forth sotto voce on the merits of the corrida. He had stayed at La Consula on his previous visits to Málaga. I dearly wished he and Elaine were among the guests now.

Another encounter that day made a profound impression upon me. After the corrida in the Miramar bar, Ernest received a note saying that the daughter of his old friend André Malraux, Florence, would like to meet him. The note was signed by Monique Lange, who worked at Gallimard, Ernest's French publisher. Ernest immediately went to the lobby and returned with three people, Monique, Flo, and a young Spanish writer, Juan Goytísolo, an editor at Gallimard and Monique's lover. Our paths were to cross with this delightful trio many times before the dangerous summer was over. Monique was small, dark-haired, and pixie-faced with smiling black darting eyes, full of love and energy. Flo, who worked for *L'Express,* was young and earnest, delighted and a little awed to meet Hemingway. Juan, originally from Barcelona and already a fine writer, was reticent and hung back. Between his English and my Spanish, we managed to discuss the political situation in Ireland and make some comparisons with the climate in Spain. He could not live in this country while Franco was alive, he told me. The sentiment was mutual, for his books were mostly unavailable in Spain. I felt an immediate kinship with Juan and Monique. Altogether this had been a wonderful day.

Returning to the house, we learned that Antonio had been gored in the thigh the day before in Palma de Mallorca. The wound was not as serious as Luis Miguel's, but now they were both in a hospital in Madrid. Bill and Ernest drove up the next morning to check on the patients, returning the following day. The cartel for the feria, which had been based on the two great matadors, Ordóñez and Dominguín, now had to be rearranged without them. In a strange way, with this competition removed, the remaining matators were spurred to do their best. We witnessed some thrilling work in the arena. Each day afterward we repaired to the Miramar to drink cold Campanas wine and discuss the fights.

Hotch was still with us, very much the clown, I thought, carrying his "devil box" and recording people sometimes when they least suspected it. Ernest had a phobia of being recorded and of press people infiltrating our ranks. He loved to let off steam by joking and fooling around, making up fantasies and personae for members of his entourage. Bill was "El Negro," Hotch "El Pecas" (Freckles). He had secret code talk and inside jokes, which to an outsider might suggest that he was not a serious person. But, of course, he was a serious person, specifically a serious writer. Still, within his family he could play the buffoon. When he liked someone, he became blind to their faults. A tape recorder on anyone else would have been traitorous; with Hotch it was a cause for amusement, the harmless "devil box." Midweek Hotch whispered to Ernest that he had overheard Tynan remarking that Hemingway was incorrect on some aspect of the previous day's fight, that he had miscalled one of the passes or some such thing. When we reached the Miramar, Ernest, now fortified with a couple of drinks, confronted Ken, virtually challenging him to a duel. He was making the kind of spectacle of himself the press loved and he loathed. Hotch kept a respectable distance from the trouble spot. Cordiality between the Tynans and us ceased after this incident.

While we were at La Consula between trips to the ferias, a work routine was firmly established. Ernest and I had an easy relationship, a little work and a lot of fun. As we joked, sharing our diverse backgrounds, I listened more than I spoke. I was becoming saturated in the history, opinions, and fantasies of my mentor. He was outspoken about his family, his friends, and the important events of his life. The random jigsaw pieces of his life gradually linked together in my mind. Trust was a quality he valued most in those surrounding him. As long as I was part of his household, everything he said and did was confidential material, not to be used or exploited.

People often query what exactly were my secretarial duties, but there was no job description. When I was hired, it was fortunate I was not asked if I possessed secretarial skills, for I did not. When the Hemingways first arrived in Málaga in the spring Ernest had set about writing the introduction to a new edition of his collected short stories. Mary had typed it for him, as always, but this time she had been critical of the piece. He grudgingly made changes. From the start of their trip, they had been at odds. He was disinclined to ask her to type for him again. When I came on the scene, he felt liberated from what he had perceived as Mary's tyranny. Of course, I was unaware of these undercurrents. All I knew was that I had to be available twenty-four hours a day, alert but not intrusive, sensitive to the nuances and moods of the principals around me. I needed to be a critical reader and a coherent writer, to be able to listen and discuss, to remember, and to take notes when necessary. An ability to drink heartily and endure hours of often repetitive conversations was essential. Lending a sympathethic ear, having an even temperament, and being a good follower but not a yes-man all helped. An independent opinion was appreciated, but only if offered at the right moment. My life at Summerhill had well prepared me for these duties. In my teenage years I had survived endless nights of drinking and story-telling around the turf fire. I had listened to writers and entertainers for as long as I could remember. I knew when to hold my tongue and when to speak up. The Hemingways treated me like a member of the family rather than an employee. I was more pupil than hireling.

One day Ernest asked me if I had any enemies.

"No, I can't think of any," I replied.

He persisted. Was I sure that I knew of no one who hated or was jealous of me?

"Pretty sure."

Then he showed me an anonymous letter postmarked Madrid a couple of days before. Short and nasty, it warned him that I was a fraud and that he should have nothing to do with me. I was stunned and stymied. I carefully recollected the events of my six months in Madrid. Whom had I offended? It was a sinister moment, knowing that an unnamed person wished me evil. For a week, plagued with nightmares, I kept the light on in my bedroom and made use of the time reading till dawn. Ernest did not mention the letter again.

Our host, Bill, had a cynical twist to his character. I thought perhaps he was tantalized by the naiveté of the convent-bred Irish Catholic teenage girl who had joined his household in a nebulous capacity somewhere between guest and employee—after all, I was the cuadrilla secretary and receiving a salary. When Ernest was not within earshot, he slyly attempted to embarrass me with lewd remarks. I remained immobile, pretending not to hear, but my blushes must have betrayed my discomfort. One night before retiring he handed me a book.

"You should read this," he said. "It's a classic about a young woman."

The book was *Fanny Hill.* I read it that same night. I noticed the bemused smirk on Bill's face at breakfast next morning as he scrutinized my demeanor for any hint that would reveal my newfound knowledge. Later that day I returned his book with what I hoped was a nonchalant, "Thank you. It was a pleasure."

After the feria was over we spent a relatively quiet week working and recouping. The next big fight, the second mano-a-mano, was slated for August 14. Since leaving the hospital, Antonio had spent some time recuperating at Luis Miguel's ranch, the two rival matadors training together in harmony before the next onslaught. Then Antonio came to relax at La Consula a few days before the fight, bringing along his Basque friend Ignacio Angulo, whom we called Natcho. We had no idea that we were about to witness one of the best corridas ever. Two matadors, six bulls, ten ears, four tails, two hooves—a record of statistics and a memorable afternoon. Ernest said afterward that it was one of the greatest bullfights he had ever seen. For a moment there was evidence that Luis Miguel, his confidence restored after the last *cornada,* might prove a worthy opponent. This was what Ernest had come to Spain to see. There were three more mano-a-manos ahead. His story was now assured.

Next morning, August 15, Ernest set off with Antonio and Luis Miguel by plane to Biarritz via Madrid. He later told us of a queasy moment when the pilot let the two bullfighters handle the plane. The third mano-a-mano was set for Bayonne, and from all accounts it was not a notable one. The horns had been altered and the bulls were small. Ernest stayed with Luis Miguel to see him fight the day after, while Antonio drove to Santander, on the north coast, for his next appearance. We would all meet up again two days later in Ciudad Real for the fourth duel. Ernest flew with Miguel to Madrid and then accompanied the two matadors by road to Ciudad Real, two hundred kilometers south of Madrid.

We set off from Málaga, Bill, Hotch, and I in the plush new Lancia with the Italian driver, Mario Casamassima, at the wheel. We had no trouble reaching Ciudad Real in time for the corrida. Mario had chauffeured the Hemingways on a previous visit to Spain. Ernest had introduced him as a racing driver and an aspiring television director. He came from Udine, which boasted the highest per capita ownership of Lancias, Ernest said, so we would be in good hands. Although the mano-a-mano in Bayonne was not spectacular, it proved a little more definitively that Antonio had the edge over his brother-in-law. Luis Miguel had lost some of the confidence and panache shown in Málaga. We were all on edge to see what this next spectacle would bring. As it happened, a new player was to enter the ring, and no one was more surprised than our companion, Hotch.

While Antonio had been at La Consula for a few days before the August 14 corrida, Hotch decided to show him how to play baseball using young Teo Davis's bat and glove. The matador took to the sport immediately. He showed such aptitude and enjoyed it so much that he jokingly said he should show Hotch how to be a torero in exchange. Ernest, fascinated by the idea and a man who loved playing games and acting out fantasies, immediately volunteered to be Hotch's manager.

"How are your reflexes?" Antonio asked Hotch.

Ernest, now Hotch's manager, replied that they were excellent. To prove it, he threw wineglasses and cutlery across the table at Hotch, who responded with suprising agility.

The plot did not end there.

"How about El Pecas being the *sobresaliente* at the mano-a-mano in Ciudad Real?" Antonio suggested.

Imagining it was all in jest, Hotch agreed. He was game for anything. Certainly he could train and be ready to face the crowd in six days. Never mind that if he was caught breaking the strict rules governing bullfighting, he could end up in prison for twelve months, as a predecessor had done. It is amazing what bravado a few glasses of wine can produce. The joke continued. Antonio instructed his pupil. His manager, in charge of translating and advising on bullring etiquette, never left his side. It was all *muy serio,* and everyone was caught up in the tomfoolery. Maybe not all; Mary was skeptical of Ernest's judgment. She was tired of bullfights, of the constant merriment, of the heavy drinking, of the ever-present hangers-on, and of Spain in general. She had had enough. *¡Basta!*

On the other hand, I was duly amused and not in the least confounded. My whimsical Irish upbringing allowed for plenty of codology—a form of verbal nonsense the Irish love to engage in—which I took these antics to be. Codology was rarely acted out. In fact, it was a verbal sport not intended to be acted out.

Antonio's superiority over Luis Miguel in the ring was so firmly established after the fourth fight that the competition was beginning to lack luster. The chief unknown was the possibility of a *cornada*—not likely in Bayonne, where the bulls were smaller and their horns undoubtedly shaved. A little excitement was in order. When we arrived in Ciudad Real before the fight, we found on the cartel, under Antonio and Luis Miguel's names, "El Pecas, sobresaliente." Could it still be a joke? Hotch was assigned a sword handler and led upstairs to Antonio's room. His handler started to assist his dressing in a *traje de luces* that was laid out for him in Antonio's dressing room. The two "matadors" dressed side by side. Hotch was tentative, unsure of what would happen next. I think that until the moment he headed into the ring with the cuadrilla all dolled up in his torero duds he did not believe it. This was his moment of truth. He fit into Antonio's shoes and suit so snugly that nobody questioned his legitimacy as a bullfighter as he walked into the ring in the opening procession. Only Luis Miguel noticed he was missing the pigtail. El Pecas behaved impeccably. Luckily for him, after the opening procession his services were not called upon again.

Bilbao was the next stop. Mario displayed his driving skills when we left Madrid late. It was clear that he enjoyed showing off for Ernest. He stepped on the gas and did not pause until we reached Burgos, where we ate at an old tavern that served wonderful trout and partridges. It was Ernest's favorite, and we would go back there on several occasions. This time he wanted to show it off to Mario. *La Barata,* the cheap one, Ernest had named the Lancia, as it was his custom to label all kinds of things. He was never comfortable with his wealth and felt he must joke about it to show he did not take it seriously. "I wonder what the poor folk are eating tonight," he liked to say when we were having a particularly splendid meal.

We stayed at the fashionable Carlton Hotel in Bilbao, a town noted for its serious attitude toward the corrida. There was no chance that the bulls would be anything but the best: big and sturdy, with good horns. There would be no chicanery in the ring or out of it. No chance of El Pecas appearing in the paseo. Ernest was a little chagrined when Antonio told him he would not be allowed to watch the show from the *barrera*, where he was now accustomed to standing in his capacity as honorary cuadrilla member. He would have to observe from the stands like everyone else. Antonio liked Bilbao, so Ernest did not hold the stuffy, bourgeois, bureaucratic atmosphere against the town. Antonio had influential and rich friends there, and what suited Antonio was acceptable to Ernest.

As we had come to expect, Antonio was brilliant on the first day. He absolutely enchanted the audience and came away with two ears from each of his bulls. Next day it was Luis Miguel's turn, still favoring his leg from his goring in Valencia. Again he was having trouble killing. The fourth day the fifth mano-a-mano was scheduled. Antonio was set for a slaughter. He wanted it definitively known that *he*, not Luis Miguel, was *el número uno*, the best matador in the world. And he wanted the money that went with the title and the glory. He was tired of outperforming his brother-in-law yet receiving a lesser fee. He felt confident in this town, more so because he knew he had the edge over Luis Miguel artistically and physically. He was determined that this feria would settle the matter once and for all.

On the third day Antonio fought, one could tell that his social life and the fierce travel schedule he had maintained for the last eight days were taking their toll. His performance was mediocre. For the fourth corrida both matadors were on the cartel with Jaime Ostos, who was from Córdoba and, as Ernest liked to say, "as brave as the wild boar of the Sierras of his country." We all liked Jaime and loved to watch his bravery, which sometimes appeared to border on the suicidal. Doña Carmen Polo de Franco, the caudillo's wife, sat in the presidential box. I had met her briefly in Madrid some months before. The three matadors paid their respects to her. Right afterward Luis Miguel faced his second bull—black, bigger than his first, with good horns. He was well in control, working his passes with the bull following the cape. The picador came along to do his job. Luis Miguel took the bull to the center and performed four slow veronicas, then brought the bull back again to the picador—a simple maneuver, but one that somehow went wrong. The bull, without warning, charged the horse. Luis Miguel was caught in the middle, with a horn deep in his thigh. Antonio and Jaime both closed in with their capes, steering the bull away from the injured matador. It was Antonio's job, as the next most senior matador, to work the bull and quickly put him to death. But Antonio, recognizing the bull as a champion, took his time, savoring every pass, coming closer and closer, surpassing every performance of the week with skill and grace until finally making a quick, clean kill.

He then tackled his own beast, the biggest bull of the afternoon, which looked dazed and dangerous. Antonio was soon wafting his magic, which meant he made fighting the most difficult bull look easy. He summed up his opponent's defects and set about correcting them, tailoring his movements to make the defects appear nonexistent. With this bull, Antonio was going to show his friends that he was the greatest, and when he was finished, he set up the kill in the most dangerous manner there is, *recibiendo.* Forcing the bull to charge the muleta, he thrust his sword deep as the massive, raging animal hurtled toward him. Normally the matador executes the kill when the bull is both groggy and fairly stationary. On this day in Bilbao, Antonio Ordóñez provoked the bull into charging the sword not once but three times. It was an unheard-of feat, one that would go down in the annals of bullfighting. The duel between Luis Miguel and Antonio was over. No one disputed that Antonio was the new champion. Luis Miguel's physical wound was not mortal, but his pride suffered. Moreover, his career for the season had ended.

From Bilbao, we continued on the quest, driving the relatively short distance to St.-Jean-de-Luz, in southwest France, and spending the night at the beautiful old Chantaco Hotel outside of town. Antonio was sched-uled to fight at nearby Dax the next day, an event that proved disappoint-ing after the great excitement of Bilbao. A chapter in our summer then closed with the absence of Luis Miguel and Hotch's impending departure. After the Dax bullfight, Bill drove Hotch to Biarritz, where El Pecas boarded the *rapide* for Paris and then went on to New York by air. Anto-nio was in the San Sebastian hospital. To complete the anticlimax, a bull had stepped on his foot during an unspectacular fight.

Bill, Ernest, and I spent another night at the Chantaco and left early the next morning for the long drive to Madrid. We stopped for breakfast with some newly acquired aficionado friends, the Pardos, at their hilltop house outside Hendaye, close to the Spanish border. Before we left, they surprised us with a gift: an authentic shrunken head. It was a fine specimen. Ernest ap-peared indifferent, but Bill's eyes lit up. Noting Bill's enthusiasm, Ernest agreed to our taking her, dubbing the luckless woman Lady Luck. "She'll be our mascot," Bill chuckled as he tucked her into the trunk of the car.

We passed the border at Irún and coasted through the Pyrenees, then hit the long, straight, dusty road. Midmorning, we stopped in Vitoria to find ice for the ice bag and to buy some of the local red wine, Las Campanas *clarete*. We picked up the morning newspaper and some bread, manchego cheese, and apples. Bill took out the map. Three hundred and ten miles to Madrid.

Ernest suggested that we stop for lunch at our favorite tavern in Burgos.

"All passengers aboard," commanded Bill, the driver. Ernest said that all passengers were accounted for, "even your girl"—a reference to our grue-some companion.

Bill was in a jocular mood. "She's our mascot, remember? Let's take her out of the damn hatbox." With unconcealed glee, he unwrapped the curi-ous object and propped her up on the back window ledge. We settled our-selves comfortably in the front seat with the ice bag at our feet and set off once more along the straight, flat road. Every now and then Ernest took a swig from the chilled bottle of vino and passed it to Bill and to me before setting it back on the melting ice cubes.

Lunch was exactly what we had hoped for. We set out once again, sated and quieter now. Bill was a determined driver, always hating to rest. We forged ahead. The glaring sun and the wine were beginning to have an effect. I found it hard to keep my eyes open, and when I glanced sideways at Ernest, his eyes were closing too. Bill was awake and intent upon the road. The countryside was flat and monotonous, parched after the dry summer. The sky was white, the sun a huge silvery disk. Its effect was hypnotic. *Sueño,* it seemed to say, *sueño.* There were no signs of life. The only movement was swirling dust. No animals, no peasants tending their fields, no cars in front or behind. I must have dozed off completely.

Suddenly I was thrown to the windshield. The car lunged forward. Bill clutched the steering wheel and pressed his foot hard on the pedal. We jostled to one side as the brakes screeched. Having missed the curve, the car rolled down a short, rocky incline at the road's edge, its front tire bursting as we hit a concrete road guard. With an abrupt jerk, a grinding noise, and a thud we came to a standstill in a shallow ditch. All three of us were abruptly awake, slightly dazed but unhurt, but our beautiful new Lancia, *La Barata,* was an unpretty sight, its hood badly damaged and its engine injured.

I heard myself saying, "My God, what's happening?"

It took a few seconds for my eyes to focus. We were not alone. The apparent solitude of some minutes before no longer existed. We were surrounded by peasants. Hardy, inquisitive Castellanos seemed to have appeared from nowhere. They looked on with curiosity and awe at the plight of three foolish foreigners and their luxurious vehicle. We did not move but stayed seated in the car, assessing the situation.

"I must have fallen asleep," muttered an embarrassed, incredulous, apologetic Bill.

Ernest said that we should get out of the damn box. Then he turned to me and, in a gentler voice, asked if I was all right.

I nodded. With difficulty, we extricated ourselves from the lopsided vehicle.

There was quite a crowd around us now: twenty men, women, and children, maybe more. We shook ourselves and bent our arms and legs to make sure every limb was still in working order. The people were still there, but they were not paying attention to us. Instead, they were gaping at the car, peering in and pointing excitedly with their fingers.

Still unhappy from the rude awakening, Ernest wanted to know what the hell was the matter with them. What the devil could they be gawking at? My eyes followed the gestures of the excited peasants to the backseat.

"It's that mascot of yours, Bill," I said.

"Jesus!" Ernest exclaimed as he pushed his way through the crowd and forced the back door open. He grabbed the shrunken head.

"*Señoras y señores,*" he said, bowing to the crowd with a grimace on his face.

I thought he had taken leave of his senses. It flashed through my mind that he was about to give our girl one swift kick out into the field beyond. Instead, he held her up, grimacing at the wide-eyed, utterly mystified, uncomprehending peasants and said: "I give you *la puta,* Lady Luck."

He then tucked her securely back in the hatbox in the Lancia's trunk. He said we'd had quite enough luck for one day and asked Bill what he thought. Our driver smiled wanly. He had no stomach left for humor.

We got a ride to the nearest town, Aranda de Duero, where we were fixed up with a temporary car to take us to Madrid. Bill arranged for the repair of the Lancia. As it would take some time, we were booked on the next day's flight from Madrid to Málaga, reengaging the Pembroke Coral for the interim. Before the newspapers could get hold of the story and exaggerate it beyond recognition, we cabled Mary and Annie at La Consula to say that, in spite of mishap, we were safe and would return on the morrow. And for good measure we cabled Hotch in Paris, just in case there was an item in the French press.

Antonio's next fight was in Linares. It was there, I learned, that in August 1947 the torero Manolete was gored and later died as a result of inadequate medical attention after the *cornada.* The young Luis Miguel Dominguín was on the same cartel and had witnessed the goring. We planned to spend the night in nearby Córdoba at a luxury hotel, but when we got there they could provide only a suite for the Hemingways and a double for the Davises. When we learned that there was no room for me, for a sweet moment I imagined I might find my own quarters and a respite from the constant companionship. Ernest solved the problem promptly, putting an end to my hopes. I could sleep in the sitting room of his and Mary's suite. It was a hot, sticky night. The open windows only accentuated my discomfort and my longing to be outside. I had visited Córdoba in 1956, and pleasant memories of that visit lingered. There was a gaiety in the air. The blaring and thumping of music outside, the buzz in the streets, and laughter of the citizens on their paseo beckoned to me. The fun was just beginning, but I felt confined within the four walls like a caged pet.

In general, Mary gave me a wide berth. When our paths crossed, she was always polite and solicitous, charming to the edge of sarcasm when inquiring after my welfare and comfort. I kept up a distant but polite front. I could tell that her patience was at an end with the traveling and the drinking and the undue adulation her husband was receiving, while she was barely acknowledged. For me it was just a summer job. I admired her spunk, her independence, and her outspokenness—a quality I lacked. Clearly there was tension between the couple, but also an understanding and caring that come with years of living together. Couples learn to roll with the waves as well as create waves when the sea is smooth. The Hemingways knew how to spar, but that night the marital waters were calm. It was I who was agitated. A twinge of pain shot through my jaw. I was not imagining it. I reached for the vodka bottle. I was still a rebel vodka drinker, reverting to the communist libation of my Dublin days. I drank. The heat, the noise, and the pain persisted, the first intimation of a decaying tooth. I lulled myself into an uneasy vodka-induced sleep.

Next morning, with no tooth pain and only a slight headache to remind me, I put aside my woes and entered into the enthusiasm Ernest brought to the breakfast table. He was keen to show me Córdoba, a city that stands on the right bank of the Guadalquivir where the ranches and farmlands of the Sierra de Córdoba plateau to the north meet the wheatlands and olive groves of the Campiña plains. As we left town, winding our way southward, I caught my first glimpse of cotton fields, known to me only from American folk songs. Next we passed families camping in massive melon patches to protect their produce from marauding thieves. We drove past vineyards with white grapes ripening in the hot sun, and finally reached familiar territory, olive country, the arid hilly Andalucia now so familiar. We had traversed it half a dozen times already this summer.

Back at La Consula for another few days before taking off again, I awakened one morning with a raging toothache. I hoped it was a temporary aberration, like the twinge in Córdoba, but the pain persisted. This was the real thing. I chided myself for waiting so long before making an appointment with the local dentist. I was in for quite a surprise. What a contrast I found to the smart Merrion Square office of Dr. Phillips, where my mother had taken us for our annual checkup. There everything was sterile and fresh-smelling, as the doctor peered though his rimless glasses with magnifiers attached, wearing a serious but kindly expression. In Málaga I ascended the concrete stairs to a stuffy, dingy, overcrowded waiting room, garlic breath and fear pervading the air. "Next, next," were the words most frequently uttered by the receptionist. When my turn came, I was thrust forward into the cubicle where the doctor harshly prodded inside my mouth, soon locating the offending tooth and finding two other cavities for good measure. He drilled, swabbed with disinfectant, and stuffed a wad of cotton in each cavity. "See you in a week," he said curtly. "Next."

A week! We were to leave in a couple of days for the next round of bullfights starring Antonio, the first at Logroño the next Monday. I had a bad dose of bull fever, at last understanding and enjoying the fights. I was really hooked, ready for the next bloodbath, poised to cheer on the winner and sympathize with the loser. I hated to miss the fun. Yet how could I undertake the journey, six days on the road, with nothing but a cotton ball between my nerves and total exposure?

Ernest settled the matter for me. When I told him of my dilemma, he insisted that I stay and have my teeth fixed.

There was a knock on my door the night before they left. Ernest had some reading he wanted me to do while they were away. He brought me a copy of his short stories and the pages of the new introduction he had written for them. He also had copies of *Ruedo,* the bullfight magazine, and paperbacks of Gerald Brenan's *South from Granada* and *The Spanish Labyrinth.*

La Consula was situated just outside the village of Churriana. The same year the Davises moved there, Gerald and Gamel Brenan had settled in the village in a large, rambling house with a walled garden and a retinue of servants. Cyril Connolly had introduced the two couples, who soon became friends. When Ernest and Mary arrived in Málaga, Ernest asked to meet Gerald, whose writing he admired. The Brenans came to lunch. The English writer—who had been a prominent participant in the Bloomsbury literary circle of the twenties and who had fallen in love with the painter Carrington—was now infatuated with the local beatnik generation, with their habits and especially their language, which he had learned. He was fascinated by the young dropouts, many of them English, who had settled in nearby Torremolinos. Andalucia, with its warm climate, was an inexpensive place to live in 1959. Mary was unacquainted with the genre and bored with Gerald's prattle. She did not come when Bill, Ernest, and I accepted a return luncheon invitation with the Brenans in Churriana.

I had been brought up on the antics of the Bloomsbury crowd, and meeting Brenan was a great thrill, although I tried not to show it. Instead, I listened to the two writers talk. There was an uneasiness between them. You could hardly imagine a more disparate pair. Gerald knew and cared little about bullfighting. He tried to steer the conversation toward literature and, failing that, the Spanish Civil War. Ernest preferred to talk about the corridas, physical prowess, and bravery. He disclaimed any interest in the ideologies of the left. It was the mechanics of war that really interested him and had drawn him to the conflict in Spain. I often thought in the hours I spent listening to him that he liked to make statements more for effect than for accuracy. He didn't say what he really thought. In conversation with literary figures or people he was not well acquainted with, he was a provocateur. He told the Brenans that the contemporary American writers he most admired were J. D. Salinger, Carson McCullers, and Truman Capote. When we were next in Madrid he bought me a copy of *The Catcher in the Rye.*

Gamel was a beautiful woman but already frail at fifty-nine. A published novelist, she had aspirations as a poet and longed to see her poetry in print. She was preparing a volume to send to T. S. Eliot at Faber. Their house was pleasantly shabby, bookish, and lived-in, with the garden overgrown, a wild, unruly Arcadia. I could have moved right in with the Brenans.

That August night, as he was about to leave the room, Ernest turned shyly to me and said he would miss me. He had something to hold my luck while they were gone. He handed me a furry rabbit's foot pendant with gold stem and loop. I must have blushed, partly with pleasure and partly with shame. It had not occurred to me that my absence would be noticed. I, on the other hand, having accepted that I would miss the next round of corridas, had been savoring the prospect of freedom and being alone. I held the little fetish tight, its light brown fur soft on my palm, and wished luck for them on the journey and for myself and for all those who most needed it. It was the first gift that Ernest gave me—if you didn't count a lucky pebble he had once picked up on the seashore and handed to me, saying that you never know when your luck will run out. He had told me he always hedged his bets by keeping a lucky stone close to him. To prove it, he had reached into his pocket and pulled out a handful of objects: a grubby white linen handkerchief, a rusting penknife, a piece of string, an old chestnut, and a smooth, flat black pebble that looked as if it could hop seven times as it skimmed across a watery surface. Then he had stuffed these treasures back into his trousers. That was in Valencia. Now he whispered that I should take care. The door closed behind him.

Many months later, when I transcribed the chapters of *A Moveable Feast* in the little house at the Finca Vigía, I found myself typing these words: "For luck you carried a horse chestnut and a rabbit's foot in your right pocket. The fur had been worn off the rabbit's foot long ago and the bones and the sinews were polished by wear. The claws scratched in the lining of your pocket and you knew your luck was still there."

After they left I felt a sense of relief. My yearning for the bullfights ebbed as I realized I could do with a rest from the tension and excitement. I had not had a moment of introspection since I boarded the train for Pamplona two months before. I could do with a night devoid of mandatory drinking until the wee hours, listening to stories that were already overly familiar—tales of Spain during the civil war, of the antics in the Florida Hotel in Madrid, and of the superiority of Ernest's third wife, Martha Gellhorn. Consort of generals, his ex-wife had fallen from grace because *she* had left *him;* her personality was the butt of venom and parody. Ernest could not let go of a slight or grudge, and his failed marriage to Martha never stopped eating at his guts. I was beginning to learn that Ernest stayed up as late as he could because he suffered from fearful insomnia. The only chance of keeping the demons away was to avoid darkness and solitude. But as he drank, he also became morose, inviting the demons to taunt him.

From Logroño they went to Madrid, Cuenca, Murcia, and Alicante. While they were in Murcia the wind blew and made the corrida close to unbearable to watch. As if to prove Ernest's point that this was a land of thieves, his wallet was stolen. It had nine thousand pesetas in it, which amounted to $150. It was not losing the money that disturbed him as much as the loss of the wallet, a gift from his son Patrick. He posted a notice in the local paper, appealing to the thief to return the wallet with its image of St. Christopher in it. St. Christopher is the patron saint of travelers and, as with pebbles and rabbits' feet, it was his wont to tote all the protection he could. "As for the 9000 pesetas it contained, your skill deserves that prize as a reward," the notice said. The wallet was not returned.

Teeth fortified, I joined them again in time for the trip to Ronda, a town I had heard much about because it was Antonio's birthplace. It was every bit as enchanting as described, and the aficionados had the tense energy of a crowd well disposed toward their favorite son. The corrida and Antonio's performance were among the season's best. Ronda is considered the cradle of bullfighting. Its bullring was built in 1785, one of Spain's oldest. Three successive Romeros were native sons: Francisco, born in 1698, who laid down the rules of bullfighting; his son Juan, who introduced the cuadrilla; and his grandson Pedro, who became one of Spain's greatest bullfighters. Pedro founded the Ronda School, still known for its classicism, a strict observance of the rules and the most difficult feat of all, *estocada a recibir.* Antonio Ordóñez had demonstrated all summer that he was a true son of

Ronda, and on this day, his hometown showed how proud it was of him. He was awarded four ears and two tails.

We rolled off again early next morning for Sevilla, then to Mérida and north to Béjar, directly west of Madrid. At Salamanca we found a message waiting from Carmen. Antonio had been jailed in Albacete for some minor infraction of the bullfighting rules. He was released by midday and given a police escort to the border of the province of Albacete, which was now stricken from our list of places to visit. We spent the next two days in Madrid and then returned to La Consula.

A letter from the author Juan Goytísolo awaited me there. It was post-marked Barcelona, where his family lived. He was planning to return to Almería with his friend Vicente, a photographer, and would be in Málaga on the twenty-third or twenty-fourth of September. Could I get away for a couple of days to join them on a trip to Ronda or Cadíz? Juan was twenty-eight, the same age as Antonio, but I found him much easier to converse with. We had similar feelings about the politics of our native lands. Juan's first novel, *Juegos de Manos* (The Young Assassins), had come out in 1954, but just this year it had been translated by M. E. Coindreau into French and published by Gallimard, Ernest's publisher, where Juan was busy bringing Gallimard's Spanish department up to date. In France he was hailed as "an elder, the front-rank man in the new literary generation." Now considered Spain's greatest living writer, he has long disclaimed his early novels as of no value. Still, I had procured a copy of *The Young Assassins* and read it avidly.

I was excited at the prospect of getting away for a couple of days and being with people closer to my own age and interests. I expected Ernest would feel the same way when I showed him the letter. He read it silently, expressionless. Then his face clouded over, and softly he told me that if I wanted to go, I must do so. I should disregard the fact completely that he needed my help right then. To get back to writing and handle his correspondence without my help would be not only inconvenient for him but a downright hardship. Without my being aware of it, it seemed, I had become indispensible. Of course, if I really wanted to go, he would manage without me.

I saw how it was. I had been working a little more than two months, and less than six weeks remained until the Hemingways returned to their home in Cuba. I had taken a week off to have my teeth attended to. It was a part-time job. I would probably never have such an opportunity again. Although I felt Ernest was being unreasonable, and that irked me, I was slightly bemused that he did not want me to leave. I would have the rest of my life free, I reasoned, to do exactly as I pleased and see whomever I wished. So I said cheerfully: "I'll write Juan and tell him I can't get away right now, we're busy with the bullfight stuff. I can see him another time."

Ernest asked if I was sure that was what I wanted to do.

"Quite sure," I lied. And there was peace in Eden.

About this time Ernest announced that he had invited Antonio and Carmen to visit Cuba and then to travel with the Hemingways to Sun Valley in time for the hunting season. Mary's reaction was to plan an early return on October 4 so that she would have a month to prepare the *finca* for their visit. I think she welcomed the excuse to get away after a summer that had increasingly become a nightmare for her. Ernest seemed oblivious to her needs. Having had no prior experience of the couple, I assumed their behavior was status quo. Many couples I knew existed between alternating states of war and amnesty. From what I had observed in Irish marriages, a wife's wishes were rarely taken into consideration.

I minded my own business, absorbing everything I could: the literary chatter and gossip, the art of bullfighting, the tragic history of Spain, the intensity of wars as experienced by Ernest, and his views on courage and cowardice, on friends and enemies, and how each should be treated. I laughed at the jokes, which were fresh to my ears, and practiced being a sympathetic and interested listener, ever present and attentive no matter how long the day. When required to, I was able to provide the necessary information or right response. There were moments when I wanted to escape, when I felt I needed a respite from the constant frenzy. Sometimes I longed to be with young people of my own choosing or craved solitude. In spite of those moments I couldn't imagine anyone having a better time than I did that summer.

On one of our trips—perhaps the first one from Madrid to Málaga—the talk was mostly about writers. Ernest spoke of Evan Shipman, a keen man for the horses who had once tutored Hemingway's son Bumby. There was talk also of the *New Yorker* writers, Dorothy Parker, John O'Hara, Lillian Ross, and E. B. White. Ernest admired Parker's wit, O'Hara's short stories, Ross's reporting, and White's finely honed essays. Scribner's always sent along copies of their young authors' books to the *finca*. Ernest was an avid and a prolific reader, going through about three books each week and re-membering what he read. He was never hesitant in his opinions, always forthright, often praising younger, more inexperienced writers and being harsher on his contemporaries. There was banter about Mr. Tolstoy, Mr. Dostoyevsky, and occasionally, perhaps for my benefit, Jimmy Joyce, his old pal. I racked my brains to contribute to the conversation. I had read none of these American writers. Although I knew Joyce, my knowledge of Russian literature was almost nil. Ernest bought me a copy of *War and Peace* when we were next in Madrid. Then it occurred to me that I did know an Amer-ican writer, who by all accounts was a famous one. Also he had been a com-munist, so I thought I might gain a point or two by mentioning him.

"I've only met one American writer," I piped up when there was a mo-mentary lull. "That is Max Eastman."

There was a definite silence—disinterest, I thought—so I decided to elaborate a little.

"He and his Russian wife, Eliena, were good friends of my family and stayed with us one summer." I had never discussed my family, so there seemed no point in saying it was at Summerhill Hotel and they were guests there when I was fourteen years old. They were indeed friends of the Dunnes. I remember so well Max with his shock of white curly hair, tall, bulky stature, and affable disposition. And Eliena, an accomplished artist, had left us a watercolor of the Sugarloaf Mountain to remember her by. They had rented a Volkswagen Beetle and looked a strange pair in the little Bug, petite Eliena and large, lumbering Max. If they passed my brother Peter and me on the road, they always stopped to offer us a ride. It had been fun to climb into the backseat and answer Max's questions about the idiosyncrasies of the Irish. Perhaps he felt he would get the true perspective from a couple of kids. Ciss's sister, Nan, and Max had a particular bond. A civil servant, she was a fiery union member with socialist leanings who had achieved much for the equal employment rights of Irish women.

Even our animals had loved the Eastmans. I remember that Eliena and Max were in number eight, with a bay window overlooking the garden. At breakfast time one morning, I noticed little Cuala, the cairn terrier, patiently sitting on the gravel beneath the window, looking upward. *Strange,* I thought. Then bits of toast and bacon came flying out the window as the terrier jumped on her hind legs to catch her treats.

To Peter and myself, the Eastmans were the best of fun, and it was a sad day when they had to leave. It did not occur to me to buy and read one of Max's books. His being a writer was entirely incidental. Less than two years later, Max wrote us that Eliena had died of cancer.

I now tried to convey some of my delight with Eastman to my travelling companions. The silence was deafening. Ernest said nothing. Bill muttered something about the weather or the crops as if he had not heard anything I said. When we next stopped, Bill took me aside.

"I thought your days with the cuadrilla had ended," he said. "You've just had a lucky escape. I imagined we'd be leaving you by the roadside to fend for yourself. Max and Ernest knew each other, all right, but they are no longer friends, and that's an understatement."

It was a while before I learned of a past incident at the Scribner's office when the two writers had come to fisticuffs. There could hardly have been two more dissimilar people than Max and Ernest. By his own account, Max, the son of Congregationalist preachers, was a timid, cowardly child. He had not spent his childhood hunting and fishing. His chief interests were writing and, early on, socialism. In his twenties, he became editor of *The Masses,* an unpaid job that he relished and that he used as a forum for his pacifist leanings. He was vehemently against America joining in the First World War and stood trial twice for his beliefs. Ernest could not wait to join the forces, and to that end, he falsified his age by adding one year, hoping he would be eligible for service. Ernest had not made it into the army, but had served as a Red Cross ambulance driver instead. Max neither understood nor cared to know about such things as bullfighting, and it was a remark in his review of *Death in the Afternoon* (in the June 7, 1933, issue of the *New Republic*) that caused the fracas, published under the damning title of "Bull in the Afternoon." While Max did not feel he was attacking Ernest personally, the latter read between the lines and sensed that his manhood was being questioned. At Scribner's, a furious Ernest was determined to prove he had hair on his chest. I was in touch with Max when I arrived in New York in 1960. He replied with a friendly letter hoping that I would come and visit him. I felt I should let him know that I was working for Ernest at the time, so I wrote telling him so. After that I did not hear from Max again for some years. Ernest, on the other hand, never mentioned Max, nor held my good opinion and fond memories of Eastman against me.

In Logroño, our merry band passed a Gypsy encampment. Ernest had a fondness for Gypsies, which I shared. I had read my countryman Walter Starkie's books about Spain and viewed Gypsies in a romantic vein. I had been to the caves in Granada with my uncle three years before and witnessed them dancing flamenco. I was mesmerized by the haunting music, the wailing and stamping of feet, and the solemn faces, especially of the women. An English folk song we sang as children was "The Raggle-Taggle Gypsies O."

Three Gypsies stood at the castle gate
They sang so high, they sang so low,
The lady sat in her chamber late
As she listened to the raggle-taggle Gypsies O.

Starkie noted that the Gypsies he met were unanimous in their praise of Logroño as the most charitable and hospitable city in all Spain. I told Ernest that Irish Gypsies were called tinkers, and every year we expected them to turn up in their colorful caravan pulled by sturdy ponies and followed by a couple of donkeys and shifty mongrels. We brought out our pots and pans. There was no one like them for repairing all kinds of tinware. "Lock the doors, the tinkers are here," old Mazy Dunne would hiss as the snotty-nosed children in their rags gaped wide-eyed through the kitchen window.

Now, as we talked of Gypsies, Ernest asked me if anyone had ever read my palm. No, I replied. I have always had a fatalistic view of life: what happens will happen, *que será será*. I'd rather not know until I must. He said he was an expert at reading hands. A Gypsy woman he knew had shown him how. He took my hand in his and held it firmly with my palm turned upward. He moved it back and forth slightly to follow the lines and held it high so he could see them better. Then he let it go without a word.

"What do you see?" I asked jovially. "A long life, riches, romance, children?"

When he didn't reply, I noticed tears in his eyes. He said he couldn't tell me. No, he wouldn't tell me. He was pensive, aloof, and overcome with emotion. I was uneasy, quite disturbed. Had he seen an early death, perhaps a violent one? In the months ahead, whenever I looked back on this scene it made me feel reckless, this new unknown. I must live life to the fullest, for my days could be numbered.

CHAPTER SIX

Provence and Paris: Life as a Moveable Feast

*T*OWARD THE END OF September we visited Provence. Ernest was excited to show me some places where he had spent time as a young man. We would travel throughout the south of France, to Nîmes, Arles, Le Grau-du-Roi and Aigues-Mortes, and then drive up through the Loire Valley to Paris to see Mary off. She had decided to first stop in Madrid to shop and then later take the train to Paris and meet us at the Ritz. She was truly through with bullfighting and was intent upon returning home to Cuba to prepare for Antonio and Carmen's visit.

We drove up the full length of Spain, stopping in Madrid for the night. Ernest had the manuscript of *The Garden of Eden* with him, intending to do some revisions and to make a decision about the ending he had in mind. We had become familiar with the roads, winding and twisting; wretched trucks held together with string and wire, emitting foul black smoke, chugging up the hills; the flat plains scorched by the sun, the vineyards now ready to yield their fruit. We stayed, as always, at the Suecia, and I had a brief chance to check in with my friends. Ernest had given me an elk's tooth as a gift upon his return to Málaga when I had my teeth fixed. Now I had a pendant made of it, with a gold fitting to match the rabbit's foot so I could wear it on a chain. Thinking Ernest would be pleased at the distinction I had paid his token, I was surprised by his negative reaction. He did not like his gift being tampered with; he felt altering it a betrayal. The tooth was a good-luck omen like a chestnut or a pebble, to be kept near at hand but out of sight.

The contrast between France and Spain was sharp. At the first town we stopped in on the other side of the border, Ernest was recognized as some-one famous. "Mr. Steinbeck, you're my favorite author. I've read your book *From Here to Eternity* at least twice" was the chirpy greeting of a fortyish American. Ernest accepted such nonsense with good humor, nodded, and walked on. At least the fan had *everything* ass backward, not just his identity. But many more people recognized him for who he was, and this pleased him immensely. The first objective of our trip was to see Ordóñez fight in the am-phitheater, the famous bullring in Nîmes built by the Romans in the middle of the first century and capable of holding twenty-one thousand spectators. A number of aficionados we had encountered along the bullfight circuit and who had now become Ernest's friends were also sure to attend. After our discussion about Juan's visit to Málaga, Ernest sent Monique Lange enough money so that she, Juan, and Flo Malraux could join us in Nîmes, where we planned to stay at the Hotel Imperator. There our friends met us and Ernest held court late into the night in the beautiful garden restaurant. The ambi-ence and the company provided a jolly finale to the corrida season. As soon as our little group dispersed that first night, Ernest handed me a package and asked me to read it and let him know what I thought.

When I opened the manila envelope what I found inside was an almost completed version of *The Garden of Eden*. I read page after page of the ex-traordinary doings of Catherine and David Bourne, none of which made the slightest bit of sense to me. A heap of codology, I could hear Ned Dunne say-ing if I had tried to explain the book to him. I read it through. I could not claim to have met people like them nor to understand what they were after or why. Certainly it was entertaining, if repetitive, sometimes to the point of te-dium. However, I needed to evaluate what I had read in order to give some opinion in the morning. What did I really think of it? I was irritated at how the story drifted along. Catherine was blamed for all the mischief, while in-nocent David was just a passive participant. I wanted to give him a kick and say, "Wake up! Do something or let me escape from this grim fairy tale." What a strange trinity they turned out to be. Catherine as the wicked stepmother and her two daughters rolled into one; Marita, the quintessential Cinderella, pleasant and pleasing to everyone; and David, Prince Charming incarnate.

Ernest wanted to visit Aigues-Mortes and Le Grau-du-Roi, to drive through the country, rekindle memories, savor the ambience, sharpen his characters, and seal their fates. As I worked for him over the next year I was to learn just how close the character of David Bourne was to his creator. I can say from observation that Ernest lived for his writing. Writing was the core of his existence, and when his writing ability finally faltered, he saw no reason to continue. I did not realize it the first time I read the book, but it became apparent to me over subsequent months that David Bourne *was* Ernest Hemingway. Like David, every morning Ernest got out of bed, sharpened those pencils, took out his copybooks, and wrote and wrote; happy, tired, hung over, ebullient, depressed, whatever his mood, it was cast off, discarded. As the creative juices began to flow, he entered another world, and if we were lucky and his words were good enough, he left them for us to enjoy forever. When I say pencils and copybooks, it could also have been pen and foolscap, or the hesitant typeface of his Royal typewriter. The bottom line was that he wrote. It was sacred, it was fulfilling, and it was an act of hope. Once when we were driving through Alicante we stopped to buy a melon from a vendor at the side of the road. A couple of impish ruffians came over with ingratiating smiles and their hands out, begging for a few pesetas. Ernest took a ballpoint pen and a sheet of paper and handed it to the smaller one, who had black dancing eyes and a shaved head. "Take this, maestro," he said. "With it you can make your own fortune." I can still see the befuddled look on their faces. They were too surprised to beg again. They stared at us in puzzlement as if they had been visited by extraterrestrials.

Catherine, I realized even then, was a composite of several people. Zelda Fitzgerald came to mind. I had already heard Ernest speak with anger at her jealousy over Scott's writing, and how he despised Scott's weakness in allowing it. Catherine also had some of the elements of Ernest's second wife, Pauline. She too had been an heiress, and her money freed the writer to live a more extravagant and carefree life, to enjoy the champagne and caviar in his own home, not at the table of the fawning rich. Ernest had told me of Pauline's experiment with dyeing her hair blond in 1929, both as a declaration of sexual freedom and as a birthday surprise for him. Catherine was also reminiscent of Hadley, Ernest's first wife, who once lost her husband's precious stories. The loss of the writer's work through his wife's actions was an experience Hemingway would never forget and probably never forgave. Already in the few months I had known him, I had heard the story of Hadley's effort to please him by bringing his writings, both originals and carbons, to Lausanne. In a careless moment she had left a briefcase unattended and it was stolen from the train. No copies remained to show for the many months, if not years, of arduous writing.

Hadley was devastated, but Ernest was even more so. It was a situation akin to when a couple loses a child; there is sometimes a pervasive, unspoken rebuke that eventually undermines and erodes a marriage. The character Catherine's action in burning the writer's stories and clippings is deliberate, but still it is parallel to Hadley's mishap because its outcome was the same. In real life it was worse because the lost stories were never reconstructed. Unlike Ernest, his character was able to restrain his temper and to write even better than before. But in real life Ernest saw it differently: once the story was written and lost, there would be no second chance. Only some of these thoughts came to me at that first reading.

Whatever I said to Ernest the next day about his book, he took it in good humor. Back then, I was not aware of the magnitude of his success and his appeal to readers worldwide. I didn't have the built-in reverence his name evoked for young and old alike. I did not worship at the Hemingway shrine. I think Ernest found this refreshing. He enjoyed watching my reaction to reading his work for the first time. That day as we drove along the narrow Provençal roads he sought out a suitable spot to stage a fatal car crash. I can remember my surprise at watching the novelist at work. I had pegged creative writing as an armchair occupation, but here we were, Bill and I, sitting in the car on a lonely country road in the south of France as Ernest physically paced out the distance, then mentally calculated the speed needed to effect the collision and the circumstance necessary to provoke it. He sought to ascertain in accurate detail the impact of the car and motorcycle crash that was to take Catherine's life. To my knowledge, this ending was never written, but at that time, as Ernest pondered the final scene, he was determined to leave no detail unexplored. As far as I know, he did not return to work on the book and was still dissatisfied with the manuscript at the time of his death.

There was a little bit of Eden in our sojourn in Provence that late summer of 1959. We ate and drank, sang and danced, revisiting youth and innocence. I can remember the warmth of the sun's rays as we stretched out on the beach, the grit of the sand and the autumn chill on the water as we swam in the cove where Ernest and Pauline and David and Catherine had swum before us.

It was raining in Aigues-Mortes when we arrived. The town's name added to the melancholy, dead water; its large towers and a fortified curtain wall stood erect in a mournful landscape of ponds, sea marshes, and salt pans. Ernest said it was the finest walled town left in France. It was also the spot from which Louis IX of France sent off his crusade to Palestine in 1248. From Aigues-Mortes we visited Le Grau-du-Roi, a small fishing village at the mouth of the channel connecting the salt marshes and the sea just five miles below at the extremity of the Rhône delta. Here at a small pension Ernest and Pauline had spent their honeymoon in May 1927. It was here too that he finished "Ten Indians" and "Hills Like White Elephants," which he mailed to Scribner's in New York that same month. Ernest often spoke to me of Pauline, who was now dead. He emphasized that, like me, she was Catholic, and he had rejoined the faith to marry her. He told me the story of how he had inadvertently been baptized in 1918 by a Catholic priest in Italy, as were all the fallen troops thought to be in danger of death. He had an interest in the religion but had not taken it seriously until he fell in love with Pauline. Ever since, no matter how he had faltered as a practitioner, he had never failed to fulfill his Easter duty. His only quarrel with the Catholic Church was that he believed animals have souls, and if he was to be damned for that, then so be it. As far as he was concerned, his Black Dog was up there in heaven with all the faithful; if he wasn't, it was not a place Ernest wanted to be. I never knew to what extent he was being serious when he made remarks like that, but I think at the time for him it was the truest statement he ever made.

We ambled through the beautiful van Gogh country, stopping in Arles on our way back to Nîmes. Next to writing, Ernest loved paintings more than anything, and van Gogh's rated close to the top of his list. Many times I had heard him exclaim how he would like to be able to write as well—or, as he put it, "as good as"—van Gogh or Cézanne could paint. It was a thrill to drive through the countryside in the waning of the summer, sharing his enthusiasm and delight as he compared the reality to canvas, life to art. A few days later in Paris I had the reverse experience when we walked through galleries of the Jeu de Paume recalling the landscape we had so recently enjoyed as we gazed at the great Impressionists' canvases.

It is hard to believe that van Gogh arrived in Arles eleven years before Ernest was born. His presence is as indelibly there as Ernest's is in Cuba today. Other painters Ernest liked to talk about as we drove through Provence were Cézanne, Gauguin, Matisse, and Dufy. He spoke with enthusiasm, in pidgin English and a mixture of French and Spanish, as if all life were a game, a contest, a puzzle. When he praised his heroes of the brush, it was unlike any other discourse I had ever heard: life was fun, everything was relevant, and it was good to be alive. It was so unlike the didactic teachings I was used to. By and large he knew the text, but he improvised life every step of the way. His appreciation of painting dated back at least to his early twenties. In May 1924 he had written to Ezra Pound from Paris, "I have been down in Provence and discovered it ain't no place for a writer. But I wish to hell I could paint." He went on to say, "I made a pilgrimage to Van Gogh's whorehouse in Arles and other shrines. A six day trip on 250 francs including railway fares and a seat at the corrida in Nîmes which ain't bad in these modern times. Nîmes, Arles, Avignon, Les Baux, St. Remy and home." Now, thirty-five years later, we also spent about a week in the area and followed a similar route, taking in the bullring at Arles, but not van Gogh's whorehouse. The amphitheatre is slightly larger and older than its cousin at Nîmes. Although we did not see a corrida there, Ernest delighted in discussing the architecture and history of the arena. We also stopped to admire the Pont du Gard, the wonderful Roman bridge and aqueduct that lies between Nîmes and Avignon. Ernest was excited and awed by the engineering feat, still in use two thousand years after its construction.

The cypress trees gave way to sloping vineyards on either side of the road, home to the grapes of the fine Tavel rosé wine. Once we were in Provence, Tavel became the mainstay of our journey, as the rioja had been on the other side of the Pyrenees. "A great wine for people that are in love," Ernest had written. Indeed, there was a gaiety and lovingness in his disposition these few days as he recalled and revised his youth in his new novel. Always an uncorked bottle lay in the cooler on the backseat of the Lancia. Each Provençal outing was punctuated by a long draw from its mouth, which passed from lip to lip. Olives, cheese, breadsticks, and sometimes a sweet raw onion staved off hunger between meals. No matter how severe the Midi sun, there was no chance of being either famished or parched while in the company of the wandering Hemingway.

Traveling with Ernest was never dull. He was a man of extremes. When he enjoyed life, as he did on that trip, he enjoyed it to the fullest, and he had the gift of being able to impart his pleasure and enthusiasm to those around him. He unleashed his imagination and could be deeply sensitive. He tended to exaggerate greatly, and mostly this was fun and enhanced every activity. But there was a dark side: an enemy was a deadly enemy, usually for keeps. A grudge was jealously guarded, and loyalty in friendship was demanded. He had the most inquiring mind of anyone I've ever met. Although his knowledge was vast and diverse, he constantly deferred to those around him, asking their opinion and valuing the answer. He often drew upon Bill Davis's knowledge of Spain, architecture, and modern art. He used to tell me that I was a lot smarter than he was but that he knew more because he had been around longer. Although he had been on these roads many times, it was as though he were seeing Provence for the first time. He noted the changes with interest, not ennui. He might not have liked what he saw, but he analyzed and processed the changes instead of dismissing them. Each day was a new adventure, and I often felt that I was the aged and jaded one when I could not muster up enough enthusiasm for visiting yet another scene from his life or literature.

It was sad to say goodbye to our friends in Nîmes, especially Antonio, for I did not know when or if I would see him again. Juan accompanied him back to Spain, where they planned to meet up with Luis Miguel. But Monique and Flo promised to see us in Paris. The corrida season had truly ended for us, and Ernest turned his attention to the trip ahead. He was excited about our first visit to Paris together. He liked nothing more than to show off his city to new companions. Bill and I were as receptive as Ernest was to the prospect of his being our guide, and we knew Annie would feel the same when we joined her at the Ritz. Ernest said that Paris was the city where he had learned to write. Living there provided the inspiration for his first novels.

As we neared the capital, his enthusiasm grew. He recalled using the Ritz Hotel as his headquarters after the city had been liberated in 1944 during the first flush of his love for Mary. Then, with prompting from Bill, he spoke of his old friend Scott Fitzgerald and what a shame it was that he had become a rummy, had sold out to Hollywood, and was no longer able to write. Gertrude Stein came in for her share of criticism, but she and Alice B. Toklas were Bumby's godmothers, and there was a time when Ernest had respected her talent and opinion. He never spoke ill of "old Jim" Joyce, although he too might have been classified as a "rummy"; still, Joyce never lost his ability to write, and for Ernest, that was the most important thing. Ernest told us of boxing at the gym and going to the races, and of how poor and happy he and Hadley had been in their little apartment above the sawmill. As we neared the city, he sang, "Dix bis Avenue de Gobelins, that's where my Bumby lives," a song he had invented to teach his little son to memorize his address in case he ever strayed from home.

Approaching Paris while listening to the stories of those early days, we were not indifferent to our surroundings as we sped through the beautiful

Loire Valley, with its fabled châteaux. Ernest promised that we would drive more slowly along the river road on our way back to Spain, picnicking by the banks and taking our own sweet time. Nor did we neglect the culinary possibilities and delights en route. Bill knew a number of good places to eat. There was also a particular restaurant an hour or so outside the capital that Ernest was keen to try, so we stopped there for an extravagant lunch on the final leg of this journey.

After Bill parked the car we walked together across the gravel to the arched wooden door, Ernest leading the way. As we entered, the maître d' came forward beaming and bowing. "Ah, Monsieur Welles," he said, "*bienvenue.*" A cloud passed over Ernest's face. "Hemingway's the name," he barked. A horrified expression was quickly supplanted by profuse apologies, more bowing, and renewed welcomes. "A table for three?" We were given a fairly secluded table where we were attended with tremendous flourish, commencing with a complimentary aperitif. From this vantage point we observed the reverend shuffle that accompanied Orson Welles's appearance. He was seated at a table with a single place setting, in good view. No menu was offered; he had evidently arranged his luncheon courses the day before. With pomp and circumstance the wine was brought for his approval. He sniffed, swirled, and tasted to his satisfaction. A plump capon was served, and with serviette tucked neatly under his chin, he attacked the fowl with a fond ferocity. He was oblivious to all but the edible and was as serious as a presiding judge.

Ernest recalled an earlier encounter with Welles that had not ended satisfactorily. During the Spanish Civil War, Joris Ivens had made a film of Hemingway's *The Spanish Earth,* which Welles had been chosen to narrate. He made a preliminary recording, but Ernest found his intonation unacceptable. Then the young novelist Prudenica de Pereda, who had worked earlier with Ernest on another documentary of the civil war, *Spain in Flames,* wanted the part. As it happened, Ernest ended up doing the narration himself. Welles shared Ernest's interest in Spain, was sympathetic to the Republican side in the war, and became an expert on the art of the bullfight. He too was a staunch supporter of Antonio Ordóñez—his last wishes

were that his ashes should be buried at Ordóñez's *finca* in Ronda, a wish
Antonio later honored, inviting Orson's close friends to a short private ceremony. The relationship between Hemingway and Welles over the years
had not been cordial, each making jibes about the other whenever the opportunity arose; now Ernest was working up to his uneasy fighting mode.

Ignoring Ernest's approaching tempestuous mood, I piped up bravely
that it would give me great pleasure to be introduced to the actor. Ernest's
anger and unease quickly dissipated. He declared that this presented no
challenge at all. When Welles was ready for coffee, Ernest called the waiter
and asked him to bring Mr. Welles a brandy with his compliments, at the
same time handing him a scribbled note asking the actor whether he would
care to join us. Welles conferred with the waiter, then held his snifter up and
toasted us. Within minutes he was at our table, and a lively, funny conversation with much gaiety ensued, all of us relaxed and in good humor. Orson
Welles bore an uncanny likeness to my uncle Patrick. Apart from their facial
resemblance, there was something about their girth, expression, and turn of
phrase, not to mention supercilious intonation, that was similar. Welles did
not scare me, but I couldn't imagine our ever being friends. He was far too
conceited and self-important. He told us about the movie he was making
and mentioned his small daughter Beatrice, who was the light of his life.
There was discussion about the corridas, and everyone was in agreement
upon Antonio Ordóñez's skills and artistry. Before we parted, we set a time
to meet again in a couple of days for lunch at the Ritz in Paris.

Ernest was cheered by the encounter, deciding that Welles was a fine
character after all and he must join our new club, which Ernest then invented on the spot. Orson would be inducted at our next meeting. A symbol of membership would be a Swiss army knife, and I was to remind him
to buy several when we got to Paris so that they could be presented to any
newly invested members.

I had been to Paris before, but this time it was different. I settled into my
stylish room at the Ritz Hotel after we were greeted by Charlie Ritz, scion
of the hotel family, who was also a great fisherman. He was a smallish, elegant man, gracious, most hospitable, and quite delighted to see us. Mary

and Annie had preceded us and were also happy to see us and anxious to hear our news. Ernest was keen that not a moment be wasted. Though he had so much on the agenda, first we must have a welcoming toast at *le petit bar* on the rue Cambon side, presided over by Bertin, the bartender. He recommended the kir, white wine and black-currant cordial, which I hadn't heard of before. Cool and crisp with a mellow taste of forest fruit and brambles, this became the preferred drink of the group. Ernest and Mary were greeted heartily by Bertin, and in a short time several friends who had already received word of the Hemingways' arrival came to pay respects. "How do you like it now, gentlemen?" Ernest said, beaming as he raised a glass in toast.

Ernest had tucked a manuscript that he referred to as "The Paris Sketches" into a worn, well-labeled leather briefcase and brought it to Spain. One day in August at La Consula he handed me several chapters, which I read, thinking how wonderful it must have been to be a poor writer living in Paris in the twenties. Now that we were in Paris, Ernest rechecked the places and scenes he had written about the year before in Cuba and Ketchum. He told me that the idea for the book had come to him in 1954, when he was recuperating from multiple injuries sustained in the two African plane crashes. Being confined to his room, with his movements restricted, had given him time to cast his thoughts backward. This brush with death and subsequent pain and immobility reminded him of his mortality. What came to the forefront of his mind were the days of his youth in Paris, his life and friends there, and how it had later turned out for him and for them. He had never written a memoir, but as he thought about each incident, writing it down became a necessity.

That first day in Paris we went for a long walk, supplemented by an occasional taxi ride. He paused now and then to point out a particular spot or to relate an episode that had just come to mind. Passing the house where Joyce had lived, he recalled how often he had brought the Irish novelist home after an evening's drinking, helping him up the stairs because Joyce's vision was already poor. Nora would open the door and say, "Well, here comes James Joyce the writer, drunk again with Ernest Hemingway." Ernest chuckled with glee as he told it. On the way back to the Ritz we stopped at Lipp's for a beer. On later excursions it would be the Deux Magots or the Closerie de Lilas, where we ordered a glass of muscadet and cassis. Ernest thought back to the time when he passed so many hours at these cafés, nursing one drink because he did not have money for more and it was too cold to write in his small apartment, or baby Bumby's crying distracted him. As the Irish proverb goes, hunger is a great sauce. For Ernest in those early years, hunger was good discipline.

One morning we walked down the rue de Castiglione and turned right, toward the place de la Concorde. There, across the street, was the Jeu de Paume, the little art gallery that housed the Impressionists, the same Manets, Monets, and Cézannes that the young Hemingway had gone to see nearly every day at the Luxembourg Museum. Ernest drew our attention to his favorites and in particular to one Cézanne that had influenced his early work. He said then, as I had heard him say before, that he always tried to write as good as the best picture that was ever painted. I think he meant that he tried to see things in a way no one had seen them before, to present with his pen and words as great artists did with their brushes and paint, a challenge to the world to think and feel differently, more deeply, and with an open mind. It was fun to recall the scenery we had just seen the week before and now observe it immortalized on canvas.

In the early days when he couldn't afford to buy books, he had borrowed them from the rental library of Sylvia Beach's bookstore, Shakespeare and Company, on the rue de l'Odéon. We walked along the rue de Rivoli to number 224 and browsed among the books on the shelves of the Librairie Galignani. Inside, Ernest, knowing that I was sorely lacking in my knowledge of American writers, purchased a number of books for me, which I still have. Among them were John Steinbeck's *The Short Reign of Pippin IV, The Man with the Golden Arm,* by Nelson Algren, John O'Hara's *From the Terrace,* and Pound's *The Cantos.* That day he also bought me *Madame Bovary* in French, Stendhal's *The Red and the Black,* and Lawrence Durrell's *Bitter Lemons,* which he highly recommended.

Le petit bar at the Ritz Hotel became a familiar haunt. Seldom empty, by noon it was so crowded one could scarcely hear oneself amid the chatter and the clinking of glasses. Bertin, bespectacled and ruddy-faced, alert but unintrusive, busied himself behind the bar. Here we would rendezvous religiously before lunch or dinner, and here Ernest was sought out by old friends, acquaintances, or members of the press. Most of the characters who appear in "The Paris Sketches"—later published as *A Moveable Feast*—were no longer in Paris. The people who came now were of a different era. An exception was Luis Quintanilla, the painter. He had done the pen-and-ink sketch for Lillian Ross's infamous portrait of Ernest, which appeared in the *New Yorker* in 1950. All of Quintanilla's early work had been destroyed by the bombs and artillery of Franco's army. He exiled himself to Paris and later New York. In 1938–39 Ernest had written a preface to *All the Brave,* a volume of Luis's drawings of the Spanish Civil War, with text by Elliot Paul and Jay Allen. The preface, dated March 10, 1938, and datelined Key West, begins:

A year ago today we were together and I asked Luis how his studio was and if the pictures were safe.

"Oh it's all gone," he said, without bitterness, explaining that a bomb had gutted the building.

"And the big frescoes in University City and the Casa del Pueblo?"

"Finished," he said, "all smashed."

"What about the frescoes for the monument to Pablo Inglesias?"

"Destroyed," he said. "No, Ernesto, let's not talk about it. When a man loses all his life's work, everything that he has done in all his working life, it is much better not to talk about it."

I liked Quintanilla and could tell that he and Ernest shared a history and mutual respect. He had drinks with us several times, and I talked with him as much as I could. Luis told me that he and Ernest first met in Paris in 1924. In 1931 he painted the writer's portrait. Ernest wrote of that portrait in *Death in the Afternoon.*

Luis seemed to lament more the loss of Ernest's letters to him than his own paintings. He told me that an important revelation in the correspondence was that whereas Ernest was indifferent to politics in general, including that of his own country, Spanish politics interested him profoundly, especially after the proclamation of the Republic. Ernest had many illusions, and his position was apparent in his frequent letters to Luis when the Spaniard was in jail. Those letters offered insight into Ernest's character. Their loss was deplorable, he said, for so often people label Ernest as apolitical.

"I read those letters to my fellow prisoners, and they served as an encouragement to us, for Ernest had confidence in the integrity of the Spanish people, whom he felt would react against fascism, as happened two years later. He also wrote to me on literature and art; his critical commentaries were usually humorous and amusing, written in Spanish, picturesque but clear."

There in the Ritz bar Ernest discussed with Luis the idea of his illustrating *For Whom the Bell Tolls,* a project that never came to fruition. Later Ernest gave me a copy of *Gulliver's Travels* with Quintanilla's splendid woodcuts, and one of the pen-and-ink studies for the *New Yorker* piece that Luis had sent him.

Another person who joined us at *le petit bar* was the poet Jacques Prévert, with his long face, piercing eyes, and whimsical expression. Ernest bought me a copy of his poems, lyrical, haunting verses that I still enjoy. Florence Malraux came too, serious and restrained. She was keen to discuss her father, André, with Ernest. Flo, whose mother was Jewish, had been greatly hurt by her father's desertion of her. She sought comfort and reassurance from Ernest, and he was sensitive to her needs.

One of the few people still around who appeared in *A Moveable Feast* was Georges, the head bartender at the Ritz. Tall, thin, elegant, always a welcoming smile on his angular face, he was a man who could be relied upon to impart any amount of information on a variety of subjects.

"How are the horses?" Ernest asked him one day. A visit to Paris would not be complete without at least one trip to the races, Auteuil or Longchamps, depending on the season. At this point, it was Auteuil. Well prepared, as was his habit with any venture, Ernest picked up *The Racing Form* and *Le Turf* first thing and had already studied the entries. He compared notes with Georges. Before we set out for the track, Ernest supplied himself with betting monies from his French royalties—francs that he took great delight in splitting equally among us to see who would come out ahead at the end of the day. His generosity was amazing. He told Monique that he would like to receive whatever royalties Gallimard was holding for him. A messenger arrived with a large envelope. Ernest asked Bill, Annie, and myself to join him and Mary in their room. As we entered, he popped the cork of a chilled Champagne bottle and poured us each a glass. Then he ceremoniously opened the large, fat envelope and let a vast amount of cash fall upon the bed. He proceeded to count it and divide it into five piles, handing every one of us a bundle of francs. "This is your gambling monies," he said. "Good luck." Those old thousand-franc bills seemed more like Monopoly money than the real stuff. We could only accept and play this game, yet another of Ernest's games.

It was time to say goodbye to Mary, who was anxious to return to Cuba. There had been tension between her and Ernest, and even after she left, a cloud of gloom remained as he mulled over her unreasonableness. He grudgingly conceded that he was partly responsible for her disgruntled state. He was pensive as we again headed south, only four of us left, Bill driving with Ernest beside him, Annie and myself in the back. We took the scenic route through the Loire Valley as he had promised, detouring first to visit the beautiful Gothic cathedral at Chartres and view the renowned thirteenth-century stained-glass windows.

Chartres was an important landmark for Ernest, and his mood lightened as he told us how he and Archie MacLeish had cycled there from Paris in 1926. The year before that, on his first visit to Chartres, he had been preoccupied with finding the right title for his first novel, *The Sun Also Rises*. He insisted on taking Morley Callaghan and his wife to see the cathedral when they were in Paris in the twenties, and later passed through Chartres on his way to "liberate" Paris in 1944. Although Ernest claimed to prefer the cathedral at Santiago de Compostela in Spain, he was proud to show off Chartres's splendors to us that fall day in 1959.

We spent the night at Poitiers. After dinner we lingered over coffee and Courvoisier, recapping our travels and planning for the time ahead—less than a month left in Madrid and Málaga, then back to Paris, where Ernest was scheduled to sail for New York on the *Liberté*. Finally, all talk exhausted, we retired. Shortly afterward there was a rap on my door. Ernest asked if he could come in. He settled in the stuffed chair by the window, an old man, world-weary, eyes half closed. He looked up at me and said he wanted me to come to Cuba in January, to stay with them at the *finca*. He told me he could work well only when I was around, he needed me, he hoped I would come.

I was taken by surprise. Had he discussed this possibility with Mary, or had he thought of it just now? What about my own life? True, I had been enjoying myself, but it was always with the understanding that this was a temporary situation and that I would return to my work and friends when the hijinks were over. I never for a moment envisioned prolonging my role as *la secretaria*. I looked at him and saw his sad face straining for hope. I answered cautiously, "I don't know. I shall have to think about it."

He suggested that I think carefully. My coming would mean everything to him—his life, his work, the future, our future. He closed his eyes and told me in a whisper that if I did not come, he would have no reason to go on. He said he had often contemplated suicide, but never more seriously than at that moment. Life without me at his side, he told me, was *nada*.

My first feeling was anger. More than once he had spoken to me contemptuously of his father's suicide. He had called him a coward and said that killing oneself was the ultimate act of cowardice. I could not imagine that he was serious. Was he toying with my feelings, subtly blackmailing me to get what he wanted? What exactly *did* he want? I was baffled, but then I thought of the good times we had had that summer. People had come and gone, as they do in life. Why not me? I had not signed on for the long haul. Yet I could see that he was in pain. He was pleading with me to help. I had no idea that I meant anything to him more than good company, and for that he did not lack. It seemed incredible that it would make any difference whether we met again or not. And what if he really did kill himself? How would I feel then? What had I to lose by doing as he asked? I couldn't bear to see the sadness on his face, that forlorn, dejected look, a sadness beyond human reach. I told him then that I had no idea my being around was so important to him. I would see what I could arrange. He moved toward me, smiling wanly, and wrapped his arms around me in a big bear hug. "Sleep well, daughter," he whispered, and was gone.

The next day he was in better spirits. The gloom had lifted. He told Bill and Annie I was thinking about going down to Cuba. They agreed that it was a splendid idea and said how lucky I was to have such a chance. We all became quite jolly. After arriving in Madrid, we checked in at the Hotel Suecia and then walked around to El Callejón for dinner. I took some time off to look up old friends and mull over whether I should go to Cuba or cut the ties. Ernest was now acting as though the matter had been decided. I was shaken by what I took to be his declaration of love, his neediness, and his intended suicide if I did not comply. A wise Irish friend helped make up my mind. He said, "You're young. What have you got to lose? You're enjoying life and have a unique opportunity, which you will look back on with gratitude and pleasure. 'Tis an old story that men of a certain age become infatuated with the young girls on their horizon. As sure as anything, in due course Hemingway's affection for you will wane, and you can go on your way, nothing lost, everything gained. God go with you, girl."

With Bill at *La Barata*'s wheel once more, we discussed Madrid and Paris, new and old friends, as we made our way south to Málaga. Now the forseeable future was secure, Ernest determined, he would set to work right away on his bullfight piece for *Life*. On October 10, with Mary gone and a new, unspoken pact between us, Ernest started to write. Each day he arose early, went to the stand-up writing desk Bill Davis had provided for him, and put down what he had experienced since his arrival in Málaga four and a half months before. When he had finished writing, I joined him to take care of the mail that was accumulating. He loved to tell me about the people who corresponded with him, how he knew them and what they meant to him. For instance, Lenny Lyons had copies of his *New York Post* column, "The Lyons Den," mailed weekly no matter where Ernest was. He spoke of Lenny with great affection, and I learned why later in New York, where I came to know Lyons well. Harvey Breit, of the *New York Times,* was another correspondent whose newsy letters always bucked up Ernest and prompted him to send a speedy reply.

Life back at La Consula then settled into a pattern of work, long, leisurely meals, and short excursions to the beach to see Gamel and Gerald Brenan or into town to have tapas and drinks at the Miramar Hotel. Ethel de Croisset came to visit, a charming lady who had been a friend of Pauline Hemingway when she worked at *Vogue* in Paris in the twenties. She brought news of Cyril Connolly's marriage and, in his mid-fifties, the famous writer's impending first-time fatherhood. The day after the wedding, on August 27, the eccentric Cyril had left his bride behind in England and traveled to Venice with Ethel and her mother.

I felt I had made the right decision. There was a jauntiness to Ernest's step now, and a kinder, more relaxed, funnier personality emerged. He loved to talk about his home in the tropics, of the good people who worked on the *finca* and who were his family, along with the animals, his many cats, and the fighting cocks the gardener, Puchilo, bred. He told me he would teach me to fish for marlin and swordfish in the Gulf Stream from his beloved boat, *Pilar,* instruct me to use a shotgun and a rifle without flinching, and show me how to choose a winning rooster in the pit. He spoke of jai alai games at the Fronton in the old days and the many varieties of mangoes I could eat, of coconut ice cream, *coco glacé,* served in the shell and doused with rum, which he knew was going to be my favorite dessert, and the warm, smooth water of the swimming pool where he exercised each day after writing. His spirits soared as he anticipated the winter, spring, and summer ahead. He was writing well and imbued with joie de vivre.

Sometimes he fantasized that we would have a life together. His days with Miss Mary were over, he said. She no longer cared for him and had strongly hinted that she would divorce him. Once he sorted things out, we could get married and have the daughter he had always longed for. I made no response. I could not imagine such a life for myself or for him. He reasoned that I might consider his former marriages an impediment, but he was a serious Catholic too. He pointed out that he had only once been married in the Church, and that was to Pauline, who was now dead, leaving him free to marry again. I could not and did not take what he said seriously. It was just another game, akin to the many games he liked to play—secret clubs, nicknames, imaginary assaults on enemies, and all the rest of his childish fantasy life, which for the most part, was charming, harmless, and endearing, but never to be confused with reality.

Ernest ordered a set of his books from Scribner's and inscribed each one of them to me on October 18 before we left La Consula. He asked for the book that had brought us together, the one I had received in June and which had prompted me to go to the feria at Pamplona, *Guerre à la Tristesse*. Inside he wrote: "To Valerie this book which Juanito delivered for all good luck with gratitude to him and love Ernest Hemingway. July 7—October 18—minus 8—18/10/59." He had counted those few days we had been apart, whereas I had looked upon them as days of liberty.

CHAPTER SEVEN

Partings and Promises

*A*s we set out to visit Paris a final time in the Lancia, harmony, satisfaction, and hope allowed us to engage in lighthearted banter. It was agreed that after Ernest left, I would drive back to La Consula with Bill and Annie. I would spend a couple of weeks there, then go on to Madrid to collect my belongings and to Ireland for Christmas. I would travel to New York after the first of the year, joining the Hemingways in Cuba in early January. Life could not have been better. We spoke of returning to Spain the next summer. The Lancia would stay at La Consula until our return. It was not the end of the cuadrilla, but a seasonal interlude.

Paris was as magical as before. The Ritz did not have a regular room for me, so I was assigned an attic room designated for guests' maids and valets. I loved my new quarters, where I could view the rooftops, the spires, and the open sky, observing the busy pigeons at work and play. I was among the gods, close to heaven in the theater that was Paris. Like the air, the walls up here seemed thinner, for each morning at approximately the same time I was awakened by the telephone ringing next door. A mature Frenchwoman's throaty voice answered, and there ensued a discussion of the day's horses, presumably with her bookie. As I listened, first just to see if I could understand the French and then to make note of the content of the conversation, I started jotting down what I heard. I have had a lifelong habit of writing down odds and ends, a habit formed in my convent days when silence was a way of life and the only source of communication or sorting out one's thoughts was with pencil and paper. I now found that the information I was receiving was pertinent. We were going out to the racetrack again, and I recognized the names of the horses. I was able to put the information to good use and surprise Ernest and the Davises with my newfound ingenuity in choosing winners and evaluating the field.

Ernest dreaded his reunion with Mary in Havana. He knew he would have to make amends and smooth everything over while Antonio and Carmen were visiting so that there would be no unpleasant outbursts. He thought a trinket from Cartier might do the trick. Mary had hinted that a pair of diamond earrings could supply the dash of appeasement needed, so we made a little pilgrimage to the august jeweler. Ernest donned his tweed jacket and a tie, looking awkward and ill at ease. We were ushered into the sanctuary by a courteous and elegant salesman. Ernest drew close to the counter and in muted tones explained his mission. Bill, Annie, and I kept a respectful distance. As Ernest looked at the customer to his right, he saw a dapper, dignified Frenchman, the antithesis of the flustered author, obviously adept at his task and completely in his element. But wait, didn't he look a little familiar? As the man turned his head, there was no doubt in anybody's mind. It was Georges, the head bartender from the Ritz.

Georges greeted us all effusively. "*Un petit bijou* for my niece," he proclaimed suavely.

"*Un bijou* for Miss Mary," Ernest countered with a nod. Salutations, bows, and smiles were exchanged.

"Lucky niece," said Annie.

"Hmmm," mused Bill, slightly incredulous.

Ernest became more chummy now, more himself. The task had lightened and his confidence returned. After a cursory look at the earrings, he declined. The gift would be a diamond pin. The transaction was completed, and we took our leave.

At Hermès, Ernest bought each of us a gift: mine a black cashmere sweater with short sleeves, a V-neck, and collar, a scarf for Annie, and a tie for Bill. We lunched on sausage, potatoes, and cold beer at the Brasserie Lipp across the Boulevard St-Germain and then went to Shakespeare and Company, where we emerged laden with books. I had tucked under my arm a special French edition of *Death in the Afternoon*, Leo Lania's *Hemingway*, and a handful of other titles that are still scattered in my library. When we returned to the Ritz with our packages, Ernest wrote in the Club des Libraires de France edition of *Mort dans l'après-midi*, "To Valerie remembering all the summer and the fall and where we went and what we saw and felt. Best love and luck, Ernest."

It was time to say goodbye. Ernest, prone to illness and accidents, had picked up a germ in Paris and was now nursing a cold. He took his health problems seriously and wherever he went always brought with him the equivalent of a full medicine cabinet. We drove up to Le Havre to see him off. It was a lonely figure, as solitary as a bereft waif, we waved to as he became lost among the passengers bound for New York aboard *La Liberté*. We headed back to the hotel, subdued and contemplative. Bill was never a talker, and Annie was clearly sad. I had expected to find the parting a great relief. However, my feelings were mixed. On the way back we tried to joke and re-create the jolly atmosphere, but *tristesse* and gloom overwhelmed us. In Paris there were telegrams from Ernest full of gratitude and longing. Mine, dated October 27, said simply, "Thanks lovely presents sleep well love = Ernest =." That night we dined at Pruniers, determined not to lower the standards nor to forget, but an absence couldn't be restored or ignored. We felt a hollowness, as Ernest would have put it. On October 30 we cabled him on board ship, "Hemingway SS Liberte FFL. Without you Paris sad but thinking of you helps love valannibill."

My memory of the drive back to Madrid and Málaga has dimmed, for the days without Ernest's company were sterile. Only with his absence could I appreciate the intensity of his presence. Around him everything came to life, for better or for worse. There was an urgency and vitality that even in the darkest or most tedious moments did not ebb. I had grown accustomed to the excitement and had completely forgotten just how bland life could be without that pivotal figure. When we arrived back at La Consula I found a letter there:

À BORD LIBERTÉ LE 30/10/59.

My Dearest Val.

Rougher than we ever thought. Not the weather. It only blew two days (force 8-9) then moderated as we ran out of the storm yesterday before daylight. But I can't get along without you. I knew it before. But now I know it for keeps.

You have been very good about taking care of though because always when it would be impossible you would be there wonderfully tactile and with the secret smile, you know the one, the freely given after work one. You took such good care to make things so we could get through this and were so wonderful always when we knew how rough things were.

This is a very good ship in a heavy sea. We made 22 ½ knots in the worst of the weather and are going to get in at Daylight of Nov. 2 giving more time to get things done in N.Y. Am busy staying in bed and taking anti-biotics to knock bad chest and head cold with fever that probably started when it turned so cold in the night in Paris and I did morning exercises in the gale blowing in from the garden. Had fever of 100 at noon which isn't bad—Think was worse yest but only went to Dr. today. Went down to lunch but will eat dinner in the cabin as did last night. Can't sleep nights but think of you and that you're sleeping well and say my prayers and so far every night sometime have been able to see you and it be the same as when we said goodbye.

So if you do make that with magic please keep it up because without it _____

Have been reading the technical and critical bull books I

bought in Madrid—(shipped some out west and brought 10 or so.) They are a mixed bag. Some extremely good—There is such an infinite lot to learn always about that strange business. Think Will Lang though was satisfied, or anyway pleased, with the 1st ½ of the Life piece and with your help I'll write the second half well. I depend on you in so very many ways and the letters that we do with fun are almost impossible for me to do alone.

—They brought dinner and this is later. The Andalucia book is beautiful. Thank you very much for it and for the wonderful scarf. I'm writing on the back of the scarf box from Sulka with the To EH from V. I read that and what you wrote in the Andalucia book. The cabestro bell card is packed—and what's packed nobody knows where that is. So that's what I have from you to read.

They've taken down the ropes on the decks and in the passage ways and the sea makes a good sound now along the plates—sandy through the porthole—you would have loved it when we had the full force of it when we had passed Southern Ireland. It had the steep hills of the western ocean with snow blowing off them like a blizzard.

Val I miss you too much—I'll stop now and write some more tomorrow. Good night that word we are familiar with from EH to V.

Good night—Sleep well—Moi aussi—you—You very dearest and loveliest

It's cold this morning, Saturday, and we must be getting off the Banks of New Found Land. Slept well at the start but woke at a quarter to three—chest and head nonsense still on but am taking the stuff regularly and should knock it today if I stay in bed. I always love you as much in the morning when I wake as I do at night when I go to sleep—could see you very clearly in the white part of the night and in the dark part too

Love

Ernest

I'll try to get in good shape fast and write a non sad letter But triste
and hollow and non existent is what it is when you're not there and
starting off this day I don't know how to make it. But we'll make it.
How can we not? Let's not talk about (it). I'll think about how you
sound when you say we.

EH

BACK IN DUBLIN after almost a year, it was as if I had never left. Friends
I ran into on O'Connell or Grafton Street would stop me and say, "Haven't
seen you in a while, how have you been?" As promised, I stopped by Angle-
sea Road to visit the Behans and report on my year in Spain. Brendan was
there alone and he made a pot of tea, which we drank in the kitchen. He wore
a crumpled white dress shirt and his navy trousers were held up with a pair of
braces. His jet-black curly hair was uncombed and his piercing blue eyes
sparkled with mirth and mischief. A small man whose diminutive hands and
feet were overshadowed by an extensive girth, Brendan had a sonorous voice,
with the lilt of pure Dublin in it. Sober, as he was at that moment, he was a
most entertaining companion, incorrigibly mischievous and hilariously
funny. He was never at a loss for words, mingling Irish and English with a
dash of Spanish and French in a torrent of sentences that revealed an amazing
breadth of knowledge and insights. I had brought a couple of his books, *The
Quare Fellow* and *The Hostage*, both plays, and asked him to inscribe them.

When I told him of meeting Hemingway, who had enjoyed reading
Borstal Boy, I learned that Brendan was equally a Hemingway enthusiast. I
mentioned my imminent trip to Cuba to work for the American writer, and
he exclaimed, "Why in the name of Jaysus would you want to work for
America's greatest writer when you could work for Ireland's best instead?"
Then he told me that he had some good news himself. Joan Littlewood,
who had successfully staged *The Hostage* in London, was now planning to
take the show to Broadway in the autumn. "I can easily get you a job with
the *Hostage* company," he said. "Forget about the ol' man and Cuba, and
support one of your own."

Ah! The ironies of life, where opportunities present themselves in the wrong sequence. I had a keen interest in the theater. Working with Behan and the *Hostage* company was something I would have given my eyeteeth to achieve, but the offer came in the wake of my commitment to go to Cuba. We chatted for a long while about Spain and the theater, literature and Ireland, and the new horizons ahead for both of us. Brendan made me promise that I would attend the first night of *The Hostage* in New York no matter where I was. I imagined that by then my sojourn with the Hemingways would be at an end and I would have returned to a normal life.

During this period I stayed at my mother's place on Seapoint Avenue, a neat row of brick houses entered by steep stone steps and overlooking the Irish Sea. She was of mixed emotions at my new adventure, stoically emphasizing that she would never stand in the way of opportunity for any of her children and that I must make my own decisions. With a view to doing some laundry, she had looked through the suitcase I had brought from Spain, and found there a crisp new blue-and-white checkered man's short-sleeved shirt of large dimension, which filled her with trepidation. When we had stayed in the Hotel Suecia in Madrid Ernest had, as always, great difficulty sleeping. If we retired at a reasonable hour, which was never before midnight in Spain, he would ask me to come to his suite for a nightcap, and we would talk and sip wine or whiskey, sometimes for several hours, until he grew drowsy. At some point he had given me the shirt, a match of the one that he used to sleep in. He said if I wore the mate, some of my solid sleeping habits would be transferred to him. Ernest thrived on such little games and secrets. I never wore the shirt. It and various affectionate notes disappeared from my belongings. I made no comment, nor did my mother, but I could feel her tacit disapproval.

On November 30 the Davises received a telegram from Ernest. He had some bad news to report. He told them that Mary had shattered her left elbow in a fall while hunting. She was operated on and needed extensive therapy. This would be helped by swimming and fishing in Cuba. They planned to leave Ketchum for Havana early in January, skipping their intended visit to New York. Ernest and Mary both wanted me to join them in

Cuba in late January. The Davises were to relay the entire message to me in Dublin. Annie wrote me the details, and then I received a letter from Ernest. He said I should put off my arrival in Havana until the latter part of January instead of the beginning. Mary was in great pain and needed him right now, and equally he needed me. If he was not good to Mary when she needed him, he would not be good to me, he reasoned. I was thankful. Whatever brought Ernest and Mary together in harmony was what I truly wished for all of us. In a perverse way, the accident seemed like a godsend.

CHAPTER EIGHT

Cuba, 1960

I ARRIVED IN HAVANA on January 27. Ernest was there at the airport to meet me, accompanied by Juan, his chauffeur. When I stepped off the plane at Rancho Boyeros, a blast of warm air brushed my skin, soothing like a healing balm. It was my first visit to the tropics, and in some mysterious way I felt an immediate kinship with my newfound island. There was no mistaking the familiar figure as I emerged from the plane—his large frame loosely clothed in khaki shorts and a checkered short-sleeved shirt, the brown moccasins, and the round, bearded face with a shock of white hair smoothed under the peaked cap. Ernest was impossible to miss, and already the small crowd had spotted him and was edging in. As I came down the metal steps I picked out his face, anxiously peering at the descending passengers. His wide jaw broke into a smile of recognition as our eyes met. He introduced me to Juan, trim and respectful in a gray chauffeur's uniform, cap in hand. The three of us set out in a red Chrysler for the twenty-mile trip to the Finca Vigía, or Lookout Farm, which sits on the periphery of Havana in the suburb village of San Francisco de Paula.

I shall always remember my first glimpse of Cuba. The city of Havana seemed not much larger than Dublin, but more regal, more exotic, with a greater variety of architecture—colonial, baroque, neoclassical, art nouveau, and modern—a profusion of lush foliage overhanging the stone or stuccoed walls, and towering trees providing welcome protection from the glaring sun. Both cities nestle by the ocean, but the sweeping majesty of the Malecón, Havana's seaside boulevard, with its view of the harbor, the mighty sea, and Morro Castle, with great waves cascading over the stone wall and onto the road, far outshone anything in my native town.

Gradually we left the city behind and passed onto the Carreterra Central, the main west-east road that courses the island. I perched my elbow on the car door and through the open window took in the sights: stately houses giving way to the occasional wooden shack, clusters of royal palms swaying in the breeze. As we entered the village of San Francisco de Paula, shacks with palm-leaf roofs lined up side by side, opening onto the street. These shops, bars, and little cafés were doing a leisurely business. We turned right to see, one block away, the padlocked wrought-iron gates of the farm, isolated from the village only by a high wall, which served more as a challenge than a deterrent to local youths, whose sport was to scale the wall, especially when the writer was away on his travels, and steal as many as possible of the eighteen varieties of mangoes that grew on the grounds.

Miss Mary greeted me on the broad steps leading up to the beautifully proportioned house, which had been built in 1887 by a wealthy Catalonian immigrant. Large windows and French doors, symmetrically placed, kept cool air flowing through. "A house on the top of a hill where there was always a breeze," Ernest had described it to his editor, Maxwell Perkins, in 1939. A giant ceiba tree shaded its entrance, silently taking possession of the house as its gnarled roots slowly crept under the foundation, unsettling the tiles on the living room floor which added a quaint irregularity most noticeable when traversed barefoot. The tree's knobbly shape fit in precisely with the faded and peeling whitewashed walls. Inside, a slightly decaying air of mildew, humidity, and tiredness pervaded the atmosphere. The large, simply hewn furniture with faded chintzes sat on straw matting. Low white bookshelves left ample wall space for the splendid paintings collected by Ernest as a young man in Paris, displayed alongside antlers and bullfight posters. Magazines, newspapers, a cocktail buffet, and a turntable on a stand completed the furnishings. No swagger, no pretense—this was a house well lived in, a writer's house. René, the butler, just a few years older than myself, gathered my bags and showed me to the little *casita* above the double garage at the bottom of the steps.

My quarters were spacious and comfortable. The *casita* had been used by Hemingway's three sons when they spent their childhood vacations with their father. It had also been home to many illustrious guests over the years. The young woman Ernest had been so enamored of years earlier, Adriana Ivancich, had stayed there in 1950, chaperoned by her mother. Her brother, Gianfranco, whom I had met at the birthday party in Spain, had been a frequent tenant. After some years in Havana, he had married a Cuban girl, Cristina, and brought her back to Venice with him. Gary Cooper had slept in the little house, as did Luis Miguel when he was courting the film star Ava Gardner. She had lunched at the *finca,* swum in its pool, and joined the Hemingways in downtown Havana for drinks and dinner at El Floridita. The guests who had immediately preceded me were Antonio and Carmen Ordóñez, just three months before. In November Antonio and Carmen had left the *finca* with Ernest and Roberto Herrera, Ernest's friend, factotum, and sometime secretary. They had driven to Ketchum, Antonio and Roberto spelling each other at the wheel of the new station wagon. Apart from seeing the Idaho house the Hemingways had bought the year before, the party had planned on duck shooting there. As soon as they arrived, however, Antonio received a telephone call from his sister in Mexico. She intended to leave her husband and urgently needed him to help her make her getaway back to Spain. Before they had a chance to try out the hunting, they were on their way again. Shortly after that Mary had the accident that incapacitated her left arm.

I settled into my new life happily. The upstairs of my aerie was a large square room fitted with twin beds, a chest of drawers, a desk, and a couple of chairs. A bathroom was carved out of one corner. Windows were all around at regular intervals, perpetually open and protected by screens. At night, the air was cooler. It took me a while to become accustomed to the nocturnal noises, particularly the patter of a myriad of tiny lizards scampering up and down the screens (mainly on the outside) making a music all their own. There were crickets and night owls, mysterious rustles and stirrings. An occasional lone squeal or growl rent the air, sending a shiver down my spine. I had the sensation of camping out; because the mattress was level with the window, my head was bathed in the caresses of cool breezes and the sky was my canopy. It often startled me to wake up suddenly in the dark and feel the sharp stirring of the nocturnal life all around.

By breakfast time the heat was rising and the rhythmic beat from the village radios became audible. I was soon humming the jingles for Hatuey beer and Partagas cigars. At nine o'clock there would be a rap on the door downstairs. René or Marta, Mary's maid, brought my breakfast of fruit juice, black Bustelo espresso with a jug of steaming hot milk, and thick toasted bread with butter and guava jam. "*Buenos días,* Miss Valerie. How are you today?" René would ask with a grin from ear to ear. Marta was more circumspect. She smiled a little warily as she put down the tray quietly and hurried away. I ate in the lower room, which was also my workroom. It was darker because of the foliage around it and the slanted stone wall that protected it from the view of the big house. Inside, the walls were lined with books, and along with my breakfast table there was a large old desk with a typewriter. These were my waking, working quarters. After breakfast I took a turn around the grounds before settling down to work. Later, after I finished my typing, bearing one of the books Ernest had prescribed under my arm, I strolled through the garden or meadow, answering the greetings of the gardener and his helpers with a bright "*Muy buenos,*" and finally settling under a mango tree. Ernest had told me that if I wanted to be a writer, first I must read all the great writers.

Our life fell into a daily rhythm, a pattern of alternating serenity and excitement, of earnest application and sporting fun, and finally of tensions brought on by the weight of the work, Ernest's declining health, and the changing political clime of the island.

Every morning Ernest wrote standing up in his room, carefully pecking out the words on his Royal typewriter. He was finishing the Paris sketches, fine-tuning the chapters he had already written and incorporating his notes from the previous fall. After Antonio and Carmen's sudden departure from Idaho, Mary's accident, and the indifferent duck hunting, he had taken up the manuscript again, adding to it since I had last seen him. In the spring of 1960 in Cuba he went over the text carefully a final time, and when he was satisfied with each chapter, I would retype it. His next project was to reread the first half of his long article for *Life* magazine, started at La Consula, describing the 1959 bullfighting season in Spain. Here he often called upon my memory of the little details he had asked me to note when we were on the road. The manuscript grew and grew until it became book-sized. It would later be sharply edited and published as *The Dangerous Summer.*

After writing, he went down to the pool to swim. Once it had been the center of jolly gatherings, with international guests frolicking in the water or lounging poolside, nibbling tapas and sipping on ice-cooled drinks to Dixieland music or Frank Sinatra's crooning. Mary told me her birthday present to Ernest one July was a truck full of ice offloaded into the pool. It was one of the most successful presents ever. Presents and birthdays were an important element in *finca* life. That year the pool was used for serious exercise only. Ernest's practice was to complete a half mile a day, lap by lap, with a steady breaststroke.

Just as we ate our breakfasts individually, I can't recall more than one of us using the swimming pool at a time. It was an unwritten law that Ernest always swam first when his morning's work was done. Next Mary came down the shaded path to the pool in her robe, towel in hand. When I saw two towels stretched out to dry upon the wooden chaises by the pool, then I knew it was safe for me to take the plunge. A morning swim was expected: a house rule not enforced but desired. Mary had told me that there was no need to wear a swimsuit; it wasn't done. My convent background and quaint ways amused her, and I felt I was being challenged. I had not been a swimmer when I first met the Hemingways. Hotch had taught me the basics in the pool at La Consula, and, being a fair athlete, I picked up the strokes quickly. I preferred walking or reading, but not to have taken advantage of the pool in the humid, sticky climate would have been foolish. As to swimming in the buff, it had never occurred to me. I, who had worn a chemise in the convent bath until I was eleven and had never exposed my flesh intentionally before, approached the matter gingerly. At first I imagined one of the gardeners peering through the foliage with a leer, or perhaps just happening to cross to the tennis court at the moment I let my terry-cloth robe fall to the ground. However, feeling the water surge against my skin as I moved from end to end in the tepid water was keenly liberating. Stroking the water to a serenade of birdsong or, at dusk, black bats skimming the surface seemed the most natural thing in the world. Swims at noon and before cocktails in the late afternoon became the most soothing and refreshing moments of the day.

At first Mary was far from friendly. She later told me that her resentment stemmed from the fact that Ernest had not discussed my visit with her in advance, but this neither rang true nor was borne out in her written recollections. In any case, I paid scant notice, did my work, and kept my distance. Gradually she started inviting me to join her on little excursions to town or helping in the garden. Going to the market in old Havana became a high point of our week. As her distrust diminished, she accepted having a female companion around, and we began to laugh and joke together. As soon as Ernest thought we were becoming too chummy, he stepped up my workload, which was light enough that I could not complain. I began to divide my time almost equally between them. In the late morning or early afternoon Ernest and I met in the library and he dictated answers to his personal correspondence, which I often wrote down in longhand and he signed. A few business letters were typed. More general letters were left to my discretion to answer or not as I pleased, and I did this in the *casita* along with the typing. When he felt inclined, he discussed what he had written that morning, or asked me to type out the pages or to help him recall some minute detail in the sequence of events of the past summer when we were following the corridas in Spain. He was a voracious reader and seemed to have a photographic memory for what he read. I learned a great deal. No university course could have taught me as much.

Ernest was meticulous about having his papers in order, sometimes to the point of paranoia. He had known it would be difficult for me to enter Cuba with a work permit, so he recommended that I request a visitor's visa, which would last ninety days. This meant that I should say to anyone who asked that I was visiting the Hemingways as a friend, not there to work as his secretary. In keeping with the plan, he said that he would pay me at a later date in the United States or Europe. My salary was the same $250 a month he had offered in Spain, and since all my needs were taken care of and I was treated as a guest—or, more accurately, as a member of the family—this was more than generous. On January 30 I was issued a *carnet de extranjera,* a small blue identification booklet with photo and finger-prints, showing that my address in Cuba was Finca la Vigía, San Francisco de Paula. My black hair and hazel eyes became brunette and gray, and on paper I gained an inch in height. Ernest kept the *tarjeta* in his desk. As I now write, I have before me the letter from the Ministerio de Gobernación, Dirección General de Inmigración, answering Ernest's written request to grant me ninety more days in Cuba.

On Thursdays Mary and I went with Juan in the yellow Buick convert-ible, "Mary's car," to the market in old Havana to shop for groceries, house-hold items, necessities, and a few little luxuries. Other days I helped her tend the kitchen garden, where she grew many varieties of vegetables. As food became scarcer with the inroads of the revolution, Cuba's political leaning toward socialism, and the Soviet Union's support hampering the availability of imports, especially from the United States, this produce from Mary's treasured garden increased in value. Lily, the hair stylist, came every week. If I was not busy, Mary extended to me the luxury of a shampoo and manicure. There was also a seamstress who appeared regularly to mend and fix all manner of garments and linens. Mary decided my European clothes were far too dull for the tropical climate. We purchased bright fab-rics at the market, and with great delight Mary set about designing flam-boyant suits and dresses of bright-colored silks and flowery cottons for me to wear around the *finca.* Our everyday outdoor footwear was canvas and rope *alpargatas* purchased at the market for a few cents. In the evenings, the three of us sometimes walked to the top of the hill behind the ruined cowshed to watch the sun set. Above the silhouette of the city Mary showed off her flowering fence post trees, and displayed her horticultural knowledge as she proudly pronounced their Latin name, *Gliricidia sepium.* The panorama before us was always a delight.

CHAPTER NINE

A Week of Suppers

D INNER WAS ALWAYS PRECEDED by two drinks: Scotch and soda, Gordon's gin and tonic water, a martini, Bacardi rum with soda and a squeeze of fresh lime, or one of Mary's favorites, Campari, vodka, soda, and lime. There had been a time when among the dinner guests were the great writers, film stars, and sportsmen of the day. Jean-Paul Sartre had sat at that table, as had Errol Flynn, Spencer Tracy, and the Oscar-winning director Freddie Zinnemann. However, by 1960 the political climate in Cuba had changed. Wealthy Americans had already left the country before or after their possessions were nationalized by the government. Visitors hesitated to come to a place where their reception was unpredictable. That year, only close friends of the Hemingways visited, and there was a distinct pattern to the week.

On Mondays Dr. José Luis Herrera, nicknamed "El Feo" (the ugly one), and his younger brother, Roberto, usually came to dinner. Their presence was not confined to that day alone. They were an integral part of the household. Their visits were as frequent as they were summoned, Feo for medical consultation, Roberto for odd jobs and good fellowship. Spanish by birth, their father had been court chamberlain to Alfonso XIII, but they had left their native country after the civil war, in which Feo had participated as a surgeon on the Loyalist side. Although as I understood it Feo did not have a license to practice medicine in Cuba, he was employed by the military in a medical capacity. Unofficially he was Ernest's doctor, and since their return to Cuba in January, he had visited almost daily (in spite of his heavy schedule) to spend half an hour massaging Mary's injured arm with an electric vibrator. Monday evening began with the ritual of taking his friend's blood pressure and discussing current ailments or medical worries. Ernest had a lifelong obsession with health—probably a legacy from his physician father—and this was complemented by a proneness to accidents and illness. Feo, a dedicated revolutionary, felt at ease with the new political situation in Cuba. He had known Castro during his medical student days. There was a great mutual respect, and he was soon to become chief of the medical section of Fidel's army. Ernest loved to probe discreetly into the military and political developments, and Feo, equally discreetly, gave some insight into the movements of the government and his own opinion as to the successful development of the revolution.

Roberto too was a longtime visitor to the *finca*. He did not have his brother's brilliance, but he had been present at almost every important event or crisis in Hemingway's life, even before Mary came on the scene. He was one of the eight-man crew on the *Pilar* during Operation Friendless, the wartime submarine hunting escapade that Ernest directed in 1942. He had helped nurse Ernest's son Patrick back to health after his mental breakdown in 1947. On and off, he had acted as secretary to Ernest or as his chauffeur when in the United States. His loyalty could be counted upon absolutely. Both brothers were of serious disposition and devoted to Ernest and Mary. Dinner conversation mainly entailed Ernest's recalling their adventures together, discussion of the Spanish Civil War, and mulling over the present state of Cuba and what the future might hold.

Tuesday was Dr. Carlos Kohly's evening. A physician, Cucu was a fishing and shooting club pal of Ernest's whose American wife, Joy, had shown Mary around Havana when she first came there in 1946. Cucu was short and slightly portly, with jolly brown eyes shielded by glasses, and a smuggish smile. He had that male self-assurance so common in Spain, where boy children, *varones,* are treated from birth like little princes. He and Ernest discussed sports and medicine. I heard that Cucu had once taken care of the *finca* when Ernest was away for an extended period. Something had gone missing, I cannot remember what, and it turned out that Cucu had allowed some friends to stay there and they made off with "souvenirs" of their visit. Since then, Mary had become somewhat distrustful of him. But with the continued series of ailments and injuries from which both Hemingways suffered, a doctor who regularly visited the house was a valuable friend to have, and Cucu maintained his status.

Ernest took Wednesday and Saturday afternoons off to go fishing on the *Pilar,* starting out at Cojímar, where she was docked. I always accompanied him. Mary was still concerned about risking further injury to her elbow, so she rarely came, certainly not more than half a dozen times that spring. On Wednesday night there were no scheduled guests for dinner, unless businessman Lee Samuels came over. However, Lee was more likely to appear during the day, and his presence was always welcome. In 1950, Ernest had agreed to write a short preface for *A Hemingway Check List,* a bibliography of Ernest's published work that Lee had prepared and which was published by Scribner's in July of 1951. Lee was an American, a tobacco importer, who was also an avid Hemingway fan, and over the years he had put together an impressive collection of the writer's work. Business brought him back and forth between Cuba and the United States. At the onset of the revolution he wisely moved the bulk of his business to Florida, but he continued to visit Cuba while the Hemingways were there. He and Ernest mostly discussed literature and especially Hemingway's own work.

Lee had one foible that irked Ernest. He said that he had never found a book by a woman worth reading. At first Ernest lent him various books by his favorite women authors, Isak Dinesen, Dawn Powell, and others. Each time Lee returned the books, he said as far as he was concerned they did not measure up. Then Ernest had an idea. He lent Lee Cecil Woodham-Smith's *The Reason Why.* It was the story of the tragic charge of the Light Brigade during the Crimean War, the title taken from Tennyson's poem: "Theirs not to reason why. / Theirs but to do and die: / Into the valley of

Death / Rode the six hundred." It was first published in the United States in 1954. Lee reported that it was a fine book and he enjoyed reading it. For months Ernest never let on to Lee that Woodham-Smith was a woman. He just reveled in the pleasure of bringing up the book whenever they met and letting Lee pour on the praise. Finally he made his move. When Lee repeated that he had never been able to read a book by a woman, Ernest asked innocently, "You enjoyed *The Reason Why?*"

"But of course."

"And Cecil Woodham-Smith is a writer you have no trouble reading."

"Certainly not."

"And since she is a woman . . ." The two men were friends enough to weather this storm. It became one of Ernest's favorite tales, pointing to the fallibility of self-styled literary experts.

If we dined alone on Wednesdays, after dinner Ernest and I walked to the top of the hill and then down again to the village, where we stopped at one of the open-air cafés for a Bacardi and soda with a squeeze of fresh lime. We each carried a staff to secure our foothold in the dark against the twigs and uneven ground or to ward off unwelcome critters. He was totally relaxed and loved to reminisce about his childhood, particularly escapades with his sister, Ursula (Ura), who was his favorite. Perhaps in some way having me by his side brought him back to a time of innocence and hope. Ura, the third Hemingway child, three years Ernest's junior, was the closest of his siblings. All his life he spoke of her with affection and wrote of her in his letters as "my lovely sister," "my best sister," "my nice sister." On those evenings, he was tender, soft-spoken, and funny. We laughed a great deal. We always paused at the hill's apex, where the distant lights of Havana below winked at us while all around the air vibrated with the rhythmic thumping from amplifiers in the little bars of San Francisco de Paula. Some nights we might read the sky, Ernest's hand lightly touching my shoulder. Or if it was totally dark, he embraced me with his huge, warm, all-encompassing bear hug, my unruly black hair pressed against his chest. Then we walked onward in silence. It was the only time we touched, except when he placed his bare feet over mine under the dining room table at lunch, engaging in his mysterious and expressive foot-speak. A change gradually came over me. Rather than feeling resentful and smothered by his affection and possessiveness, as I had in Spain, I grew to treasure our moments together, to cherish the harmony, tranquility, and intensely private life we lived now instead of the extroverted, celebrity-hound-provoking frenzy we had experienced in Europe. I fondly imagined all of us living together in this paradise, this Garden of Eden, Ernest, Mary, and me, René and Juan, Marta and Ana the chubby laundress, the cook, Puchilo the gardener and his hirelings, with nothing to break the perfect circle. What an absurd dream!

Thursday night Phil Bonsall, the American ambassador, usually came to dinner, and it was on a Thursday that this dream of Eden showed its first signs of shattering. Ernest loved to talk with Phil, a direct connection with his homeland. Quintessentially American, although he had spent little of his adult life in the States, Ernest eagerly followed all that was happening in his native country: domestic and foreign policy, the military, sports, the underworld, and all kinds of intrigue. With each Thursday's visit we saw that Bonsall was becoming increasingly uneasy about the relationship between the United States and Cuba and about the tenuousness of his own situation. On one visit in the spring his face was grave. He brought Ernest an important though informal message from Washington, D.C. The U.S. government was seriously thinking of breaking off diplomatic relations with Cuba. Hemingway was a U.S. citizen, but he was also a resident of Cuba, and he remained the island's most conspicuous, high-profile expatriate. Washington's wish for him was not only to cease living in Cuba but to openly voice his displeasure at Castro's government and the Cuban regime. Ernest protested: this was his home, he was a writer, he saw no reason to change his living arrangements, which were his life, his livelihood. The Cubans were his friends, the staff at the *finca* was his family; how could a writer ply his trade and concern himself with these changing political situations? He had seen leaders come and go, he had lived through political upheaval during his years on the island. This was not his business. His business was to write. All his life he had shown his allegiance to America without living in the country. He was recognized worldwide foremost as an American writer; his loyalty to his country had never been questioned. Phil, a sensitive, gentle, understanding man, concurred with Ernest. He had no quarrel with what Ernest was saying; he understood exactly. But, he urged, some in Washington took a different view. They did not see the situation as Ernest did. Hemingway's high-profile presence in Havana might become an embarrassment to his country. Why allow that to happen when it was within his power to use his influence for positive purposes? If the writer was not prepared to take a stand as a public figure on behalf of his country, there could be consequences. The word *traitor* had come up. Phil reiterated that this conversation was a private one, not an official communication. It was a kindly warning given by a friend, but it was to be heeded. Phil, a true diplomat, finished his spiel and smoothly passed on to lighter conversation, not referring to the matter again. Only Ernest, Mary, Phil, and I were present during the conversation. It was not intended to be menacing, but it was. Ernest appeared not to take it seriously at the time, but I could tell as each day passed that the threat of losing his home and all it stood for began to weigh heavily on his mind.

On his next visit, Phil told us sadly that he had been recalled. Diplomatic relations between the United States and Cuba had been broken. He was leaving the next day for the States. We tried to be cheerful, to laugh and say this was just a temporary measure and it too would pass. A year or so from now we would all be sitting at the same table looking back on this moment and having a good laugh. Before he left, Phil softly reminded Ernest of what he had said on his previous visit. He felt now more than ever that Ernest would have to make an open choice between his country and his home—loudly and clearly, so that the world would know where he stood. We all embraced, promising to meet again before too long, believing things could only improve. While we waved to Phil from the steps as he left, I noted the sadness in Ernest's eyes. None of us would see Phil again.

Friday at the *finca* was fight night. Boxing from Madison Square Garden was televised, and dinner was scheduled so that the show would not be missed. Ernest presided in the kitchen quarters, where the TV was located.

Dinner guests and the male members of the staff joined in. There was a token betting pool, so everyone could participate without fear of penury. It was good fun, and I learned a lot about a sport that I had never imagined would interest me.

On Saturday nights, pleasantly exhausted after a day's fishing in the Gulf Stream, we showered and dressed in our best clothes: Ernest in his guayabera and Mary and I in silks and sandals. With Juan at the wheel of the yellow convertible if the weather was clement or the red hardtop if a storm was brewing, we set off for El Floridita, a bar in downtown Havana. There Ernest was always greeted with affection and appreciation as he settled on a bar stool or stood in his corner, elbows leaning on the polished mahogany bar. Until the waiter announced that our table was ready, he held forth genially as we quaffed large quantities of Papa Dobles, Ernest's favorite double daiquiri, made with fresh grapefruit juice and no sugar. Various friends or fans came over to chat or pay their respects: all were closely monitored by the staff so that their most illustrious client's privacy was not invaded. Only at the Floridita could he rely on there never being an incident that reached the point of annoyance, as I had seen happen in other places during our travels. We ate in the formal dining room, and I was always expected to end with the *coco glacé,* the coconut ice cream that was Ernest's favorite and which he had decided would be mine too. However, I had never cared for ice cream. Coming from a damp, cold climate, I favored warmth in everything, including food and drinks, but I had no intention of letting him down. So often associations determine our tastes, and soon this did become my dessert of choice. As I now think back on those days in Cuba, I cannot imagine anything more delightful or enticing than the coconut half shell firmly packed with delicately flavored ice doused with light rum and garnished with a maraschino cherry. This was invariably accompanied by the inimitable smile of my benefactor, who could not have been more pleased if the dessert had been his own creation. A lively musical group played mariachi tunes, traveling from table to table to serenade each party. Both Mary and Ernest loved the music and requested songs during which they joined their voices in harmony if it was a particularly light-hearted evening. We returned home quite replete and sleepily satisfied.

On Sundays Ernest arose and worked as usual. At quarter to ten Juan would back the red car out of the garage, leave the motor running, and tap on my door. It was time to go to Mass at the little church in a nearby village. I was the sole passenger, with the exception of Easter Sunday, when Ernest came along to fulfill his Easter duty.

The church edifice was simple, with few flourishes. The aging celebrant was charmless. There were several families with young children, many older women dressed entirely in black fingering their rosaries, and a few men. It was similar to many Hispanic churches I had visited in rural areas, except it lacked the warmth and effusiveness I expected—the painted statues and frescoes, masses of brightly colored flowers, and dripping candles in brass stands. With Juan always waiting for me afterward, I never had a chance to meet or talk to any of the parishioners. Mass was still in Latin in those days, and all the women wore hats or mantillas and were modestly but neatly dressed in their Sunday best.

One delightful Sunday Washington columnist Joe Alsop came to lunch and brightened up our lives. What a charming person he was! As Sunday afternoons were always devoted to the cockfights, Ernest decided he should come to it with us. Afterward Joe wrote in the *Herald Tribune* that although Mary put on a splendid luncheon, "the best part of the day was the cockfight that followed." He said that "even the arrival at the rickety little Cuban cockpit was an event of sorts, with its own processional almost ritual character. Ernest led our small parade, unencumbered, as was only fitting with something of the air of being the host at a huge, exceptionally successful party. His pretty Irish secretary and the rest of us followed, bearing many wine bottles." Joe's enthusiasm earned him a place in the heart of his host. Ernest asked that when I was next in New York I should pick up some corrida books and mail them to Joe in Washington.

CHAPTER TEN

Friends, Fishing, and Fidel

LIFE AT THE *FINCA* was a luxurious sojourn with no worries, tasty meals, good company, and lots of leisurely time to read and think. I could hardly imagine a better existence. I was charmed by the warm climate, the lively and rhythmic music, the lush tropical foliage and colorful fruit, the genial people, the lazy Cuban Spanish dialect interspersed with expressive African words such as *guagua* for "bus." Yet after my initial infatuation with the island, I became aware of the invasiveness of the political situation, of an uncertainty and a grating edge that was honed uncomfortably sharper with each passing day. Too often, the blaring music from San Francisco de Paula was replaced by the drone of a now familiar voice, that of El Jefe, Fidel Castro. He talked for hours, and everybody listened, or at least everyone turned on a transistor radio. Hour after hour he talked to his people, insistently, sometimes with angry, hoarse, gutteral intonation, at other times with a softly coaxing way, as if a child were being addressed, and less often in a forthright, friendly, and confidential way. The air echoed with the strains. Even the most illiterate person, and there were many, could not avoid the admonitions, the promises, the threats, the cajoling, the ever-present propaganda. Among ourselves, Ernest, Mary, and I never discussed politics.

Whenever Ernest stopped by the *casita,* it was with a correction or addition to something I was typing. If we discussed anything but the work at hand, it was literature. Ernest was a born teacher, and few things gave him greater pleasure than to introduce everything he loved to a receptive pupil. In this I excelled. From as far back as I can remember, I loved to read and would eagerly devour all the printed matter I could lay my eyes upon. Now for the first time I read Baudelaire, Stendhal, Stephen Crane, Scott Fitzgerald, John O'Hara, Steinbeck, Salinger, Dawn Powell, Dostoyevsky, Lawrence Durrell, T. E. Lawrence. The list was as long as my waking hours. I read a number of Ernest's books as well, including *A Farewell to Arms,* which he said was his favorite. I found more to my liking in *For Whom the Bell Tolls* because I had listened ad infinitum to his tales of the Spanish Civil War. As we drove through the countryside south of Madrid, so many times Bill had asked Ernest, "Is that where such-and-such took place? There's the river, is that the bridge?" Then Ernest described the fictional scene, as well as how it had actually been in the war and how he had reinvented it.

One time Bill had stopped the car and we got out to see more clearly how that last ambush could have happened. We had looked at the spot where the fictional Robert Jordan died. I had loved all things Hispanic from the first time I set foot in Spain. Pilar and Maria and Robert Jordan had been woven into the tapestry of my dreams, and I could recall names like Joris Ivens as though they were people from my own past, just as whenever I go to a racetrack I still think of Evan Shipman, although I never met him, and the tales Ernest told of Evan going out to the track at Santa Anita in California. Ernest had an extraordinary way of making people come to life, creating heroes of his friends so that they became fictional portrayals, every bit as real and colorful as the figures of Greek mythology and just as memorable.

The young editor of the *Paris Review,* George Plimpton, had impressed Ernest with his erudition and charm when he interviewed Hemingway in 1958. Plimpton was one of the people Ernest embellished in his stories. It seemed a dream come true when I received Ernest's cable saying George would meet me in New York and show me the city before I flew to Havana. Imagine my surprise when George turned out to be not New

York's most eligible bachelor and debonair literary star but Ernest's contemporary and former sparring partner George Brown, a staunch Roman Catholic imbued with old-fashioned courtesy. In Ernest's view George Brown was the perfect escort for a young Irish girl seeing the New World for the first time. Instead of hitting the hot spots with a suave young intellectual, I lit a candle at St. Patrick's Cathedral and lunched at Schrafft's under the paternal eye of George Brown. Many years would pass before I met George Plimpton.

Ernest liked to choose the articles about himself or his writing that he wanted me to read. Along with the *Paris Review* interview, in the spring 1958 issue, one of the first pieces he gave me was a copy of the controversial profile by Lillian Ross that had appeared in the *New Yorker* in 1951. I knew he corresponded with Ross and always spoke of her in friendly terms. He never gave me the slightest hint that he had not cared for the piece. He held Lillian up to me as an example of a woman reporter who plied her trade well. If Lillian's name came up within Mary's hearing, she dismissed it with "Miss Ross, the human tape recorder. She takes everything down exactly as she heard it but is as inept as a recording machine to evaluate what she had heard." Whatever he had thought of it at the time of its publication, by 1960 Ernest was quite pleased with the portrait of himself in his jocular, colloquial persona, which he sometimes put on for his family and intimates. Baffled outsiders considered his behavior that of an egotistic, drunken buffoon. Ross's piece was pure Ernest, but it was also pure parody, Ernest's parody—portraying a playfulness that no one in the inner circle would have taken seriously. Ernest had not contemplated how adverse the reaction would be to this little joke.

The Cuban revolution and its consequences of making even necessities scarce and of driving away resident Americans and tourists curtailed the round of visitors to the *finca* in 1960. Entertainment was at a low ebb compared to earlier seasons, but there were a number of friends and visitors who came out to the *finca* or met us in town for drinks. Of the old Cuban friends, Mayito Menocal was still around. Alejo Carpentier, the novelist—

more acquaintance than friend—paid a brief visit to the *finca* that spring. Ernest spoke well of him and his work. Mayito's friendship with Ernest dated back to the thirties. A wealthy sugar and rice plantation owner from Camaguey in the province of Oriente, he was a sportsman and fisherman whose main residence was in Havana. Ernest had bought his first fighting cocks from Mayito. They were both members of the Club de Cazadores and competed in the famous pigeon-shooting tournaments there. They fished together, and Menocal had even joined Mary and Ernest for part of their African safari in 1953.

When he was at odds with his father in the early forties, Mayito junior spent time at the *finca*. Expelled from Cornell University, he needed a safe haven from his parents' displeasure. Sadly, his visit coincided with the disintegration of Ernest and Martha Gellhorn's marriage, and the young man was witness to their marital squabbles.

Mayito's boat *Tensi* was part of the fishing fleet used during the shooting of *The Old Man and the Sea*. On the day in October 1954 when Ernest learned that he had been awarded the Nobel Prize for literature, a dozen people were invited to lunch at the *finca*, on which occasion Ernest declared Mayito and his cousin Elicio Argüelles, who were both present, to be his "best friends in this country." The friendship lasted to the end. I liked it when Mayito came around. He was always cheerful and gracious, and he and Ernest enjoyed a camaraderie that was becoming a rarity as friends scattered or friendships dissolved. Mayito was hopeful about the revolution, but every sign pointed to a decaying economy in a system which would soon turn from socialism to communism, from relative prosperity to complete ruin. Hope for the future of landed gentry such as the Menocals would slowly recede.

In early March we had an unscheduled visitor. The Russian delegation to the new Cuban government telephoned to say that Anastas Mikoyan was in Havana and, being a keen Hemingway fan, he desired to meet the author—could he be invited to the *finca*? Mary obliged and set a time the next afternoon. She planned a simple tea with sandwiches and expected no more than a carful of people. I was curious to meet the Armenian politician and was not disappointed. To everyone's surprise, a convoy of six cars pulled up at the house at the appointed time. Mary was dismayed because the meager tea would not suffice and she had to do one of those conjuring tricks, like the miracle of the loaves and fishes. She produced a tasty codfish stew, bacalao, one of her specialties, which had been prepared for a future meal.

After the introductions, Mikoyan proudly presented Ernest with a set of Russian translations of his complete works. Hemingway was the most popular of all foreign writers available in Russia. This probably came from his involvement with the Spanish Civil War and *For Whom the Bell Tolls,* the novel that evolved from it. The irony of the fact that Russia ignored the world copyright laws and paid no royalties could not have been lost upon the writer. He could visit the country and spend the accrued royalties while there. However, since the law required all accommodation and meals to be prepaid, and the duties on anything brought out of the country amounted to the cost of purchasing it elsewhere, there was little to be gained. Mary yearned for a sable coat, and occasionally she and Ernest talked of going to Russia to fulfill her desire and to walk in the footsteps of his literary heroes, Dostoyevsky and Tolstoy, but it was not to happen during Ernest's lifetime. Later Mary fulfilled her wish.

Mikoyan was a short, compact man. Straight black hair streaked with gray was combed back from his forehead. He had the roundest, blackest eyes I have ever seen. They shone and danced with amusement and, I suspected, mischief. On casual acquaintance, it was hard to dislike him. He spoke to me for a few minutes, and I could see that he was pleased I came from Ireland. Like Santa Claus, he produced presents for everyone. To my delight, I received a brightly painted set of wooden nesting dolls, all yellow, vermillion, and purple. I wrote the date, place, and donor on the bottom and treasured them as a souvenir of my visit to Cuba. (A couple of years later when I stayed with friends in the States, I noticed my doll was missing from the dressing table where I had set it. My hosts told me that they would not tolerate "communist trash" in their house and had done me a favor by tossing the offending object in the garbage. Those were strange times. Fears of communism were rampant. Even the fact that I had been in Cuba was distasteful.)

We took Mikoyan and his entourage on a tour of the house. It was my chore to bring him to the top of the tower so that he could enjoy the view. All twenty of us trooped up and down the cement stairs. Then we tucked into a hearty meal and, in spite of the language barrier (we spoke through an interpreter), it was a jolly and spirited afternoon. Our spirits were strangely perked by the intrusion.

The other Russian visitor who came to the *finca* that spring, Aram Khachaturian, the composer, was three years younger than Ernest. Armenian like Mikoyan, Khachaturian was a large, handsome man with abundant white wavy hair, black bushy eyebrows, and thick, sensuous lips. He was the first composer I had ever met, and although I had not yet heard anything he had written, I knew that his reputation was international. Again we had a pleasant afternoon with our guest.

March brought a visit from Ernest's old friend Herbert Matthews. He was the *New York Times* correspondent whom Ernest had met in 1937 during the Spanish Civil War. They had worked practically side by side for the duration of the conflict but had seen little of each other in the intervening years. They renewed their friendship when the *New York Times* sent Matthews to Cuba in 1952 to study the political situation under Fulgencio Batista. He had closely followed the political career of Fidel Castro from that point on. After Batista's coup of 1952, Castro, then twenty-five, strove to bring about the dictator's downfall. He filed a brief in the Havana Urgency Court asking that the assumption of power by General Batista be declared unconstitutional. When that was rejected, Castro turned rebel. It took six years and many escapades and brushes with death before he would triumph.

Matthews was with Castro in the Sierra Maestra in 1957, obtaining an interview that was published in the *New York Times*. From that time onward, the entire youth of the island was with Castro, and Batista started losing ground. Almost every element of the country was involved in the struggle. It became clear by July 1958 that Batista would lose. The victory was a military one. Three hundred to four hundred young rebels pushed westward against an army of thirty thousand that would not fight except when cornered. The defeat and dissolution of the army meant that Cuba could have a revolution of a profound social, political, and economic type. This was what Fidel Castro had planned and what he and his followers had fought for from the beginning. Matthews was with Castro when he and his forces took over the capital after Batista had fled. It was a triumph for Castro—and for Matthews, who scooped the world with his firsthand account of the successful Cuban revolution. Matthews wrote to Ernest and Mary in Ketchum to report to them of the incident and to reassure them that the *finca* was safe.

A tall, slender man of serious demeanor, Matthews was a seasoned journalist. Ernest was so pleased to see him when he came for lunch that their animated conversation continued well into the afternoon. He was keen to get Matthews's take on the political situation and to talk over old times. Herbert was still enthusiastic about the revolution and Castro's prospects. Seventy-five percent of the people were for El Jefe, who promised decent food, education, and medical care. This was a great deal more than that 75 percent had ever imagined they would have under the former Cuban regimes. But Matthews already foresaw problems arising between Castro and the U.S. government. He complained that the *Times* was editing his reports to show Castro in a poorer light, and in some cases not publishing the material at all. He felt he was wasting his time in Havana. He wanted another assignment, perhaps in South America, where his work would be of more value. While delighted to see his old pal, Ernest was disturbed to hear what Matthews had to say.

A number of other friends from the States popped over to Havana that spring. For instance, Dr. George Saviers came from Sun Valley for a week's fishing in April. With ominous political signs ahead, and a new medical problem, that of failing eyesight, Ernest's writing had not been going well. Every day he worked on the *Life* piece, but with its increased length, he was at a loss to focus or cut it.

His one great enjoyment was getting out on the Gulf Stream, which we did regularly as long as the weather permitted. Just to get out on the ocean was tonic for him, and he liked nothing better than taking his friends on the *Pilar* and letting them try their luck with the "big ones." Gregorio Fuentes had been *Pilar*'s mate for more than twenty years. Born in the Canary Islands, Gregorio arrived in Cuba an orphan at the age of six. His father, who had traveled with him, died on the journey, and according to Gregorio's story, when he arrived alone on the island he immediately set out to earn his living, doing odd jobs for the fishermen and learning their trade. Over the years of their association, Gregorio, thirteen months Hemingway's senior, became the writer's friend, confidant, and fishing companion.

I recall joyfully the many afternoons spent on the Gulf Stream trolling for the prized black marlin, and the wonderful meals Gregorio prepared in the tiny galley, especially his *salsa verde*. Gregorio helped me land my first sailfish, a thirty-nine-pounder. Nothing since has seemed so challenging or as onerous, nor so big and weighty, as reeling in that first fish. Often Ernest and I went out alone, but when Mary's elbow was feeling strong she came along too. No matter how the luck was running, a day on the water promised to be fun. It was refreshing to have George or other friends participate. Then I was not the object of Ernest's full attention as prize student. I didn't have to be so eager to catch a fish, so focused and ambitious. I could relax, lost in my own thoughts, enjoying the water and the lulling of the boat as the engine throbbed.

By May the fishing was a little better and life on the Gulf Stream became more social. Mary was able to come out more often, and so we would stop off at La Terraza in Cojímar when we docked *Pilar,* enjoying cocktails and hors d'oeuvres of fresh lobster before heading back to the *finca.* Everyone was gearing up for the Hemingway Marlin Fishing Tournament, a highlight of the season that in past years had drawn its share of tourists. Before the revolution, many of the Hemingways' friends came over to the island in their boats and the competition had been fierce. Now all the appropriated boats from the banished Americans were handed out by the government to groups of workers, mostly amateur fishermen. Fidel himself planned to compete in one of these boats. Toby (Otto) and Betty Bruce sailed over from Key West for the week. Otto Bruce had been part of the Hemingway entourage for almost three decades, dating back to Ernest's days in Key West with Pauline in the early thirties. He had served Ernest as chauffeur, valet, companion, odd job man, and jack of all trades, and now was firmly in the category of friend. They had driven across the States on several occasions, and in 1939 Bruce was the go-between for the buyers of the Finca Vigía. At that time Ernest had just sold *For Whom the Bell Tolls* to the movies and was afraid the sellers would increase the price if they knew the identity of the buyer.

When they were apart, Ernest kept up a lively correspondence with Toby. I was familiar with his name and history. A diminutive man with penetrating brown eyes and a large nose set on a blotchy face, Toby was always attentive to Ernest, but he was able to hold his own in the repartee when the moment arose. Betty was the salt of the earth, good and easy company, a pragmatist who did not intrude yet was an engaging member of the group. Mary decided that because of her elbow this year she would not fish on her little boat, *The Tin Kid,* as was her custom. Instead she boarded *Pilar.* Everyone was in good spirits, and we were well prepared. Gregorio had the best bait available. Expectations were high. But the seas were unwilling to cooperate. During the two days of the tournament, the course of the Gulf Stream was confined to a fifteen-mile run eastward instead of its usual hundred or so miles off Cuba's north coast. The many contestants kept their boats within a small area, all using the same space and causing everyone to fish in each other's wakes. We greeted some locals as they drew alongside and then floated past us. On at least one occasion Castro's boat came alongside ours and salutes were formally exchanged. We were not having luck with the fish, but Ernest and Mary kept his old U.S. Navy binoculars at hand to check the status of the competition. Mary trained the glasses on El Jefe's boat and one time shouted to Ernest to come and look. Fidel had hooked one and was bringing him in. Ernest took the glasses and gave us a short commentary on the proceedings. Not a skilled fisherman but a conscientious one, Fidel adhered to all the rules. We listened as Ernest described how El Jefe reeled in the fish and didn't attempt to gaff it before he grabbed the leader. Over the two days the combined weight of the three fish caught by Castro gained him the first prize, a silver trophy cup to be presented by the author himself.

We kept our distance during the presentation. It was the only time Hemingway and Castro would meet. Photographers took full advantage of the occasion. They exchanged a few words and Ernest was pleased Fidel took that moment to let him know he was both a reader and admirer of his work, especially of *For Whom the Bell Tolls*. The strategy used by the guerillas in the book had given him some ideas which he put to use when he was in the Sierra Maestra, Fidel confided to Ernest. Mary, Toby, Betty, and I all shook hands with the winner, and I was pleasantly impressed by the geniality and gentleness of the thirty-two-year-old leader. No sign of arrogance, only a reverent humility and genuine delight in the presence of one of his heroes. I was quickly swept away by the converging crowds. Before I could say anything significant or even pose for a photograph, a group of young Cuban women, clearly admirers, had pressed through the ropes, pushing themselves past the guards protecting El Jefe to have their photo taken instead. He was whisked away before mayhem broke out.

Ernest loved firearms and hunting, and it pleased him that I had some knowledge of the sport. He loved to tell of the time his son Gigi, age nine, won the pigeon-shooting tournament against a group of seasoned shooters. Gigi had been a crack shot and his father was proud of that. But he had gone bad, Ernest would add sadly. Any mention of his youngest son's name now brought on an angry outburst, or Ernest just left the room in silence. One knew instinctively that it was best never to mention Gigi. I was aware he had done something to bring disgrace upon himself, but there was no one to ask about it, nor did it seem important to do so.

Gigi had once pleased his father by saying he wanted to be a writer. Ernest gave every encouragement he could as well as lots of advice. He had already seen how his tutelage, along with Gigi's natural talent, had brought his son top honors in the shooting competition. He felt there was no reason the boy could not also write. Some months later his boarding school informed Ernest that Gigi had won first prize for his short story, which would be published in the school magazine. When the magazine arrived Ernest eagerly opened it, turned to the page, and started reading. He could not believe what he saw. Word for word, the story came from Turgenev—not a single error in transcription. Ernest did not know if he was angrier at his son, the plagiarist, or at the ignorance of the school English department, which had failed to identify the true author. Knowing Ernest's temperament by now, how exacting he was with those close to him, how unforgiving, and understanding how much his children wanted to be noticed by him, I could easily imagine a young boy doing what Gigi had done. However, this did not seem to me to be a sufficient reason for a father to disown his son, nor was it, I would later learn.

I knew both these stories very well the day Ernest decided he would teach me how to shoot. He held the 20-gauge shotgun cracked open in his hand and stowed several cartridges in one of his leather vest pockets. We brought a box of clay pigeons and the handheld contraption from which to fire them. He had talked of clay pigeons, and when I saw them, I was a little disappointed to find they were completely flat and round, not bird-shaped as I had imagined. He knew that I was left-handed, so he set me up with the stock of the shotgun snugly against my shoulder, my left hand ready to squeeze the trigger and my right supporting the gun. He told me exactly how to line my eye up with the barrel, and for practice I followed some birds who flew overhead, squeezing the trigger of the unloaded gun. He told me to keep my eye moving just ahead of them until he said "now," and with his hand over mine, our fingers pulled the trigger at the same time. He spent a few minutes making sure that my stance was just right, that I leaned forward and sighted the shotgun and learned to lead the movement of the flying object he tossed from the firing trap. After the dry runs, he set the clay pigeons flying and I fired. He analyzed my movement each time until I became fairly proficient. Then he showed me how to use the firing trap and I sent the clay pigeons flying for him. It was a calm day with no wind to distort the flight pattern, and in spite of his failing eyesight, he hit every one. We congratulated each other and strolled back to the house, feeling that we deserved our rum and soda more than ever. Up to that point the only time I had ever held a gun was when the carnival had visited Enniskerry. There had been a stall with a shooting range. The guns had been fastened to a wooden ledge and one had to sit on a stool and aim at the fixed target trying for the bull's-eye. Back then, I hadn't even come close.

CHAPTER ELEVEN

Mail and My Short Foray into Society

*T*HE ARRIVAL OF THE mail was a high point of the day. Ernest received a massive amount: business mail, personal letters, fan mail, newspapers, magazines, and books. Every week page proofs streamed in from publishers hoping for endorsements to be used on the dust jackets. Scribner's, his own publisher, sent all the titles that Charlie Scribner or Harry Brague, Ernest's editor, thought he would like. At the time, Scribner's also had a wonderful bookstore at Forty-eighth Street and Fifth Avenue in New York. Igor Kropotkin was the chief bookseller, and Ernest referred to him as "the Russian." He loved to peg people by the nationality of their ancestors, although in this case it is probable that Kropotkin actually came from Russia. Ernest often asked Scribner's to send him a package of books from the bookstore. He was keen to read the new young writers, especially novelists, and could be very hard on those who he felt should do better. There was a mixture of harshness and leniency in his criticism. He loved history, war chronicles, and reading about sports. Harper and Brothers sent the uncorrected proofs of George Plimpton's *Out of My League* that spring. Ernest enjoyed it and he made a note on the cover: "Cable George plug for book. EH." There was a crop of foreign newspapers delivered regularly. It was indicative of times to come when the *Miami Herald* stopped arriving because the Cuban government didn't have the U.S. dollars to pay for it.

One piece of mail angered Ernest very much indeed. That afternoon I could see from the thunder in his expression that there would be no working session ahead. He had received a package from the Baron—his brother Leicester. He went out through the library to the patio, found the old oil barrel that sat there, stuffed some paper and twigs in it, threw the typescript on top, doused it with gasoline, lit a match, and watched the flames flare up: yellow and red tongues of fire, blue at the edges with a thin stream of smoke ascending to the overcast sky, the city of Havana hazy in the distance. Even the sight of the funeral pyre did little to dissipate his wrath. Mary and I knew it was going to be a long evening. We made our way out to our separate quarters, not to return till the smoke had settled.

Hotch was a regular correspondent; his letters, full of Hollywood news and welcome bits of gossip, usually cheered Ernest. One communication, however, inadvertently caused momentary consternation. Hotch casually mentioned something like, "I suppose you heard about Gigi's tragic death?" Hotch was actually referring to Jigee Viertel, who had set herself on fire while lighting a cigarette in the bathroom of her home in January 1960 and burned to death, but he had misspelled the name or written it so it appeared to be Gigi, not Jigee. I had become so attuned to every nuance that I immediately caught a fleeting mixture of grief and relief at Ernest hearing of what he thought was the death of his youngest son, Gregory. I found it at once extraordinarily eerie and perplexing. Then, from Mary, "Oh no, not Gigi, Jigee." Peter Viertel's ex-wife had once crossed the Atlantic on an ocean liner with the Hemingways and Ernest had flirted with her and, to Mary's chagrin, appeared to be quite enamored. Up to that point Jigee had been a teetotaler, but during the crossing she had succumbed to a bad dose of flu, so Ernest prescribed a course of whiskey sours. When Peter met them in Paris at the Ritz Hotel he was surprised to find his wife drinking and liking it. Alcohol gradually took over her life, and the marriage broke up. Peter fell in love with Deborah Kerr, and they married in July 1960. Jigee was disappointed that Ernest never got in touch with her after her marriage to Peter ended. Both Mary and Ernest were quiet that evening. They did a little reminiscing about Jigee and her downfall. Inevitable, they both said. There was the tiniest feeling of guilt on Ernest's part that he had been the one to introduce her to liquor, which in the end became her executioner.

Another piece of mail that put a further damper on the spring came from Gary Cooper. Ernest and "Coops" had been firm friends ever since 1939, when they both were invited by Averell Harriman to stay at the newly opened Union Pacific resort at Sun Valley, Idaho. The next year Coops and Ingrid Bergman played the leading roles in the movie version of *For Whom the Bell Tolls.* Over the years the two men had kept in touch and had planned various ventures together. Cooper had grown up in Helena, Montana, and they both enjoyed a love of the West and of hunting and shooting. Coops had recently converted to Catholicism; for many years, his wife, Rocky, had prayed for his conversion to her faith. Ernest felt a kinship with the actor. He was not prepared for the news he received. Cooper had just learned from his doctor that he had cancer. "You can't lick the big C," Ernest would say. "What a black-ass day this is." He sent a cheering note back to his friend, although he felt anything but cheerful.

One day the mail brought an invitation from the British ambassador and his wife to a garden party at the embassy. Mary and Ernest no longer attended such affairs, but Mary saw no reason why I shouldn't do so. I might meet some people more my own age, broaden my connections, and have a chance to observe Cuban life from a different perspective. I was game, and Ernest agreed. Mary filled in the acceptance card naming me as their representative. I put on my silks and straw hat and set off to town with Juan. I had a splendid time, enjoying every minute of the festivities. I did not realize till that moment just how closeted my life had been, how confined in a slightly unreal world. It was fun to meet a varied group of people and to assume my own identity instead of being the appendage. Before I left the party, I struck up a firm friendship with the First Secretary's daughter, Alice, who was my age, and we agreed to meet again. We planned lunch the next week at the Bodeguita del Medio with a visit to the Bacardi Rum distillery afterward. When I returned to the *finca* I told Mary of the friends I had made and of the pending date. She was pleased that her little plan had worked.

CHAPTER TWELVE

Forebodings

*A*PRIL 5 BROUGHT MARY'S birthday, and a month later to the day my own. I was twenty. On both occasions the celebrations were low-key. Ernest and I went shopping for Mary's gift, and a couple of weeks later Mary picked out a yellow straw saddlebag with a circular bamboo handle for me from both of them. On my day we went fishing and ate dinner at El Floridita, where I had my required *coco glacé* for dessert with a lighted candle upon it. I was serenaded by the mariachi band as I blew out the flame and made a wish. Ernest was proud and wistful and Mary urged us all to sing the songs they had enjoyed so much: "*Bésame, bésame mucho*" and "*Yo soy como yo y no como Papa quiere.*" It was a perfect day.

In spite of the serenity we had achieved, I noticed a dark cloud drawing over our lives. Although Ernest and I had a close and loving relationship and a harmony had developed between himself and Mary that previously had eluded most of their marriage, he showed signs of agitation. Perhaps it started with his eyesight or the nagging knowledge that the Cuban political situation and its consequences would bring a future uncertain and uncontrollable, or it might just have been that his life's long battering and bruising had weakened his spirit. Whatever it was, my presence, the salve he had counted on, was no longer working its magic. No matter how hard he tried, the writing was cumbersome and, just as he was convinced his eyesight was failing, Ernest was also losing his sharp and unerring editing faculty. In desperation, he asked Hotch to come down to the *finca* in late June to help. Hotch's presence was always invigorating because of his clownish sense of humor, his good spirits, and his obvious affection for Ernest and friendship with Mary. Although Ernest's eyesight had never been very strong, he depended upon it for reading, for fishing and hunting, for sizing up situations. He despaired that it would fail him irrevocably. His relaxation had always been reading. Eye trouble brought with it worry and strain. He arranged to see an eye specialist. Mary thought a new prescription might do the job.

One spring night I was startled to consciousness by a shout, a deep male voice calling out, "Don Ernesto, Don Ernesto, are you awake? With respect, we salute you." I heard a strumming of guitars and the shaking of maracas followed by a harmonious rendering of several tuneful Latino songs, a tenor voice straining above the harmony. I was enchanted as I shook myself awake and pressed my face against the window screen. In the soft moonlight I saw three figures in troubadour costume pouring out their hearts in musical tribute. They must have climbed over the forbidding wall, unless they had an accomplice among the staff who had provided a key to the lock on the iron entrance gate. While I wondered who had sent them and whether some great new adventure was commencing, I faded back into a deep sleep bestirred only by pleasant dreams.

Next morning I stepped sprightly over to the house hoping to hear a cheerful story. I immediately saw that Ernest was less than pleased. He suffered dreadfully from insomnia. Anything that interfered with his sparse sleep was unwelcome. Damn fools, he called them, and said that if he could get his hands on the person responsible, that chap had better watch out. Could it have been a plan to unnerve him? he wondered. Without sleep, he couldn't work. Without work, he couldn't survive. Tantamount to murder. Nothing about the night's escapade gave him the pleasure I felt surely was intended. We never learned the name of our benefactor.

As the weeks went by, there were more nocturnal interruptions, although of a different sort. One morning Ernest asked me if I had heard the planes the night before. I had to admit that I had not. They had come over so low, he wondered how I could have missed them; U.S. planes, burning the sugar cane fields. This was bad news. He became obsessed with the subtle form of attack from his homeland. He voiced his anger more at the loss of sleep and its consequence than at the malevolent intent and the destruction being wrought upon an already ravaged land. There was no mistaking that the United States was serious in its retaliation to Castro's hostilities and leanings toward its archenemy, the USSR. Ernest must have pondered Phil Bonsall's warning and wondered what his next move should be. If things continued along the lines they were going, the Finca Vigía, home for a third of his life, would soon be a memory for the author. His animals, his books, his paintings, and all else that he held dear were there. The prospect of such a loss was too painful for Ernest to contemplate, yet each night, as his sleep was interrupted by the marauding planes, he had ample time to review his narrowing options. The noose was tightening.

One day early in June Mary and I were about to leave for Havana to browse through the market stalls and indulge in our weekly shopping spree. Juan had brought the car out front. We were lighthearted, anticipating the bargains we might find. Ernest came to the top of the steps and called out to Mary by her pet name, Kittner. He told her to go on ahead. However, he had work for me. Mary and I looked at each other and shrugged, and I waved goodbye to her and ran up the stone steps. "Shall I get my pad?" I asked. He shook his head and said that I wouldn't need it.

Nothing seemed particularly urgent. I began to wonder why he had asked me to stay. We worked for a while, but I could tell that his heart was not in it. He seemed distracted, distant. I sat quietly, waiting for his next instruction. Instead he put his papers aside and looked at me sadly. Then he told me that he had wanted to talk with me when we could be alone. I nodded. He said simply, "It won't work." Did I remember when he had asked me to come to Cuba and we talked of having a life together? I looked at him quizzically. Well, he continued, his gaze fixed on me, he'd received the report from the eye man. Much worse than he thought. It was not just the eyes. It was the whole system. He was truly finished. There was no future for him. There was no future for us.

I felt strangely relieved. The situation did not seem at all grave to me. I had had no expectations when I came. I did not consider there was a future, only each day as it dawned. I had never imagined Ernest without Mary, or Ernest and me together. I was content to be a part of the household for as long as I was needed. Even that I had expected to be temporary. I knew I would have the rest of my life to live as I pleased. Rather lightheartedly I said, "All I want or expect is to be a friend, and I don't mean a fair-weather friend. Your health, good or bad, should not change anything between us. I shall stick around for as long as you need me." It was clear he thought I didn't understand. He meant that it was time for me to make my own life. When he had asked me to come to Cuba, he told me he was on the verge of suicide and the only thing that would make his life worth living was having me at his side. I had agreed to come. My presence saved him for a time, and he was grateful for that. But life is a bitch, and his luck had run out. He knew what he had to do. It was inevitable. But he would not do it as long as I was around. And he could not do it until he knew that I was settled.

I protested angrily. "I can take care of myself. What I do with my life is my own business. If you plan this cowardly way out, I cannot stop you. But you should know better than anyone else that no man is an island."

He leaned closer to me and in that confidential half-whisper of his urged me to listen carefully. He had made up his mind and there was no going back. He said that he loved me and always would. The one way I could show him my friendship was to try to understand. We were in this together. It was our secret. No one else need learn of it. We would go on just as before. We must not let Mary know. He was counting on me to help him through the months until we left the *finca*, until we parted. I should make my plans. There was no point in arguing. Our eyes met and I silently assented.

What I had just heard was completely irrational. It seemed like a nightmare of gibberish. It did not occur to me that the sickness he suffered from might be a mental one. I knew that when Ernest spoke in confidence he was to be heeded. This was no joking matter, no whim. He had clearly re-hearsed his speech and given it a lot of thought. I had been pleased at how smoothly everything had gone in the months since my arrival. I had gained Mary's confidence and seemed to have a calming effect on both of them. The terrible fights, accusations, and recriminations witnessed in Spain were merely a memory. Life had been tranquil between them. The only flare-up in my presence had been one evening when Mary returned from somewhere. Ernest and I had dined alone and were in the living room af-terward sipping whiskey. He was sitting cross-legged on the grass mat at my feet, lost in the telling of one of his stories in that almost-whisper of his, when Mary burst in, loudly greeting us. She stopped short when she saw Ernest and, like a schoolmarm, pursed her lips and hissed at him through clenched teeth, "Get up at once. You are making a fool of yourself!" He had been raising himself to his feet when he saw her, out of respect, not fear, but her admonition made him tense, and I knew a battle was about to begin. I had said goodnight hastily and retired to the tranquility of my quarters and the uncomplicated company of my furry friend Pelusa, the little black kitten the staff had presented to me on my saint's day, March 17.

Hotchner arrived at the end of June. I was relieved to see him, hoping his presence would calm Ernest's fears. They would work together to shorten the bullfight piece and discuss other projects Hotch had in mind for converting various Hemingway works for television. Ernest had always shied away from transposing his works for film or television. On the occa-sions he gave in, perhaps lured by the lucrative side of the transaction, he was furious at the outcome, feeling his work had been ill represented or misused. The exception seemed to be when he allowed Hotch to collabo-rate with him on converting several short stories into television movies. Hotch was a persuasive person, and Ernest trusted his judgment. From the moment of our interview early in the month, Ernest was distant and de-tached from both Mary and me, from his work and the daily running of the *finca*. It was as if he had opted out and was in a semitrance, just going through the motions. I kept my distance but also took every opportunity to show my support and was always amenable, hoping that he would come out of this funk, this "black dog." I welcomed Hotch's visit and wished his presence would work some magic.

There was a restaurant in Havana that Ernest particularly liked and which had remained continuously in operation from his early days in the city. It was El Pacifico, a Chinese establishment in a tall, narrow building whose two top floors had once served as a whorehouse that was a popular after-dinner destination for certain customers. As we ascended to the dining room in the open elevator cage, Ernest had many unlikely stories to tell of bizarre adventures that had taken place in the building in former days. I think it was there that we were dining with Hotch on a late June evening in 1960 when suddenly Ernest pointed across the room and asked if that wasn't someone, a young lady, who had joined our cuadrilla briefly the summer before in Spain. Very little escaped Ernest's scrutiny despite his poor eyesight. Hotch, who was sitting next to Ernest, leaned toward him and whispered something in his ear. I watched as Ernest's face clouded over with a thunderous glower. His mood changed abruptly and he was quarrelsome and irritable for the rest of the evening. Next day when we were working together, Ernest said, fairly casually and without looking at me, that I must promise him I would never have anything to do with that person again. He was referring to the young lady we had seen the evening before. He knew that we were pals and had corresponded occasionally. I frowned but did not question him. Sometime later I learned the young lady had come to Havana for an abortion. I was surprised at how vehement Ernest was about the worthlessness of our friend's character and how quick he had been to condemn her. Perhaps it put him in mind of Martha Gellhorn, whose name never failed to evoke his rage and ridicule and whom he blamed bitterly when they couldn't have children, because, he suggested, of the many abortions she'd had. I could never distinguish truth from exaggeration or downright invention with Ernest, but I thought he had strange standards regarding young women, whom he classified as either saints or sinners. This outburst seemed completely out of character. Needless to say, I have continued even to this day my association with our cuadrilla friend, and the Havana incident has never been mentioned between us.

Contrary to my hopes, Ernest was not bucked up by Hotch's visit. Very little editing actually was accomplished. Ernest would have liked to withdraw his article from *Life* but was worried that the magazine would sue him if he did. Every tiny thing became a worry for him. Unaware that there was an insurmountable problem in the author's mind, *Life* scheduled publication of "The Dangerous Summer" for September so that it would hit the stands before the corrida season ended.

Ernest decided that he must go back to Spain to see Antonio and Luis Miguel fight one last time in case any significant changes needed to be noted in his article. He was concerned that he had been unfair to Luis Miguel, who would find his recounting biased; that the bullfight people would tear him to pieces for statements he made about the paring of horns and other illegal practices; and that the Spanish aficionados in general would despise him.

Fear became his daily companion. In the afternoons as we sat together in the library, he voiced these fears. I tried to reason with him; failing this, I concurred and sympathized. Each day a new fear was added. He was concerned about his finances. Taxes were always a hidden enemy, waiting to attack. He never knew what his royalties would amount to, so he tried to keep the maximum needed in his tax account. He had a good reason for this fear because in one recent year, his lawyer, agent, and accountant, Alfred Rice, had grossly miscalculated, falling far short in his estimation of taxes due, which resulted in Ernest receiving a hefty fine and having to borrow to meet the extra money owed. He never completely trusted Rice after this fiasco. He told me once that in his opinion Alfred grew leaner and meaner with each year, becoming more like Cassius in his cunning and his calculations. Yet he was not prepared to fire him.

I had learned along the way that most of Ernest's fears were based on some concrete incident. It was not just a matter of paranoia. When I joined the cuadrilla in Spain he had told me that his one job specification was that I should not write about what took place within his household. I remember learning sometime later that a journalist named Milt Machlin of *Argosy* magazine came to Havana and made a point of meeting Hemingway casually at

El Floridita. He charmed the author and received an invitation to dine at the *finca*. They had a jolly evening amid heavy drinking. Ernest had behaved in his rambunctious, no-holds-barred way, speaking his mind on every subject and every person. Finally Juan had taken a very inebriated Machlin back to his hotel. The next morning, as Mary was straightening the cushions on the sofa, she found a rumpled notebook. Not recognizing the handwriting, she started reading and, to her dismay, found devastatingly nasty notes on the previous evening written in a drunken, partly crypto shorthand. Machlin had planned a true character assassination of his newfound "friend."

While Hotch was still at the *finca*, having difficulty persuading Ernest to accept the cuts he suggested, Mary brought up the subject of a manuscript that was in the bank vault. She thought it might make good movie material, and she suggested to Ernest that he let Hotch read it. Since the fishing was poor, the two men went off to Havana to the bank and brought back the typescript, which was tentatively named "The Sea Chase." It would later be published as *Islands in the Stream*. Hotch read it eagerly and agreed with Mary that it could be turned into a film. Ernest was not so sure. He would have to look at it again, he said. He turned to me. His eyes were bothering him, he said, so he asked me to read a couple of chapters out loud. I did, but he was still unsure. There were some things he needed to do to it. He would finish the Paris book first and then take a look. That is, he added uncertainly, if he could still see well enough to write.

CHAPTER THIRTEEN

Farewell to the Finca

*A*FTER HOTCH LEFT, ALL our thoughts turned toward leaving Cuba. It was decided we would take the ferry to Key West from Havana on July 25 and head for New York City after checking out the Key West property and visiting a few friends. When Pauline died in 1951 she had left the house equally to her two sons, Patrick and Gregory, and to her ex-husband. They had tenants renting, but Ernest was keen for me to see the house and glimpse another chapter of his past. After a week in New York Ernest would return alone to Spain to complete the *Life* article about the bullfight duel, in case the season had brought any new developments. If he needed me to join him, I would be poised to leave. Those last few weeks he was withdrawn, ill at ease, incapable of making a decisive move and sticking to it. Still, he tried to put up a cheerful front.

When we were alone, he asked me what my future plans were. I procrastinated, hoping against hope his dark mood would pass and the pace of our lives would pick up again. As promised, I gave no inkling to anyone of the ominous conversation that had taken place in early June. I endeavored to put a positive and cheerful face on things while inwardly steeling myself for the parting and for whatever tragedy might lie ahead. Mary was involved with the household management, supervising the packing and giving the usual instructions for the months they would be absent. I decided to make the most of my last three weeks in Cuba, reading under the mango trees, swimming naked in the tepid pool with bats skimming the water, writing letters to friends, and wondering what the future might hold for me, for each of us. I had no doubt that my chapter with the Hemingways was drawing to a close.

There had been a time when I looked forward to my freedom, but now, as the moment approached, I felt as if a millstone were tied around my neck, dragging me downward. How could I leave with the knowledge of Ernest's self-imposed death sentence? How could I plan a future when the crystal ball showed there was none? Was this the sadness Ernest had felt when he read my palm eleven months before, that afternoon in Spain when the tears welled in his eyes? How could my life and my future have value when his life was valueless? He still had much to give. Could I allow him to throw it all away? Was it within my power to intervene? If anyone were expendable, I should have been that person, not he. Was it my business to try to prevent the inevitable? Alone in the *casita* I mentally argued the case back and forth until I was weary and my head ached. I alternated between feeling that I was hopelessly tied to Ernest and responsible for his destiny and that I had done all I could and should wash my hands of the situation. It was no longer my business. I had kept my part of the bargain and now must make a clean break, escape from this madhouse and return to my own life, putting behind me the fears and phobias, suicide threats and deft manipulations of an aging egomaniac. Back and forth I wavered—to stay and save the day or to go and start anew.

In spite of my dilemma, I put on a cheerful face in front of the staff, behaving as though I considered myself a permanent member of the family who would return with Mary and Ernest in the late fall or early the next year. They were to look after my kitten, Pelusa, for me, and I would leave some personal items behind in the *casita* to show my intent to return. In our own ways, we were each deluding ourselves. There would be no return to life at the *finca* as it had existed for the past twenty years.

Ernest's sixty-first birthday passed quietly on July 21. Mary and I drove to town together and bought token gifts. The three of us went through the motions of gaiety, but deep down there was a hollowness through which echoed an indomitable sadness, a song of despair. Ernest was in no mood to celebrate. It would be his last opportunity. The Champagne we drank to future health and happiness turned flat and sour as soon as it touched my palate.

Key West was the second place I visited in the United States. We took the ferry over from Havana and landed there on July 27. It was not so unlike Cuba in tropical landscape, weather, and shoreline except it lacked the sweeping majesty of the Malecón and everyone spoke English; the poor man's Havana, Ernest might have called it. We stayed in a motel and ate with Toby and Betty Bruce and Charlie and Lorine Thompson, they recalling late into the night the old days of fishing on the Keys and hunting in Africa and me listening. Charlie Thompson had joined Ernest and Pauline on their 1933–34 safari and was featured in *Green Hills of Africa,* a book I had yet to read. It was dedicated to Charles and two others.

We visited the house at 907 Whitehead Street, which had been bought with money from Pauline's rich uncle Gus and with proceeds from *A Farewell to Arms.* Ernest proudly pointed out the swimming pool, now empty and with its paint peeling, but which at one time, when filled and elegantly surrounded by prancing peacocks, had brought moments of solace to his life. Sloppy Joe's Bar—noisy, smoky, and filled with locals—was a mandatory stop. Trunks with Ernest's belongings, mostly papers, had been stored there in the basement since 1939, when Ernest moved out of Whitehead Street, his marriage to Pauline at an end. He had intended to send them over to Cuba but never got around to it. Perhaps he didn't like to sever ties altogether, for he had left a similarly filled trunk behind in Paris too.

Ernest decided to fly to New York, and Mary and I followed him by train, occupying three compartments, one each and one for the luggage. Toby drove us to Miami, where we saw Ernest off at the airport. Everywhere we went someone stopped Ernest to greet him. They knew him or recognized him, or thought they did. At the airport we were stopped yet again, this time by a man of medium height with thinning brown hair and a distinctive mustache. From their greeting he appeared to be a friend. The noise level was high with the loudspeaker system blaring, but I gathered his name was Tom. A short, amiable discussion followed on such topics as the state of Cuba and the fate of mutual friends there. There were some cursory literary comments, and then we went on our way. I did not pay too much attention since for me this was just another of the constant interruptions.

The next day Mary spoke of Tennessee Williams. "You've met him," she said.

"No, never," I replied, "but I would love to. He's my favorite contemporary American playwright."

"Yes, you did meet him," Mary said with exasperation. "You spoke to him at the airport in Miami when we saw Ernest off."

"That was Tennessee Williams?" I blurted out, kicking myself for an opportunity lost.

"Of course. Who did you think it was?" Mary snapped impatiently.

Ernest's writings and photographs and many other items we had brought over from Cuba had been repacked by Toby Bruce and sent off to the Hemingways' house in Idaho. The New York apartment was no more than a pied-à-terre that could accommodate only the meagerest of belongings. There would be no room there for me. I was to stay at the Barbizon, a hotel for women on Fifty-ninth Street and Lexington Avenue, a short walk from the East Sixty-second Street apartment. That way I could join the Hemingways for meals and be available when needed until Ernest left for Spain on August 4, at which point I planned to move to Long Island to stay with Ciss Dunne's brother Lar and his wife, Helen. In spite of the depression Ernest was suffering, that week in New York with him was packed with activity and fun. He couldn't resist showing off his town and his special haunts. It solidified my affection for the city that would become my adopted home, where three of my four children were born.

One afternoon Ernest and I took a cab to the Metropolitan Museum, where he was keen to show me the Winslow Homers. He had a great affection for this painter and could spend hours looking at the works, which brought him back to the Caribbean and the simple life of the fishermen. As we walked up the wide marble staircase he pointed out the name of Pauline's legendary uncle Gus, Gustavus Adolphus Pfeiffer, chiseled in the stone as one of the benefactors of the museum. Gus's guile and business acumen had made him a fortune heavily based on the patent of Sloan's Liniment. Ernest had dedicated *A Farewell to Arms* to him and always held him in high esteem. Not only had Gus helped them buy the Key West house, but he had funded Ernest's first trip to Africa in 1933. *Green Hills of Africa* came out of this safari. Again, Ernest told me that if he had not been a writer, he would have liked to have become a painter, and that his objective as a writer was to invent with words a world as real and innovative as that a painter conjured up with his brush. We walked through the twentieth-century galleries, viewing the Impressionist paintings and the work of the Cubists, painting that was contemporaneous with his early writing. Then we sat down on a polished mahogany bench, silently absorbing what our eyes beheld, each of us lost in our own thoughts.

Mary and I saw Ernest off at Idlewild Airport on his way to Madrid. After giving me a farewell hug, he said that he wanted me to join him as soon as it was feasible. I nodded. I was having a good time in New York and was not eager to leave right away. I could not foresee then that I would spend most of my life in the United States. I thought this was just to be a temporary sojourn and that I should make the most of it.

I then took the train out to Long Island to stay with the Dunnes. In addition to meeting the crème de la crème of Great Neck society, well-heeled hearties who laughed loudly and boasted of their cars and sailboats, I was introduced to the concept of barbecues, mixed drinks called cocktails, and the country club, where the right kind of people met and amused themselves after serious exercise by sipping cocktails and discussing their latest acquisitions. It was as foreign to me as any way of life I had yet encountered.

I was only there a couple of days when Helen asked me to persuade Mary Hemingway to be the guest of honor at her local women's club luncheon to launch a new charity on August 8. The concept of a women's club was one that Mary heartily despised, but for some reason even she couldn't later explain, she agreed. I went to the city and brought her back with me. I could see immediately that she regretted coming—her tolerance for petty tittle-tattle was nil and her propensity for nasty outbursts of impatience great. I watched her uneasily, recognizing the danger signal of pursed lips underscoring a deep frown. Just before things had a chance to go awry, Mary was called to the telephone. After she hung up, she beckoned me aside. The call had been from Greta, her housekeeper, she said. There was an emergency and she had to get away immediately, and she hoped I would come with her.

"What's up?" I asked. She told me that Hotch had called from Maine. He had heard a disturbing report on the radio that Ernest had collapsed at the Málaga bullring and was in serious condition. Hotch asked Greta to let Mary know at once and then to wire Málaga for confirmation. Upon hearing this news I told Helen firmly that there had been an emergency and that I would explain it later, but now Mary and I must return immediately to the city. We were ushered out stealthily so as not to attract the attention of the photographer or newspaper reporter. All the way to town we feigned good humor, cheering each other and speculating on the circumstances. Mary wondered whether she would be able to get on a flight to Madrid that evening.

Back at the apartment, we called the AP and UPI news services. Neither could confirm the news. The Davises had no telephone at La Consula, nor did the Brenans in Churriana. UPI called to report that the news item had originated in Stockholm, but they could tell us nothing further. Mary called CBS and put Ned Calmer on the trail. They had received a news flash that read, "Hemingway Stricken," but had no details. Mary checked in with UPI again, where their latest report read that Ernest had left Málaga and was on his way to Madrid. Then Ned called back. AP had just received a dispatch filed at Churriana: "Ernest Hemingway took time to deny reports that he was stricken." The doorman called to say a cable was on its way up. The RCA message from Granada read, "Reports false enroute Madrid love Papa." Mary poured us each a stiff gin and tonic, and we danced around the room. I suggested we go to the Stork Club, where we had last been with Ernest, but Mary said for that we would need an escort, so instead we telephoned several close friends who might have heard the news to tell them it was a false alarm: Hotch in Maine, Toby and Betty Bruce in Key West, and Charlie Sweeney and Dorothy Allen in Salt Lake City.

The incident made me uneasy. I could not get back into the swing of Long Island life. Nothing seemed important except knowing firsthand that Ernest was all right. He had sent another cable saying that Annie Davis had written inviting me to join them in Spain, but he cautioned that the corrida schedule was complicated and his movements uncertain. He advised that I wait until I heard from him before traveling. Whereas once he had been decisive, uncertainty had now become Ernest's way of life. I knew I must get back to Europe as soon as possible. I could take no pleasure in waiting for the next disastrous news bulletin.

I booked a flight to Paris for August 20 and arrived at Orly on the morning of the twenty-first. Mary had seen me off and noticed that the writer A. J. "Joe" Liebling was traveling on the same plane. She introduced us, and we had a lively conversation and drinks in the lounge before embarking. I noted in a letter to her that I did not see him again during the flight. Mary replied, "Liebling, who is getting on, doubtless preferred the sweet murmurings of Morpheus to the gay conversation of a young Irish biddy." When I had settled in, I cabled Ernest in Madrid, "Paris chez Monique love Val."

CHAPTER FOURTEEN

Spain Again

WITHIN A FEW DAYS of my arrival in Paris I received a cable from Ernest, asking me to come to Madrid on August 30. I took the train and had my passport stamped at Irún. Ernest was there at the station, a somewhat diminished, dejected figure lacking the energetic spirit and joie de vivre of a year before. In the few weeks since I had last seen him, he had lost weight and appeared to be distracted, although clearly he was pleased to see me; he had feared I might not turn up. I can still see his smile stretching from ear to ear, baring the even, ivory teeth, but his eyes lacked their previous sparkle. As he hugged me, he whispered that he was damned glad I was there. He had missed me terribly.

In the taxi on our way to the Suecia Hotel, he brought me up to date on the events of the previous three and a half weeks. He was not happy with the current corrida season. He was filled with fears and indecision, much intensified since I had seen him off at the New York airport. He was tentative and ill at ease, tending to look over his shoulder as we passed through the lobby and entered the elevator in case someone was eavesdropping on our conversation. Angst was his inseparable companion. The *Life* article, in two sequential editions, was about to hit the stands. Ernest expected Luis Miguel to be upset at what would be construed as a biased portrayal, so he was avoiding an encounter with the matador. Antonio had suffered a concussion at Bilbao the week before, and about the same time his wife, Carmen, had had a miscarriage. There was not a glimmer of hope on Ernest's horizon.

At the hotel, Bill Davis joined us. The hitherto unflappable, easygoing Bill now seemed ill at ease too, not the happy-go-lucky man of a year before who had slavishly acted as chauffeur and guide, companion and congenial host. This Bill was more alert, on guard, wary, keeping his distance from Ernest yet always at attention. We dined at El Callejón, a reasonable walk from the hotel. Ernest chose calf's liver and bacon accompanied by a Marques de Riscal rioja and flan for dessert. While we stayed in Madrid, this became our habitual bistro and perpetual menu. Ernest never varied his choice of food. We ate alone, the three of us, rarely inviting anyone to join our table.

For a month we followed the corridas, stopping at La Consula in between. As we set out on the road in the cream-colored Lancia, *La Barata,* I felt Ernest's body tense beside me. He hardly dared relax and kept his eyes trained ahead for the most part, or he fell into a sullen reverie. Bill, who had always been the listener, now tried to keep a conversation going. The topics were general, for if he became in the slightest way specific, Ernest appeared suspicious and challenged his intention. Bill coaxed him to relate his previous adventures in Spain and France, which Ernest seemed reluctant to do, so our driver filled in the silent moments with tidbits of news and gossip of mutual friends or personalities they both knew, items that would have roused Ernest to piquant responses a year before.

On that first trip south in 1960 we stopped to fill up the gas tank and buy a few necessities. Ernest nudged me to fall back a bit and let Bill go ahead. Had I not noticed? he whispered urgently to me. Did I not see what he was doing? I struggled to understand. "Bill, you mean? No, I don't think so. I didn't notice anything unusual," I said. Ernest then said Bill was trying to kill him. In fact, he was going to kill both of us. Couldn't I tell from the way he was driving? He had almost succeeded the year before, and now he was giving himself a second chance. "I don't think so," I repeated, aghast, for I knew this present fear to be entirely in Ernest's imagination. Bill had great stamina but was indeed a haphazard driver. Previously his style had not bothered Ernest. In fact, he had seemed to enjoy the spontaneity. I had never heard him at any time before suggest that Bill was to blame for our mishap on the road from Burgos. He admonished me to watch carefully and not to let him doze off while we were in the car. I assured him I wouldn't. "I think you're mistaken about Bill," I said, "but I'll keep my eyes open, don't you worry."

Annie was at La Consula waiting for us, and I was glad to see her. Ernest had cut down on liquor and was being careful with his diet. He feared that he had the beginning of a kidney infection. In his traveling pharmacy he had a gallery of pills to ease his ills, but nothing could erase the tension or restore his well-being. He lacked energy and was apathetic, disinterested in everything, and brimming with imaginary woes. He was more apprehensive than a bullfighter before a corrida. No amount of reasoning could quash the demons that danced the dance of destruction and death before his eyes. In contrast to the year before, he wished to see no one for fear that the *Life* article had caused anger or worse. He retired early but continued to be plagued with insomnia. He asked me to stay by his side at night until he fell asleep, just as his sister Ura had done when he came home to Oak Park after the First World War. For hours we talked. I tried every ploy and wile I knew to ease his fear.

He was obsessed with suicide, but he needed to know what I planned to do with my life before he checked out. I felt that if he wanted to obliterate himself, then he had no claim on my future, or any future for that matter. I agreed to return to the United States after I had visited Ireland for a short while. One of Ernest's concerns was how he would pay me for the months I had worked for him in Cuba. He wanted to make sure that he would not be penalized for employing me in Cuba when I did not have a permit to work there. He was meticulous in his plan so that the money could not be construed as earnings. Over and over again we discussed the various scenarios.

I had no fears about the Cuban government, but I knew I must find a plan that was foolproof and would satisfy Ernest's requirement that the money be passed to me without suspicion.

Ernest had bet on the Johansson-Patterson fight the year before and had made a tidy winning on the Swede, who had triumphed at long odds. Hotch had access to this money, and it was being held for some emergency or special fun. Now Ernest decided that he would pay me for my secretarial services from that fund so that the amount would not show up anywhere in his own finances. He still felt he needed a cover for giving me the money if he was ever probed. He asked me if I had thought of attending university. Given all I had heard him say about college educations, college professors, and his pride in never having been tainted by either, I had no desire to pursue a higher education. It seemed like a step backward. In the course of our many conversations I had spoken of my interest in the theater. My main quest in returning to New York was to see *The Hostage* on Broadway. Later, when Ernest brought up the subject of the money with Hotch, it was Hotch's suggestion that the money go "towards Val's enrolling in the Academy of Dramatic Arts in New York." So it was decided. Ernest asked Hotch to give me the money when I arrived in New York.

I was anxious to return to the States. It weighed heavily on my mind that I had promised Behan a year before I would attend the first night of *The Hostage* at the Cort Theatre in October, and I did not want to break my promise. Brendan had been in touch with me, and it was flattering that he counted on my presence to celebrate his international success. As the time drew closer it was clear that I would not be able to fulfill this promise, so I asked if Lar and Helen Dunne and Mary Hemingway could go instead, and said I would explain to him when we next met. Brendan amicably agreed. I couldn't leave Ernest at that critical moment. I had to do all in my power to dissuade him from his suicidal determination, and that could not be put on a timetable. It would take as long as it took, and if I was successful, no event of whatever magnitude would be of equal importance.

I have little recollection of the itinerary, the incidents, or the details of our trips that September. Ernest's black mood and my efforts to dispel it were all-consuming. Bill and Annie were as bewildered as I was. We traveled to Ronda, Jerez de la Frontera, Salamanca. We saw many of our aficionado friends, but my memory of that month in 1960 is as flat as it is vivid of the year before. Ernest perked up slightly when he saw young Paco Camino fight with courage and style, for here was a possible successor to Ordóñez, but when the first copy of *Life* arrived by airmail, his fears and doubts returned, along with anger and indignation. *Life* had double-crossed him, he was sure, in their choice of photographs, making him look a fool and, with sinister intent, sparking a feud between him and the matador brothers-in-law. He did not seem to consider the one area where he was likely to receive unabashed criticism, perhaps deservedly so. That was for his remarks about Manolete's "cheap tricks" in the bullring to please the crowd. Manolete was revered by the aficionados, almost sanctified. Any criticism of his art by a foreigner was likely to be met with hostility. When the second *Life* article came out, Ernest stayed out of the spotlight and, as if anticipating abuse, sometimes became unpredictably quarrelsome when he was thrust into company.

Before he left New York in late July Hotch told Ernest that Twentieth Century–Fox was interested in making a movie of the Nick Adams stories. They were offering $125,000 for the rights, with an additional $75,000 for Hotch to write a screenplay. Ernest, generally opposed to having his works filmed or televised, was now feeling financially pinched because of all the uncertainty in Cuba and the fear he would not be able to write again, so he summoned Hotch to Madrid to see if the deal could be completed.

El Pecas arrived at the Suecia Hotel on October 2 on his way to London to see Gary Cooper, where he was going to discuss the possibility of Coops playing Colonel Cantwell in *Across the River and into the Trees*. We had just made our way back up to Madrid from La Consula to see Ernest off, but he was uncertain as to his date of departure. Discussing the movie with Hotch would delay his decision by a few days. Bill, Annie, and I were all at the Suecia with Ernest. It had been a harrowing month, and we were glad that Hotch would soon be there to relieve the gloom. When Hotch did not arrive on time, Ernest imagined every sort of disaster. The three of us were sitting in his suite when Hotch walked in. Nursing his infected kidney, Ernest was lying on the bed; his dressing gown was tied at the waist by his German World War II "Gott mit Uns" belt. Annie and I were sipping glasses of wine. Hotch wrote later, "Worry hung in the room like black crepe." While all of us hoped that seeing Hotch would be the tonic Ernest needed, I remembered Hotch's visit to Havana four months before and was less sure. Ernest did not join us for dinner, citing his ailing kidney. He told Hotch he would see him early in the morning for their business discussion.

We took a taxi to El Callejón out of habit and had a chance to bring Hotch up to date on the state of affairs. Ernest had been difficult with Bill, no matter how hard Bill tried to please him. Every small item had been blown up beyond all proportion. The entire world was out to get him, Ernest felt. Ernest's plane ticket on Iberia Airlines was in Bill's name so that the press would not hound him. He decided to take a midnight flight on a prop jet to New York, an old Constellation that took fourteen hours for the journey, to confound anyone who would look for him on a regular daytime jet. Ernest was concerned about transporting the originals of the photographs that had appeared in *Life,* for he wanted to be able to use them as proof that the magazine had double-crossed him. He feared that Iberia Airlines would not let him take them on board because his luggage would be over the limit. The Hemingways had always traveled with overweight luggage and reveled in it. Now, illogically, he felt he would be barred from embarking. Hotch made every effort to take things in hand, to allay Ernest's fears. He called Iberia to ascertain that Ernest's luggage was within the limits, that he would be accepted. But the matter was not settled until Bill went out to the airport and returned with a written statement to the effect that there would be no problem with Ernest's traveling arrangements, luggage and all.

Making preparations for my own getaway, first back to Paris and then on to Dublin, I could not find my passport. I looked all over my room without success, then asked Ernest if by any chance I had left it in his suite, since we spent a good deal of our time there. When it was not visible at first glance, he became inordinately upset. He imagined that it had been stolen,

*Thomas Reginald Smith
and Millicent Danby on
their wedding day,
December 5, 1936,
in Blackheath, London.*

COLLECTION OF
VALERIE HEMINGWAY

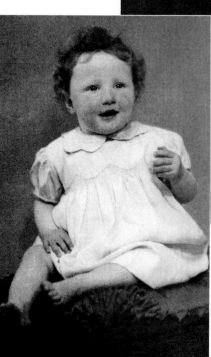

*Valerie Danby-Smith on
her first birthday, May 5,
1941, Dublin.*

COLLECTION OF
VALERIE HEMINGWAY

Valerie Danby-Smith on her communion day, June 1, 1947, at Dominican Convent Cabra in Dublin.

COLLECTION OF
VALERIE HEMINGWAY

Valerie Danby-Smith and Rev. Patrick Danby (Uncle Patrick), Estoril, Portugal. June 1956.

COLLECTION OF
VALERIE HEMINGWAY

Ernest Hemingway and Valerie Danby-Smith at the Choko Bar, Pamplona, July 1959.

Group photo in Pamplona. Photographer Cano hams it up (upper right) for his admirers. Behind Cano is Bill Davis, who is next to Ernest Hemingway, Valerie Danby-Smith, prisoner Mary Schoonmaker, and Juanito Quintana standing sideways.

Mealtime at La Consula, Málaga. Left to right: host Bill Davis, Rupert Bellville, Ernest Hemingway, Mary Hemingway, and Juanito Quintana. May 1959. COLLECTION OF VALERIE HEMINGWAY

Ernest Hemingway's sixtieth and Carmen Ordóñez's thirtieth birthday party at La Consula, Málaga, July 21, 1959. Left to right: Carmen and Antonio Ordóñez dancing, Ernest Hemingway, Valerie Danby-Smith, and guest on bench. CANO. COURTESY OF JOHN F. KENNEDY LIBRARY

Valencia, July 1959.
At the bullfight.
Left to right: Annie Davis,
Mary Hemingway,
Valerie Danby-Smith,
and Bill Davis.
CANO. COURTESY
OF JOHN F. KENNEDY
LIBRARY

Málaga, August 1959.
After the bullfight.
Left to right: Bill Davis,
Juan Goytísolo, Annie
Davis, Valerie Danby-
Smith, Florence Malraux,
Ernest Hemingway,
Antonio Ordóñez,
Nicole Pardo, and a guest.
COURTESY OF JOHN F.
KENNEDY LIBRARY

Paris, October 1959.
At the races. Left to right:
young lady, Monique Lange,
Florence Malraux, Nicole Pardo,
and Ernest Hemingway.
PETER DUFFIELD

Spain, October 1959. Ernest Hemingway poses in front of his Lancia "La Barata" before buying an ice cream.

Finca Vigía, Cuba. Photo by Valerie Hemingway, March 1999. The house had not changed since she first set foot in it in January 1960. COLLECTION OF VALERIE HEMINGWAY

Living room of the Finca Vigía, Cuba. Photo by Valerie Hemingway, March 1999. Now the Museo Ernest Hemingway, the interior was exactly as it had been in 1961 when she last saw it. COLLECTION OF VALERIE HEMINGWAY

Cuba, 1960. Ernest
Hemingway caught Valerie
Danby-Smith and his wife,
Mary, hamming it up in the
garden of the Finca Vigía,
1960.

COLLECTION OF
VALERIE HEMINGWAY

Havana, 1960. Relaxing on the Pilar.

M. HEMINGWAY. COURTESY OF THE
JOHN F. KENNEDY LIBRARY

Havana, 1960. Ernest Hemingway and
Valerie Danby-Smith pose after a day's
fishing in the Gulf Stream.

M. HEMINGWAY. COURTESY OF THE
JOHN F. KENNEDY LIBRARY

Havana, 1960. Fidel Castro accepts the Hemingway marlin fishing contest trophy from Ernest Hemingway. COLLECTION OF VALERIE HEMINGWAY

Idaho, 1940. Patrick and Gregory "Gigi" Hemingway after a day's duck hunting. Even as a young boy, Gigi was a crack shot.

Idaho, 1961. The "Block House" has a wraparound deck that gives a spectacular view.

Idaho, 1961. A view of the "Block House" from the long driveway.

Idaho, November 1961.
Snowshoeing. Mary
Hemingway (center),
Valerie Danby-Smith
(right), with friend.
COLLECTION OF
VALERIE HEMINGWAY

Idaho, November
1961. Clara Spiegel
takes a tumble.
VALERIE HEMINGWAY

Dublin, circa 1960. Artist Seán O'Sullivan and Brendan Behan view a portrait of Behan.

Cape Cod, 1966.
Gregory and Valerie Hemingway
shortly before their marriage.

COLLECTION OF
VALERIE HEMINGWAY

Miami, 1967. Gregory, Lorian, and Leicester Hemingway at
Leicester and Doris Hemingway's Miami Beach home.

VALERIE HEMINGWAY

New York, 1972. Vanessa and Gregory Hemingway on the occasion of Vanessa's second birthday.
VALERIE HEMINGWAY

New York, 1976. Book launch party for Gregory Hemingway's Papa: A Personal Memoir *at the Hemingway African Gallery. Left to right: Norris Church Mailer, Norman Mailer, Gregory Hemingway, and Brian Gaisford.* COURTESY OF BRIAN GAISFORD

New York, 1978. Left to right: Edward, Vanessa, Seán, Valerie, and Gregory Hemingway, and George Brown. NANCY CRAMPTON

Cojímar, Cuba, 1999. The centenarian Captain Gregorio Fuentes lights a cigar for Valerie Hemingway.
COLLECTION OF VALERIE HEMINGWAY

New York, 1990. Left to right: Edward, Valerie, Vanessa, Seán, and Brendan Hemingway at a surprise party the children organized for Valerie's fiftieth birthday. BRENDAN HEMINGWAY

Missoula, Montana, 1995. Gregory "Gloria" Hemingway and son Edward.
COURTESY OF
EDWARD
HEMINGWAY

that someone, probably at the behest of the FBI, was trying to target him and, by snagging my passport, would prove he was guilty of a myriad of illegal actions: corrupting a minor (I was twenty and there was no basis for this fear), employing an alien without the correct papers, and any other imaginary charges of which his failing mind could conceive. Even though the passport did turn up, he continued to be convinced that it had been stolen and would be used for some sinister plot against him. Those last days were excruciatingly painful. Ernest took to his bed and delayed his flight day after day.

It became apparent that there was no way of getting through to Ernest. If he was determined to die, there was nothing I could do to prevent it. What was strange in retrospect was that none of us, including Mary back in New York, recognized his condition to be caused by mental illness, and so we did not seek outside help. Ernest was so much of a mentor, controlling all our lives so tightly, that we did not for a moment contemplate that his mind was going, that it was medical help he needed more than anything. We barely discussed his condition among ourselves. I said nothing to the others about his suicidal intentions, although he had openly made statements such as "They might as well shoot me now," or that he expected the plane would "go into the drink." Each of us was still in awe of him to some extent and did not doubt that he could control his own destiny.

It was dark when we arrived at Barajas airport. We still had plenty of time. As Bill opened the car door, there was a chill in the air. He and Hotch accompanied the skycaps into the terminal with the luggage to attend to the details of checking in. Annie said she must find the loo. Ernest sat beside me in the backseat of the car, his arm lightly over my shoulder. A drizzle dimmed our view, curtaining us from the world outside. Tears we could not shed streamed from the blackened sky, making patterns on the windowpane. A tremor of anguish shook me as we embraced that last time. I held him tightly, hoping that whatever strength I had would be passed on, to comfort him and to steel him for what lay ahead. I scrunched my eyes, wishing—as hard as ever I had when blowing out birthday candles—that some miracle would transform our lives, that death was not the only option, that the calendar could be turned back a year, wishing for anything but the black void that engulfed us, the *nada* of despair. I could not bear to look into Ernest's eyes, which I knew brimmed with sadness. I thought of Yeats's line "The world is more full of sadness than you can understand."

He said he hoped that the plane would go down and put an end to it all for him.

"Don't," I protested, fighting back the tears I had promised myself not to shed.

Suddenly, as if aware of my discomfort, he came out of himself for a moment and told me that I would be all right, I had lots to live for. Unconvincingly he added that one day maybe things would be better and we would be together again.

"Of course we will," I reassured him. "I'm sure of it."

Tears welled in his eyes. "No matter what, no matter where we are or whatever happens, I will always be with you. You can count on that" were his last words to me. Then Annie knocked on the window and we let her in.

Bill, Annie, Hotch, and I waited at the airport until the plane took off. As it edged down the runway, gathering speed and lifting into the air, we were still waving. *God be with you, Ernest,* I silently prayed. It was a subdued quartet that settled into La Barata. With Bill at the wheel we silently headed for town.

I could not bear to go back to La Consula with Bill and Annie, although they urged me to come and unwind with them in the southern sunshine. Guests would soon arrive from England and France, and life would pick up its normal tempo as we lounged poolside, Frank Sinatra crooning through the loudspeakers. There, they said, we would wash tasty tapas down with crisp white wine while exchanging the latest gossip from the bullring, the theater, the literary scene. The thought of it made me nauseous. I knew Bill and Annie were hiding their grief at their friend's decline, that they too were drained and sad. But I needed to be alone, to mourn in my own way. In my heart of hearts, I had made my farewell. For me, Ernest was already dead, and with his demise a vital chapter of my life had ended. Now that I no longer had to cajole him and feign a false exuberance, I had no reason to be cheerful, to imagine that life, not death, lay ahead. I thought back to that day in Murcia almost a year and a half before, when Ernest had read my palm. He had remained silent, and when I looked into his face, tears were trickling down his cheeks. "What is it?" I asked him. "What do you see?" But he just shook his head. He would never tell me the fate he foresaw for me that had so disturbed him. Now I wondered if my own destiny was one of imminent disaster. The uncertainty of the future made me feel restless and reckless. I had to get away from Spain as fast as I could, away from the bulls, away from the pall of death and deep gloom. I quickly made my way back to Paris and took the first possible flight to Dublin.

A year had passed since I had been home. The success of Behan's play on Broadway was on the lips of theatergoers everywhere. There was great pride in Dublin's own. *The Hostage* had opened to appreciative reviews in New York, and when friends learned I was headed there, I was asked to bring letters, keepsakes, and cakes over with me to deliver to the author and the cast.

Again I stayed with my mother on Seapoint Avenue. One afternoon she handed me a cable that had just arrived from New York. It was dated October 13. I opened it eagerly and read, "Please keep taking care stop have good trip stop for ever go stop love." It was unsigned. I didn't doubt the identity of the sender. As I read it over I became alarmed. There was a finality to it: a farewell. My heart sank. It was Ernest's cue to me that his death was imminent. He was going to do it after all. I was certain Ernest would kill himself. I read the cable over and over, hoping that some hidden meaning might emerge, some possible sign of hope. I scrutinized the page. It had been sent via Western Union from New York at 9:12 a.m. and received at Carraig Dubh (Blackrock) at 9:05 p.m. There were sixteen words. *For* and *ever* were two separate words, emphasizing finality. *Wait just a minute,* I told myself, *don't panic.* Maybe he had meant "where ever," not "for ever." Maybe it was just an ordinary "have a nice day" communication. I put on my coat and walked briskly down to the Blackrock post office with the cable in hand. "I don't quite understand this message I've just received from New York," I said. "Perhaps you could trace it back to its origin and make sure that no words are incorrect or missing."

"We'll check for you," the woman said. "Come back tomorrow."

I returned the next day. The cable was in order. It was exactly as the sender had worded it. Ernest was saying, *Goodbye. It's no use hoping. I intend to kill myself.*

To hell with him, I thought, and took the number eight bus into town, found a pub I rarely frequented, and got thoroughly sozzled.

As much as I loved my hometown, I could never stay in Dublin. It was too confining. I had to move on. In an effort to forget Ernest, his agony, and what I took to be his imminent demise, I flung myself into the business of returning to the New World. I booked my ticket for October 21, one week after that fateful cable. Two years before, Behan had said that he could get me a job with the *Hostage* company. Perhaps he would still be able to make good on the offer. I gathered up my belongings and flew to New York.

CHAPTER FIFTEEN

Broadway Beckons, and a Funeral

I HAD OFTEN HEARD Ernest talking about the *New Yorker* magazine and its colorful writers. He spoke of the so-called Algonquin Round Table members. At the Algonquin Hotel across the street from the magazine's offices, those legendary writers gathered after a day's work to have a drink and heated discussion in the comfort of the lounge before taking the train from Grand Central to their suburban homes. If he ever joined them, Ernest did not say so. Dorothy Parker and Woollcott drank there. Harold Ross, E. B. White, Robert Benchley, and Edna Ferber had sat at that corner table in the dark velvet redness sipping their wines and spirits. That's what I was thinking of when I entered the Algonquin lobby for the first time. I was bearing messages and gifts from Dublin to Brendan and Beatrice.

Brendan met me in the lobby, greeting me with the surprising information that he had booked a room for me in the hotel, where the Behans had been resident for almost a month. He was delighted that I had arrived and was at loose ends, for he could offer me employment immediately as his general dogsbody, his right-hand person for as long as *The Hostage* played in New York. My duties were varied and diverse. I was to keep the press at bay, for Behan's name was on everyone's lips and all the media were intent upon interviewing him. I was to keep his appointments straight and make sure he turned up wherever he was supposed to, whether it was a party, television interview, rehearsal, or meal. Conversely, I was to provide a shield or smokescreen if and when he decided to play hookey. I was to keep track of his commitments with various publishers and generally ward off any trouble when he failed in appearance for duty or when he said or did something appalling. Brendan's reputation as a boozer and brawler had preceded him, and although at this time he was solidly on the wagon, there was an anxiety attached to any dealings with this comic, profane, and highly unpredictable author, especially where money was concerned. A nonappearance could mean a loss of revenue. Finally, I was to encourage him with his writing. He was engaged in several projects at the time, or more accurately he had committed himself to produce or participate in several projects, for which in most cases he had accepted a complete or partial advance. Because of his amazing Broadway success, his sharp wit, and his garrulousness he was courted by divers dubious people, pressuring him to participate in schemes and ventures, enticing him with high monetary rewards. Brendan was great for getting himself into things and not quite as smart about extrication. Of course, I did not learn all of these duties at once, only in a gradual hands-on way as the days went by. Suddenly I had a new raison d'être.

As I stood in the hotel's lobby that day, I could not help noticing that the short, stout, unquenchable bundle of effervescence that was Brendan had transplanted very well from his native Dublin to New York. Fame had not changed his countenance, with its mischievous sky-blue eyes, ruddy complexion, and decidedly crooked nose. The jet-black curly hair remained thick and unruly. He wore his habitual starched white dress shirt with long sleeves and open collar and navy woolen trousers held up with a pair of braces. His worn brown shoes were vaguely polished. His voice had the same resonance and lower Liffey inflection as he pronounced the name *Algonquin*: "Welcome to the Al-a-gonquin, *a cailín mo croí* [girl of my heart]"—often several decibels higher than need be, so that he was center stage. Publicity was a tonic for him, although as the moment struck him he might as soon hurl an insult as a compliment when approached by strangers.

I settled into room 609, a slender cell overlooking Forty-fourth Street and furnished with a single bed, dresser, and chair as well as a closet of suitable size for a monk's wardrobe. My cozy nest served its purpose, for I saw little of that room in the five weeks of my residence. It was a particularly electrifying time in New York City, or perhaps it was my youth and proximity to the central events of the time that made it seem so. Senator John F. Kennedy was about to be elected the first Irish-American Catholic President of the United States. Brendan and Beatrice were invited to everything, and my duties obliged me to go along too. I remembered first hearing of Kennedy in Spain the summer of 1959. Mary Hemingway had a great admiration for the handsome senator. She wanted to help with his campaign for president, and told Ernest so in slightly menacing tones. This was one of the reasons she found the apartment on East Sixty-second Street and persuaded Ernest to rent it, which he did reluctantly. But now, with Kennedy's goal within grasp and excitement building up, Mary and Ernest were out in Ketchum, acting out the final tragic chapter of his life. I put the Hemingways behind me. Ernest had promised to get in touch with me if his determination to kill himself was reversed, but with that final cable to Dublin I despaired of hearing from him and threw myself into my new job with all the enthusiasm I could muster. I was now the one advocating Kennedy's election and attending the Democratic Party booster parties. That glorious night in November 1960 I was at the New York headquarters, listening to the victory speech, cheering and gulping down Champagne.

Every night that fall I attended performances of *The Hostage*, and sometimes the matinees as well. The play was originally written in Irish, a language Brendan felt he could express himself in as well as if not better than in English. It was commissioned for presentation at Damer Hall in St. Stephen's Green and originally opened on June 16, 1958, to appreciative reviews. Rooted in Irish nationalism, the story was partly inspired by the capture of a British soldier by the IRA in County Down in 1955, and essentially its theme was the futility of war. Brendan transferred the action to Dublin, blending the actual house of a Madam Rogers in Nelson Street with Kitty Mulvey's legendary "hotel" in Parnell Street as the play's backdrop.

Rogers was an eccentric, genteel revolutionary known to house or befriend anyone with a connection to revolutionary Ireland. So indiscriminate was she that anyone who had been in prison received her bounty. To her mind a patriot was one who had been in conflict with the police. Mulvey's "hotel" was known for its two homosexual doormen, Fonsey and Freddy, who always gaily greeted its working girls with their temporary partners, making all feel welcome. Brendan claimed to have written the play in twelve days—probably the amount of time it took him to put his scattered notes together to meet the production schedule. The Irish title was *An Giall*. Brendan loved his native tongue and enjoyed talking and singing in it. "Irish is more direct than English," he once told a reporter, "more bitter. It's a muscular, fine thing, the most expressive language in Europe."

Joan Littlewood, who had directed Behan's first play, *The Quare Fellow*, in London with some success a couple of years earlier, told Brendan that if he translated the play, she would stage it at her Theatre Workshop in Stratford. Littlewood was an innovative director, and she had already proved that Behan's plays were precisely the material with which she worked best. They allowed for improvisation. At that point she had headed London's Theatre Workshop since its founding thirteen years before, turning it into one of the most successful and dynamic production companies in England. Brendan took her up on the offer. By September 1958 he already had companies from Paris, Berlin, and New York ready to stage the new play, which was still in the fleshing-out process. The previous year had seen Brendan busy finishing his memoir, *Borstal Boy*, which was long overdue. Hutchinson's, his publisher, was putting pressure on him. He finally finished the book in December 1957.

With Littlewood's intervention, his strictly Irish play became more eclectic, introducing four new characters, caricatures who seemed more Chelsea camp than Dublin bawdy. The show was already in production as the author was adding the finishing touches. *The Hostage* opened to rave reviews on October 14, 1958, at the Theatre Royal, Stratford East. Kenneth Tynan wrote in the *Observer* that Brendan might well fill the place vacated by Sean O'Casey. Penelope Gilliatt and Harold Hobson were equally enthusiastic. "A masterpiece of magnanimity," Hobson's review in the *Sunday*

Times began. During the months that *The Hostage* ran, Princess Margaret went to see it and was reported to have "laughed herself to tears." After Behan's death, Littlewood described him as "a marvellous, splendid, sad, shy human being and intensely proud of his craft as a writer."

Brendan's sister-in-law, Celia Salkeld, created the part of Teresa, which Brendan had written with her in mind. The show had opened at the Cort Theatre on September 30, 1960, and a couple of months afterward moved to the Ethel Barrymore. I came to know each and every member of the cast. It was like one large family, filled with squabbling and petty jealousies as well as camaraderie and good fellowship.

Brendan's philosophy was quoted on the program's title page: "I respect kindness to human beings first of all, and kindness to animals. I don't respect the law; I have a total irreverence for anything connected with society except that which makes the roads safer, the beer stronger, the food cheaper, and old men and women warmer in the winter, and happier in the summer."

One morning after my duties began, Brendan introduced me to Brendan Gill of the *New Yorker,* who had been assigned to write a profile of the playwright. They were off to Staten Island, said Behan, to see his cousin. Brendan loved to tell people that this cousin worked in a tall bank building and that his business was on every floor. Then after a slight pause he would add, "He's the elevator operator." I reminded Brendan that he had an early afternoon appointment with Mike Wallace. He had agreed to be a guest on the Channel 11 television show and would be picked up at two o'clock. "Mike Wallace?" said Brendan Gill indignantly. "You certainly don't want to appear on his show. His whole intent is to embarrass his guests. He will make you so mad that you will make a fool of yourself. He did it to Tennessee Williams only a couple of weeks ago." Gill turned to me. "Brendan won't be back till dinnertime. Take care of the Wallace people." To Brendan he said, "You are lucky to get out of that one. It would be a disaster. Let's go." And they cheerfully waved goodbye like two boys skipping school.

A little before two o'clock I found myself a strategic spot in the lobby of the Algonquin, where I could observe the front door. I was barely settled when I watched a tall, balding, anxious-looking young man come through the door assertively. He paused by the desk, his eyes sweeping the lobby and then fixing on the elevators each time they stopped. I went up to him. "Are you from *The Mike Wallace Show?*" I asked.

"Where's Brendan?" he demanded agitatedly before introducing himself as Noel Parmentel, Wallace's assistant.

"He's not here."

"Where is he? Our appointment was for two. Tell me where he is."

"I don't know, really," I said. "He went off with Brendan Gill, and I don't expect them back till dinnertime. He sends you his apology."

"Apology?" rasped the exasperated young man. "It's my job we're talking about. The show is live. Brendan agreed to be there. He has to be there. He doesn't have any choice." Then, a little ruefully, "If he doesn't come, I'll be fired."

"I'm sorry," I said, "there's nothing I can do." I started to walk away.

Parmentel grabbed my arm and held it tightly. "No you don't. If you won't tell me where Brendan is, you will have to find me someone else. I'm not about to lose my job over a double-dealing, drunken Irish playwright. You're going to stay by my side until Brendan returns or you find me a suitable substitute. If I have to, I'll drag you back with me to the studio and you can explain to Mike Wallace why you've messed up his show."

His grip was still tight, so I suggested we sit on the sofa and rationally discuss the matter. Noel went off on a tangent, raging at Behan for his fecklessness and at Gill, who had usurped his prize and who would certainly need plastic surgery after Parmentel was finished with him. I tried to appease him. There must be many other people who would love to be interviewed by such a distinguished personality. (I had neither seen *The Mike Wallace Show* nor heard of Wallace.) I pointed out that the Algonquin was filled with actors, writers, and famous people. He only had to sit still in the lobby for a few minutes and he would have his quarry.

"Who's here that you know and can introduce to me?" Noel barked.

"I don't know that I can introduce anyone to you," I replied, "but, for instance, there's Christopher Plummer right now at the desk. Why don't you ask him?"

Parmentel took a good look, narrowing his eyes, "No, I don't think so. He won't do."

As time went on, our discussion intensified. Noel became more and more agitated. "I can't believe that you would do this to me!" he hissed, having converted all his wrath from the intangible Brendans to the ever-present me. He could not sit still, getting up every few minutes to remonstrate and shake his fist. I suggested we go for a walk around the block. A breath of city air might stir our minds, and maybe we'd bump into Groucho Marx or Laurence Olivier out there.

We had coffee at a Schrafft's on the corner and a piece of apple pie—my treat. While we relaxed, I learned Noel was from New Orleans, wrote for *Esquire* and *The National Review,* and was somehow involved with movies at Pennebaker; his position was not clear, but he gave their offices as his address. He was an avid Republican with no time for the Kennedy family. But as the minutes ticked by, a satiated Noel—I suspect he hadn't eaten all day—grew agitated again as we walked briskly back to the hotel lobby, where he was determined to pounce on the first poor, unsuspecting victim he could find. No time left to be choosy. And who should walk in at that moment but Eugène Ionesco, whose *Rhinoceros* was playing on Broadway to full houses. I watched Noel steer the bewildered Romanian out of the hotel toward a taxi and wondered what kind of an interview would emerge from the encounter between the uncomprehending playwright with poor English and the allegedly predatory interviewer. I've often wished I had seen the result, but at that moment my feeling was only relief. The Brendans had a great chuckle when I regaled them with my adventures later.

While the Behans were in Ireland for Christmas I sublet an apartment on the West Side. I wrote my friend Honor Chance in Ireland, persuading her to come over.

I think you would really like this snazzy town, for a year or so, that is. There's always lots doing and if you get tired of it there's enough countryside around to explore. It's an expensive town, but you can live well on an American salary. They are very keen on Europeans in offices, particularly with English accents, having an English secretary has great snob value in these parts. You shouldn't have much difficulty finding a firm little foothold and pacing along. Wish you would think of coming. We could have loads of fun. I've found a large pleasant seedy old apartment almost beside the Park (chic), and beside the Latin American quarter (dingy), so I have the beauty of the scenery combined with the Spanish flavor. When I walk around the corner to do my shopping in the morning there is a constant yapping in Spanish by women shoppers and kids playing in the street. The laundry is Chinese, but there is Fernando's bodega, a *mantequeria,* a *panaderia* and a whole *calle* of ——*erias.* The apartment was a great stroke of luck, and if you should come you would be more than welcome to share the creaks and groans. It's an old house by American standards, and a trifle primitive by the same, but the rooms are large with high ceilings, and it's cheap, and everything works, sort of. In fact it (the apartment) belongs to a friend who works for the *New Yorker* magazine and has taken a leave of absence for several months and has sublet it to me. Tony Bailey (the aforementioned) has written one book, *Making Progress,* and has another coming out this August. He graduated from Oxford in '55. He and his wife left all their books (100s and 100s) and records (ditto) behind for me to use, also their other mod cons, so I'm well away. When they come back they'll be looking for a larger apartment as they have a bouncing one year old daughter, Liz.

Perhaps inspired by my letter, Honor came to the United States and stayed a couple of years.

The Behans returned to New York in the new year, and I continued to work for Brendan. Bernard Geis Associates was his publisher. Geis, an excellent businessman, was willing to take a chance with offbeat material and with his relatively small list was able to give his authors personal attention. He later became famous and rich for being the first to publish Jacqueline Susann's books. He was an ideal mentor for Brendan, who needed both the personal attention and the interest and direction of someone who would goad him into producing the promised manuscripts. Geis's publicity director was Letty Cottin, later Pogrebin; a lively young blonde, efficient and good-humored. She was often Geis's watchdog, assigned to see that Brendan was working and to humor him.

Religion was a subject of great interest to Brendan. He was a hands-on person, eschewing the theoretical for the practical as a matter of course. Although he altered the rules to suit himself, he was solidly Roman Catholic. He was somewhat distrustful of Protestants, but people of the Jewish persuasion fascinated him. He found them exotic and sought out their company. He was welcomed as family in many Jewish households, like that of the *Hostage* production stage manager and U.S. director, Perry Bruskin, in Queens Village. He attended Leonard Lyons's youngest son's bar mitzvah and spoke out on behalf of Norman Mailer when the famed author got himself in hot water for stabbing his second wife, Adele. Brendan loved to point out that Dublin had a Jewish lord mayor, Bobby Briscoe. Letty introduced us to several of her friends, including Paddy Chayefsky, author of *The Tenth Man* and *Marty,* and Herbert Tarr, a rabbi whose first novel, *The Conversion of Chaplain Cohen,* Geis published. Brendan was amused to socialize with a rabbi who was a fellow writer as well as the first Jewish chaplain to be sent on a Strategic Air Command extended-duty assignment.

Geis was hoping that Brendan would write another play or a book to equal his very successful memoir, *Borstal Boy.* Brendan was working on a play called *Richard's Cork Leg* at the time, which I typed for him. It was already overdue and had been promised in several directions. So Geis thought up a number of possible books that would have the Behan byline. *Confessions of an Irish Rebel* was to be a sequel to the memoir, and Geis would publish two volumes, *Brendan Behan's New York* and *Brendan Behan's Island,* both collections of essays and (when the author could not be pinned down at his desk) oral recollections from Brendan of his homeland and his U.S. experiences. Paul Hogarth was enlisted to do the illustrations.

Brendan often responded to the shout of "Author!" and appeared on-stage with the *Hostage* cast during its final curtain call. He was a popular guest on the talk shows too. Scheduled to appear on Jack Paar's show, which was being taped one Wednesday afternoon, he asked me to meet him at the NBC studios. That day I had lunched at Sardi's with Helen Dunne and some ladies who had come in from Great Neck to see a matinee. I had a generous amount to drink; martinis were in fashion then. When I turned up at the studios without Brendan and obviously slightly merry, I distinctly remember the dismay on Hugh Downs's face. I assured him that Brendan would turn up and that he would be sober. Downs was highly dubious, but I was right on both counts. I didn't accompany Brendan to Newark when he appeared on David Susskind's show, but afterward he proudly told me that, when asked to sign the guest book, he wrote only "Brendan." "They pay a dollar," he said, "and since my writing fee is a dollar a word they received fair value."

The Hostage was scheduled to tour after it closed in February, so I started looking for a regular job. My first choice was *Newsweek* magazine. I put my resumé together and applied there. John McAlister, the news desk editor, was enthusiastic but had nothing available. He asked me if I would consider working for his friend Samson Raphaelson, a playwright, until there was an opening. "He needs someone just like you to help him." The only problem was, he told me, Rafe liked to work at night. The hours would be from 7 p.m. to 1 a.m. Since I was involved with the theater, perhaps those hours would suit me. I was a night owl and not in the least fazed by the proposed schedule, so McAlister telephoned Raphaelson and arranged an interview.

My new job was a short walk from the Baileys' apartment. It was the antithesis of working for Brendan. No two playwrights could have had a more different modus operandi. Brendan bounced from topic to topic, his mind leaping all over the place. Rafe, as he preferred to be called, was punctilious and thorough. It fascinated him that I had lived in the Hemingway household, and he was the first person who urged me to record in writing everything I had heard and seen there. It would be of immense interest to the world at large and a service to literature, he suggested. At the time I disdained the idea.

Rafe had had resounding success as a Broadway playwright in the 1920s. Starting out in the advertising business, he had ventured into theater, and his play *The Jazz Singer* had wowed audiences. In 1927 it was made into what is considered to be the first talkie movie, starring Al Jolson, with his legendary rendition of "Mammy." That year the movie won the Academy's special award for technical achievement.

I knew nothing of this when I first stepped off the elevator into the Central Park West apartment, where I was greeted warmly by Dorska, Rafe's Russian-born wife. A former Ziegfeld Follies dancer, she had retained her trim figure and blithe spirit. We worked undisturbed in the study, where Rafe described to me his ambition to recapture his early Broadway success. In the thirties he had teamed up with the famous German director Ernst Lubitsch as screenwriter, and many of the nine films they made together are classics today. In the late 1990s his script for *The Little Shop Around the Corner* was remade into the popular *You've Got Mail.* Rafe was not around to see the reincarnation, but Dorska, now in her nineties, was picked up from that same Central Park West apartment by a Paramount limousine and brought to attend the premiere of the movie, starring Tom Hanks.

In the fifties, Rafe had taught a graduate course in screenwriting at Columbia University, using his own films as models. He is still considered among Hollywood's most successful screenwriters, but like many writers, he felt that his Hollywood contributions were just temporary aberrations in his literary life, accomplished for no other reason than financial necessity. In the spring of 1961 he lamented that he would be remembered only for his film scripts, and he wanted to get back to the theater before it was too late. As he dictated each scene to me, he was deeply immersed in the plot and action, and his enthusiasm was exhilarating. Rafe would insist on walking me home each evening, often with a light rain falling. He said he needed both the air and the exercise. As we walked along Central Park West, he spoke animatedly and gesticulated with his umbrella to emphasize each of his points. While he was oblivious to our surroundings, I could not help being acutely aware that his gestures brought taxi after taxi to a stop, and when we ignored them and walked on, I felt the fury and frustration of the driver as he sometimes honked his horn in annoyance. However, I soon began to enjoy the theatrics as part of our evening ritual.

I started out as a *Newsweek* researcher in April. It was a particularly exciting time for the magazine. Barely one month earlier—following the death of Vincent Astor, whose family had owned the magazine since 1937—*Newsweek* had been bought by Philip Graham of the *Washington Post*. Graham had achieved his position at the *Post* by virtue of being its owner's son-in-law. He saw the *Newsweek* purchase as an opportunity to mold something of his own, to further his personal ambitions. The prospect excited him. He poured his energy into reshaping the weekly, which then placed a poor second to Henry Luce's *Time* magazine. Even a newcomer could not mistake the electricity in the air, the sense of challenge, exuberance, and confidence as a new regime took shape. There were powwows, conference calls between Washington and New York, conspiratorial whisperings around the office, and a general alertness among the editors in anticipation of what the change might bring next.

The *Newsweek* offices were at 444 Madison Avenue, a towering building in the mid-fifties, as high up in the world as I had ever been. I was assigned to the news desk, where editor John McAlister greeted me that first morning. I was immediately introduced to his assistant, Al Wall, to whom I would report. I loved everything about my new work. Each day started in the clipping room, scanning regional and foreign newspapers and magazines and removing all pertinent references with a nifty paper cutter while concurrently checking the wire services. In this room, each new AP or UPI story unfolded, cryptically relaying the latest world news to the clackity-clack of mechanical printing as the long paper roll overflowed to the floor. These I gathered up, severed, read, and, if warranted, rushed to the appropriate editor. I became familiar with most departments and their personnel and struck up an acquaintance with the editors, especially in the sports department. There were desks at which I lingered. Gordon Manning was a Hemingway enthusiast, so we got along well, exchanging pleasantries and news items. Sports editors Barry Gotterer and Dick Schaap shared my interest in boxing, and the fact that I had met Archie Moore and Gene Tunney with Hemingway merited me their unused press tickets to Madison Square Garden.

Thursday was my favorite day. On that evening the magazine went to press. We stayed at the office as long as was necessary until we had closed all departments—put the magazine to bed, as we used to say. It often meant snatching a sandwich at the desk, tanking up on coffee, and puffing on and stubbing out a pack or more of cigarettes, since in those days almost everyone smoked. We rarely finished our work before one in the morning. If we worked through the evening, we were given a stipend for dinner, and working after 11 p.m. merited taxi fare home. The money was a welcome addition to my $55-a-week salary, and the rush of that evening—more intense than the daily sessions—heightened my sense of achievement. I felt an integral part of the outcome.

On June 23 I wrote to Bill and Annie Davis:

Brendan is back in town today after a month in Hollywood, a visit to Mexico to see a bullfight, and a general survey of the West Coast. I went out to see them in San Francisco for a weekend (in May) which *Newsweek* thought so adventurous of me they allowed me a couple of extra days. San Francisco is a wonderful city. I thought of you, Bill, starting your brilliant career there as a cabbie, no wonder the Spanish mountainy cobbly roads are no challenge to you. We went down to the Fisherman's Wharf and ate seafood facing the Golden Gate, and nimbly handled our chopsticks in the Chinese quarter. We marched in protest behind Enrico Banducci from the courthouse to the Hungry Eye after he had spent a night in jail for contempt of court. Afterwards we stayed to watch the show, Brendan as much a part of the performance as the audience. We stopped by the City Lights bookshop close to midnight and before the witching hour all the neighborhood beatniks had surrounded Brendan, eagerly listening to every word he said. *The Hostage* closed to a packed house and cheering audience. Brendan did a jig on the stage by request. We dined on steaks and Burgundy afterwards accompanied by songs, accordian and fiddle music and the popping of as many champagne corks as you would ever want to hear of an evening. There were many farewells as the company parted, some of the actors had been with the show from its inception in England.

There was one incident I did not mention to the Davises. After the closing party for *The Hostage,* which took place at the Mark Hopkins Hotel, where the Behans and I were staying, I retired to bed exhilarated but completely exhausted. I was awakened a short while later when Brendan let himself into my room with a key he must have acquired when he made my hotel reservation. I learned then that the romantic fantasies he had hinted at during the preceding months were not just attempts at lighthearted flirtation. It was a night that would change my life forever.

I KEPT MY WORD to Ernest that I would not get in touch unless I heard from him directly. There was only silence. Mary had come back to New York a couple of times. She made a point of inviting me to the apartment and confided her worries about Ernest's health. I knew he had been in the Mayo Clinic from the end of November until late January and was readmitted in April. Only later did I learn that he had made several suicide attempts starting in November. He was being treated with electric shock therapy. Mary was at her wits' end, hoping against hope that there would be an improvement, that his depression would ebb and he would find a renewed will to live. She even asked me if I would come out to Idaho that summer because, in her desperation, she thought it might cheer him up.

On June 30 I wrote to Honor in Dublin.

Life with the Hems discontinued, as you can guess. He has not been so well, only left the hospital this week, I hope cured for good, but hasn't been doing any work since we left Spain last October. Mary spent almost a month here recently, which boosted my social life beyond all ordinary status. She seemed delighted to have me around as often as possible and has even asked me to spend one of the summer months in Sun Valley with them. I'm not sure that it is a good idea as I am no longer part of the Hem "cuadrilla" but parted with them on the best of terms. Maybe I should leave things that way in spite of the temptation of a cool month in the mountain air. Besides, I have got a job. Say, did you read that properly—I, yours very truly, unruly Val, have a job. *Newsweek* magazine!

Two days later, full of good spirits, I was spending my first Independence Day weekend with Lar and Helen Dunne in Great Neck when we heard on the radio that in the dawning hours of July 2, Ernest Hemingway shot himself at his Ketchum home. A distraught Mary called me to confirm the report. I heard the heartbreak in her voice, the disbelief. She wanted me to come to Idaho for the funeral. I said I would do so if I could.

I was numbed rather than stunned. I had waited eight months for this headline, knowing as each day went by that the moment was drawing closer. I was determined to separate myself from the deed. I had promised Ernest I would stay in New York in case he got better and needed me, but I did not expect that to happen, and as much as I could, I had put him out of my mind. When I had seen Mary a couple of weeks before, she had discussed her concern for Ernest, who had not been getting better. Hotch had recommended a sanitorium in Connecticut, where celebrities were taken care of and their privacy protected. But Ernest was not a good patient. Being an invalid was a role he refused to accept. He understood medicine. The Mayo Clinic had validity in his eyes, but being an invalid did not. As far as I could tell, he was not seeking a medical solution. I had hoped for a different outcome, but instinct had told me to expect the worst. I could not cry for Ernest. He was at peace. Demons would no longer disturb his sleep. The more I thought about it, I wanted to mourn alone. I had no wish to attend the funeral. Admittedly, only family and close friends were invited, but I had little in common with them. My memories were not for sharing.

As soon as he heard, Brendan telephoned me and told me to meet him at the Algonquin. He had truly admired Hemingway as a writer and was saddened by the news. His words gave comfort. When we met, I told him that although Mary had asked me to attend the funeral, I was ambivalent about going. His reaction was that I absolutely must attend, and he was horrified that I even considered avoiding it. It was inconceivable to him that I would forgo paying the ultimate respect to a friend. For the Irish, funerals have a special significance. People attend not just to support the living; there is a kinship with the spirit of the deceased, who, now in a different world, assumes powers denied to humans. One prays to the soul of the dead person as well as for it.

Newsweek was happy to give me the time off, but it was expected that I would bring back a story. This too put me in a bit of a quandary. Mary could not accept the fact that Ernest's death was a suicide. She had informed the press that it had been an accident. The funeral was by invitation only. No members of the press were to be admitted, absolutely none. She was adamant about that. Under those circumstances I did not feel I could turn up as a close friend and then report back to *Newsweek*. Mary herself had once been a successful journalist. She was the first woman to have a *Time* magazine cover story. She would not have hesitated to sacrifice a friendship, temporarily, for a scoop. I was different. I aired my fears to Brendan. "You must go," he said. "You ought to be there. Look here, I would go if I could. I want you to bring my condolences to Mary." He reached into his pocket and pulled out several twenty-dollar notes "for my air ticket" and pressed them into my hand. "And I want you to place a wreath on Ernest's grave for Beatrice and me," he continued, and started writing the following inscription on Algonquin letterhead: "*Timcheall an teaglach gac oice, / Maireann an scealuí go deo* [Around the hearthstone every night / The storyteller lives forever]." He signed it and added "*Lá na Saorse* [Independence Day] 1961."

I arrived in Ketchum on a small prop jet filled with Hemingway relatives. Among them were Ernest's sisters Marcelline and Sunny, and Leicester, his kid brother. Hitherto these had just been names to me. Now, as I heard them talking, I began to identify each one, trying to recall what Ernest had told me about them. It was my first trip to the American West, a region I had only seen in cowboy movies. I was not disappointed by what I saw. In those days, Ketchum had one wide main street, dry and dusty, with hitching posts outside the stores, and it was not unusual to see a horse patiently waiting there, rope secure. Dogs roamed about freely. Stores and houses were made of hefty logs. In the Mint Bar, the clientele, with neatly stacked round silver dollars in front of them to prove their solvency, sat in the gloom sipping their beers and puffing on Winstons. The sheriff, like Gary Cooper in *High Noon,* wore blue jeans and boots, a cowboy hat, and his identifying star. His demeanor was amiable, but he sported a pair of pistols sitting in the holsters on his hips. People said "Howdy" and "Yep" and "You bet," and were as friendly and welcoming as their counterparts were curt and rude in New York City.

I was staying at the Christiania Lodge, owned by the Hemingways' good friends Chuck and Flos Atkinson. As soon as I checked in, I telephoned Mary. She was distinctly cold. By now she had realized that I was working for *Newsweek,* and she regretted her invitation, deciding she should avoid me at all costs. When the family met at the house or at a restaurant for meals, or went on a tour of the countryside, I was excluded.

One other person was clearly in the same boat. That was Gregory Hemingway, known as Gigi or Gig, Ernest's youngest son. Gregory and Ernest had had a falling-out ten years before, when he was nineteen. They had only seen each other once since then, when Gregory took his first wife, Jane, and baby daughter, Lorian, to visit his father in Cuba on their way to East Africa, but much vitriolic correspondence had passed between them. When I was with the Hemingways, Gregory's name was never spoken by Ernest or Mary. If someone inadvertently mentioned it, they were met with a stony silence. As far as his father and Mary were concerned, Gigi did not exist.

Now, because Ketchum was such a small place and we were both obvious outcasts, Gig and I were thrown together at every turn. Faced with Mary's snub, I bitterly regretted coming. I tried to amuse myself by exploring the little town and its environs. I didn't drive, so I walked from Ketchum to Sun Valley to see the lodge and the ski hill, which I had heard Ernest describe. He had loved the place from the beginning, its hunting possibilities, and the local people who became his friends, especially Lloyd (Pappy) and Tilly Arnold. Pappy was the official photographer who took wonderful pictures of the Hemingway family over the years. And Clara Spiegel, from Chicago, who had married into the catalog family, was one of the spunkiest ladies I've ever known. Of course there was George Saviers, the doctor, whose son Fritz would soon die of a heart condition; the nine-year-old boy had received the last letter Ernest wrote. Bud Purdy and his wife's ranch was the scene of many hunting escapades. As I wandered around, piecing these memories together, Gig pulled up in his car and asked me if I wanted a ride. I pretended not to notice him, but when he insisted, I declined. He persisted, and finally I hopped in. Upon getting to know this youngest son, who was charming, intelligent, and excellent company, I put aside all the negative things I had heard about him, the sinister hints and innuendos. We became fast friends. When we left Ketchum we both flew to Salt Lake City, where we were to change planes, he for Florida and me for New York. We stayed at the airport drinking and talking for several hours, each missing our scheduled plane until we caught the last possible flight out.

The funeral had been brief. As I entered the cemetery that day I handed my invitation card to the guard at the gate and was allowed to pass through. I took my place among the few relatives and chosen friends who silently surrounded the small plot. At the time, a suicide was denied Catholic burial, but Mary's fiction allowed the traditional graveside prayers and blessing to take place. The priest, in black and white vestments, spoke the words of the hymn "Dies Irae" as we listened with bowed heads: "Ah! that day of tears and mourning! / From the dust of earth returning / Man for judgment must prepare him, / Spare, O God, in mercy spare him! / Lord, all pitying, Jesus blest / Grant them thine eternal rest." Then he blessed the coffin and sprinkled it with holy water. Not a whisper, not a stir could be heard. Devoid of feeling, I concentrated on the ceremony. I had said my goodbye to Ernest several months before and had mourned for him then. Now, concealing a deep sadness, I felt hollow, empty, absolute nothingness; *nada, nada, y pues nada.*

Ten days after my return to New York, I heard from Mary. She said she had been under great strain at the funeral and now regretted her behavior. She was mistaken in not trusting me. Then I learned what had prompted her change of heart. She had received a telephone call from a Cuban government official with condolences and queries about her intentions for disposition of the Finca Vigía. At the time U.S. citizens were forbidden to travel to Cuba. Despite this, Mary was determined to go to Havana and deal with the matter herself. It was clear to her that without Ernest, Cuba could no longer be her home, but there were letters, manuscripts, books, paintings, and a lifetime of valuable possessions to be sorted and disposed of, and she would need help in doing so. She also wanted to take care of the servants, who would have to look for new employment. She applied to the State Department for permission to make the journey. President Kennedy personally expedited her request. It then occurred to her that I would be of great help in her mission. I spoke Spanish and was familiar with the house, its contents, the importance of Hemingway's papers, and his wishes for their disposal. Equally significant, I had an Irish passport, which allowed me to travel to the island freely. Also, I had been with them during those last good months of Ernest's life, memories of which she desperately needed to hang on to. I did not have to think twice before answering that I would go with her. Although I parted company with *Newsweek*, I told John McAlister I would send dispatches from Havana so that *Newsweek* would have the first scoop on the Hemingway story.

People who knew of my association with the Hemingways were keen to find out how I felt about the tragedy, and wanted me to enlighten them as to why it happened. Everywhere I went Ernest's death became the main topic of conversation. I had no wish to discuss it, and the escape Mary offered came just in time. To tell the truth, I was happy to have the opportunity to get away for a while and be temporarily out of circulation.

CHAPTER SIXTEEN

Havana Revisited

W E RETURNED TO HAVANA almost a year to the day from our departure, but oh, how things had changed. To be sure, the airport, Rancho Boyeros, was no different that hot July afternoon in 1961. A three-man calypso band serenaded us as we stepped down from the small Pan American prop jet, our last link with the U.S. mainland. The plane was modestly occupied on the journey over, but returning to Miami five weeks later it would be filled to an unimagined capacity with refugees fleeing the Castro regime to make a new life, taking with them only the meager possessions they could carry in their arms, nothing more.

Juan, the chauffeur, was there to greet us. He put his arms around *la viuda,* the widow, hugging her, as is Latin custom, and offering his simple condolences. Solemnly he led us to the car. We did not talk much as we drove in the red Plymouth through the flat, sprawling outskirts of the city to the little village of San Francisco de Paula. At the *finca*'s iron gates, the driveway seemed overgrown and unkempt, the house at the end of it strangely dilapidated. Standing on the great uneven stone steps that led to the entrance were the servants welcoming us home. They looked sad—more sad, perhaps, anticipating their fate than mourning their master who would return no more. "*Bienvenida,* Miss Mary, welcome home. *Bienvenida,* Señorita Valeria."

We went into the living room, tiles scrubbed and chintzes bright, everything exactly as we had left it a year before. There sat the heir apparent, Cristóbal Colón, the tabby Persian who answered more readily to the name of Stobbs, and who presided over the living quarters—as opposed to his counterpart, Ambrose Bierce, the kitchen cat. Stobbs had the dispostion of a demon, the skill of a sorcerer who could outstare the most stouthearted and was undisputed lord of the manor. In matters feline, Ernest had allowed his beloved final and faithful friend to upstage him. The past year had not treated Stobbs kindly. He did not greet us with any show of affection. Did he know that his master would never return? Perhaps not, but he knew that his lifestyle had altered radically. His presence had already lost some of its majesty, his body some of its mass. Castro's regime had been hard on cats too. Food, scarce for people, was an unbelievable delicacy for cats. Stobbs stared past us with indifference.

René, the butler, had first come to the *finca* with his twin brother from the neighboring village when they both were twelve years old. He had trained as a houseboy and graduated to valet, butler, major domo, and friend. Now twenty-nine, dressed in his white guayabera and black pressed pants, he proudly ushered us toward the dining room table, a great slab of dark native wood, and pointed to a basket of fruit set there, all greens and yellows, the fruits of Cuba; *piñas,* papayas, *platanos,* mangoes. Mary took the note and read it. "With the compliments of El Jefe"—from Castro himself. The servants, who had followed us into the house, now showed a spark of interest. They nudged and whispered. The Chief had sent his men over with the fruit and a message that he would like to visit the house in person after *la viuda* arrived. Everyone exclaimed, everyone smiled. No matter how bad things seemed, El Jefe would make them better. He had told them so again and again. What he promised would happen, of this they were sure.

"Is this true, René?" Mary asked. "Señor Castro intends to come here, to the *finca?*"

"*Sí, sí, es la verdad.* Oh yes, if you wish, he will come at the first opportunity, his emissary instructed me to tell you."

"Thank you, René." Mary smiled. "It will be a very big occasion for all of us."

Ten days, we thought, would be all that was needed to complete our mission. "My husband made his home in your country," Mary had written Castro after the funeral three weeks before. "He loved Cuba and the Cuban people and I know that he would want them to use and enjoy the Finca Vigía. In his name, I hereby give the property to the people of your land and I hope that it will serve as a center for learning and the arts." Castro had graciously accepted the gift, at the same time inviting *la viuda* back to her home for a last visit. With his permission she could take with her whatever personal papers and small possessions of sentimental value she wished. What a difficult task that would be to separate from the accumulated possessions of an entire lifetime a handful of things most cherished!

Indeed, it was a chancy business to go back to Cuba at all when diplomatic relations with the United States had been severed. Fear, anger, and scorn were everywhere; retributions and retaliations for wrongs imagined and real were rampant. Still, Ernest and Mary Hemingway had never fallen into the category of unwelcome foreigners. Rather, Cuba was proud to have a great writer, a fine man, a national—no, international—hero grace its shores. The Hemingways did not constitute the enemy. They were not a party to Yankee imperialism. They were welcome. Now Mary returned with the blessing of the U.S. State Department. The fruits of our trip—the papers and manuscripts we returned with—would become part of the archives of national letters, part of the American heritage. As Mary and I set about gathering up these papers and a few of her personal belongings we had not yet given a thought as to how we would transport them back to the United States. Castro's minister had cabled us, "You will have our complete cooperation and assistance while you are here," and we had taken for granted that this would mean when we were leaving as well.

Now the coming ten days (which would drag on to thirty-five) promised to be busy ones. A good thing too: it helped relieve our minds of the recent tragedy and numb the gnawing pain of Ernest's absence. Every crevice of the old house silently shouted his name; his image hovered like a phantom, refusing to be banished. That first morning Roberto Herrera arrived. He embraced us with tears in his eyes. Roberto's friendship with the Hemingways dated to before Martha Gellhorn was mistress of the *finca*. It was she who found the house and persuaded Ernest to lease it in 1939, in the days of their courtship. The rental was then a hundred dollars a month—an excessive amount, Ernest thought, giving him cause to grumble. With the success of *For Whom the Bell Tolls,* the Spanish Civil War novel he dedicated to Martha, and its almost immediate sale to Hollywood, Ernest magnanimously bought the *finca* for her to mark their wedding in the fall of 1940. The price had been $12,500.

Over the years Roberto had been Ernest's sometime secretary. Now he took out the key to the great steel filing cabinet in the library and, with Mary and myself present, unlocked it. There we knew we would find Ernest's last will and testament, which named Mary his sole heir and executrix, adding that Mary knew his wishes and he trusted her to make whatever bequests were necessary. Among the contents of letters and partial manuscripts we found an envelope marked: "Important. To be opened in case of my death. Ernest Hemingway." It was dated May 24, 1958. The note inside specified to his executors that none of his personal letters was to be published, nor were they to consent to the publication of his letters by others. This caused a lot of discussion between us at that time and in the years to come. It gave Mary severe qualms of conscience when she finally agreed that Carlos Baker would prepare a volume of the letters for publication in 1981. Her conscience was slightly assuaged by not personally accepting any domestic royalties. Instead she designated that the Hemingway Foundation would benefit from the proceeds.

There was one other note that caught our immediate attention. It was attached to a small bundle of letters secured by brittle rubber bands. It read: "To be burned in case of my death." Upon scrutiny, we found that all were unsent letters Ernest had written, mostly in rage, and which he saved, I think, to remind himself of how he had felt at that particular moment. It was a habit of his to dash off a letter when his temper flared over some event he found intolerable. Having unleashed his anger, he often thought better of it and put the letter away.

We drew up a list of things to be done, in order of importance. First and foremost, the papers were to be read, sorted, and packed. Those Ernest had designated would be burned; others would be left behind. There was an amazing collection of letters—happy, interesting, dull, sad, angry, and anxious ones; business letters, duty letters, letters from family, friends, fans, foes, admirers, detractors; letters handwritten, scrawled, neatly penned, typed, postmarked from the far corners of the world, dated one year or forty years before; letters in the library, the living room, the bedrooms, the garage, the guesthouse, the tower. Surely this must be the largest correspondence any man of letters had collected in a lifetime. Then there were manuscripts—fact, fiction, poems, short stories—as well as photographs, clippings, shopping lists, shoelaces, lucky stones, and rusty jackknives.

Mary decided she would attend to her own papers first while I sifted and sorted through all of Ernest's notes, letters, and manuscripts, calling upon her if I had queries. She had plenty to show for her years as a working journalist on the Chicago *Daily News,* at the London *Express,* and with *Time* magazine before she had met Ernest in London toward the end of the Second World War. Her own personal correspondence and papers were considerable. With her usual thoroughness, she planned to take an inventory of every item left in the house, a list that would be turned over to Castro when we were leaving. Another list was of personal effects to be shipped back to the United States. Mary asked Roberto to help with the inventory, as interpreter and identifier of items that predated Mary's arrival at the *finca.* I was to devote my time exclusively to the massive correspondence, along with notes and manuscripts.

I became engrossed in this monumental task, sometimes scanning and making hasty decisions, at other times completely lost in the maze of words. It was hard not to linger over every scrap, to contain my curiosity about the contents. However, identifying the importance of each piece was paramount. I wondered what had become of the writers of some of those early letters. In the case of Fitzgerald, Stein, and others it was history, but there were also those whose only shade of immortality was the piece of paper I held. What had been their fate? Sometimes I felt like an eavesdropper, privy to secrets and confidences I had no business knowing. Mary and I debated about the meaning behind Ernest's forthright note to his executors that none of his letters should ever be published. Most of the letters we were dealing with had been received, not written by him, but he also had the habit of slipping a sheet of carbon paper between the onionskin sheets of his personal letters, whether typed or handwritten, making an almost complete record. Certainly, we agreed, his biographer should be able to read these letters and use the contents to aid in telling as complete a story as possible.

Ernest had chosen Carlos Baker, then chairman of the Department of English at Princeton University, to be his official biographer, perhaps on a whim. In 1956 Baker had published *Hemingway: The Writer as Artist,* a critical study of the writer's work, which Hemingway had found bearable. This marked a significant shift, considering that he loathed academics and their critical works, especially where amateur psychology was used to elucidate a point. Baker must have passed the test, for the year before, when I sat in the library with Ernest on those early afternoons transcribing in longhand as he dictated to me, he would say: "Take this one for my biographer." Without prompting I would write, "Dear Carlos." He had determined that he and Baker would never meet face-to-face. It was clever the way he made sure Baker would hear from the horse's mouth exactly what the writer hoped posterity would read about him. To be fair, in my experience during the couple of years I worked for him, Ernest saw himself first and foremost as a writer. It annoyed him to read of his exploits in the press or in magazines, for he felt that the only worthwhile news was what he wrote; all else was irrelevant. Yet he was shrewd in creating his public legend.

News of our trip to Cuba soon reached New York, where the fate of the letters and papers were already being discussed. We were sent a clipping from the *New York Times* in which Glenway Wescott had urged that Mary be deterred from destroying any letters or manuscripts. The manuscripts were never in jeopardy, only letters, and then only after careful consideration. In years to come, the debates and arguments that ensued in favor of re-taining or destroying the letters, publishing or not publishing them, were endless. Literary experts from all over the country were quick to write to the widow telling her that surely her conscience would forbid her to de-stroy anything that would provide an insight into the essence of one of the country's greatest writers. How could she deny the value of the material and not take seriously the job entrusted to her as executrix? Sometime after we returned to the States, following discussions with people she trusted, such as Malcolm Cowley and Archibald MacLeish, a compromise was reached. With barely an exception the letters would be kept, the most per-sonal of them to be held in escrow for a period of fifty years. Before her death Mary rescinded this policy, donating all the Hemingway papers in her possession to the Kennedy Library in Boston and allowing scholars im-mediate access to them. Over the last forty-one years, only the papers left behind in Cuba were unavailable to the world, with the very few exceptions made by the Cuban government. In destroying the designated letters Mary was following Ernest's specific instruction, which she felt was her duty as executrix.

On July 27 I responded to a cable I had received from *Newsweek* the previous day. I wrote to Bill Roeder:

Mrs. Hemingway came down to Cuba at the request of the Cuban Government to discuss with them the converting of the Finca Vigía into a National Museum for the Cuban people. Dr. Carlos Olivares (Minister for External Affairs) called her at her home in Ketchum early last week to say that the Government would like to buy the property for that purpose. They would build a house on the grounds for her to live in where she could move all her personal pos-sessions. Mary, in her turn, wishes to give the *finca* as a gift to the Cuban people, the *pueblo,* and she will keep the *casita,* the guest house for when she visits Cuba. She feels she could not live here, for some time, with all its associations. In view of this she hopes, as they have been courteous so far, the Government will allow her to return to her home in America with the manuscripts, papers and a few personal possessions she chooses to keep. However, none of this has been discussed yet as officials are tied up with the current festivities. [I was referring to the national holidays, July 25, 26, 27, National Rebellion Day commemorating the attack on the Moncada Barracks in 1953.]

At present we are sorting papers and letters, an accumulation of more than thirty years; and putting the house in order for display, labeling animal heads, by whom shot, where, etc., and unearthing curios collected in travels, African spears, Cuban Aztec stone carvings and others.

The chief manuscripts and other important papers are still in the bank vault. We are not sure of exact contents but guess that the original manuscript of *The Old Man and the Sea* is among them. As the bank has been nationalized we will need Government assistance in recovering these things, but feel sure there will be no problem.

The *finca* itself is in an ever increasing state of senile decay, inhabited only by the servants in the year's absence. They kept it in good order. Nothing was missing, and no greater mishap than that the ceiba tree further uprooted the living room floor.

Mrs. Hemingway has no comment until she hears from Olivares and has a better idea of what will actually happen. We expect to be here at least another week. Will keep you informed.

Two days later, Mary and I drove with Juan to the bank in Havana. We had no idea what we would find there because all private property had been nationalized some months before, with bank safe-deposit boxes opened and valuables confiscated. We learned at the First National Bank of Boston that the contents of Ernest's box had been transferred to the Banco Nacional de Cuba, and there we were relieved to find two large bundles of manuscripts carefully bound and sealed with wax. Mary's signature was all that was needed to recover them without incident. Juan helped put the heavy packages in the back of the car, and we returned to the *finca* eager to see what they held.

To our great relief, there was the original manuscript of *The Old Man and the Sea,* which Ernest had written in Cuba eleven years before. It has been by far the most consistently best-selling of his books over the past fifty years. The manuscript of *The Garden of Eden* was there too. It brought back memories of when we were in the south of France in the late summer of 1959 when Ernest was working on it, trying to settle upon a suitable ending.

We did not expect to find *A Moveable Feast*—the last book he had worked on, and which he left close to completion. I had typed the chapters the year before at the *finca*. He always referred to it as "The Paris Book" or "The Paris Sketches." Ernest had brought the manuscript with him to the United States when we left Cuba in July 1960. We did find more than a thousand partially handwritten and partially typed pages of a work in progress, which would be posthumously published as *Islands in the Stream*. And there were short-story fragments, ideas for stories, and another mammoth work, the rambling African novel/diary that would be published as *True as First Light* in 1999 to mark the centenary of his birth. Having checked everything with satisfaction, Mary packed the booty away in her suitcase and firmly locked it.

July turned to August, and I was still working through the papers. Sometimes I toted a box of stuff outside and sat under a mango tree in the rocky field that separated the *finca* from the village. Puchilo, the gardener, was often nearby, raking or hoeing. As he passed me with his full-faced *bandido* grin, he would call out, "*Buenos días, señorita.*" Puchilo had attained a certain prominence in the village as an able trainer of prizefighting cocks, and even though he had given up his "stable," as Ernest called it, he was still a reliable handicapper, though he did not part readily with his tips. In the past I had seen him in action many a Sunday afternoon at the arena and knew the laurels his expertise had gained him. The conspiratorial tone of his greeting confirmed that we shared this knowledge.

The year before, I had idled under the same tree with a book. I had ac-

quired half an education in that spot. When the sun persiste⌐
my books and stroll along the tree-lined path to the pool, sh
and jump in. Now I avoided the deep, empty pit. It was not v
the short time we intended to stay. Besides, to buy the chlorine, a luxury
only imperialists could afford, was out of the question. Bare necessities
were available in the stores in small quantities, and only if you were lucky.

The overgrown rectangular grassy patch by the pool had once been a
lawn tennis court. It had lain idle now for many years, vestige of a bygone
era. Ernest had taken pleasure in its unkempt condition, for he had always
disdained the game, enjoying only things at which he excelled. Tennis accentuated an awkwardness that the egotist in him could not tolerate. However, the pool beside the tennis court had been an integral part of life at the
finca. Now the pool was a thing of the past, as was that grand old lady of the
sea, the *Pilar*, Ernest's beloved fishing boat.

"Val, dinner's ready" or "*Está listo, señorita*" would now bring me back
from some reverie. We still took regular breaks for meals. Marta, Mary's
maid, always served an early, light breakfast to us in our rooms; *café con
leche*, fruit juice, a soft-boiled egg, and toast. Lunch and dinner were served
rather formally by René in the dining room with a somber Stobbs sitting
complacently on the table. We retained our former seating positions: Mary
at the head of the table with her back to the French windows, close to the
kitchen door, I on her right. The wall behind me was conspicuously bare.
Miró's *The Farm* had hung there many years, in full view of its owner, who
had sat opposite. By a stroke of great luck, it was now hanging in New
York's Museum of Modern Art on an extended loan. It had been one of
Ernest's proudest possessions, a souvenir of his early, romantic Paris days
when he was poor and writing well. He had gone to the artist's studio and
chosen it, at a price that was beyond his means. He paid for it little by little
on the installment plan. It was now considered to be Miró's finest work.

This year the garden had less to offer, though what it had was more
valuable, for food was even scarcer and more difficult to come by. Two
pounds of meat were allowed each week per family, if you could find it. The
open-air market in the city of Havana had been a great place to get groceries

and other odds and ends at a reasonable price. There had been smells and noise and bustle, and you had to be prepared to bargain and to keep your eyes and ears open as well as a firm grasp on your pocketbook. But now meat and fish were in short supply; tinned goods from Russia and Czechoslovakia lined the stalls in their stead. Beans, rice, yucca, and corn were plentiful enough, but olive and vegetable oils, lard, and butter were no longer to be found. Our greatest disappointment was the lack of fish. Delectable fish had been so abundant in this coastal city. Now the regulations governing fishing boats restricted the operations of the fishermen and threatened their livelihood. There had been a rash of escapes to the United States in little fishing boats, crowded to capacity with desperate people smuggling their families and few possessions hoping to make a new life in an untroubled land. The government was on to them and determined to put an end to the illegal departures, even if the people who remained behind were to suffer as a result.

After shopping at the market we made our ritual visit to El Floridita. There we took stools at the tall wooden bar and, from habit, ordered a Papa Doble. It was quiet in that place, which once had been abuzz with social activity—another sign of changed times. Castro didn't approve of drinking, gambling, or any of the so-called vices of the capitalist nations.

Mary was a first-rate improviser when it came to culinary matters, and in spite of the dismal fare at the market, we were not to suffer one whit. The deep freeze held neatly labeled packages of marlin and dolphin and the considerable remains of a large sea turtle we had brought back in the *Pilar* after a fair struggle the year before—a surprise catch in late spring while we were trolling for marlin outside the Havana harbor. The cellar downstairs was stocked with some fine wines, and the storage pantry's shelves were laden with delicacies. "I've just been down to the cellar, and I think I can say we're the luckiest pair on this island. Wait till you see the goodies I've found!" Mary shouted. I followed her down the stairs. The pantry shelves were filled with tins of palm hearts and pickled mushrooms, brandied peaches, baba au rhum, and a slew of delights from Maison Glass and Charles of Madison Avenue. "I had quite forgotten about them," she exclaimed, brightening considerably. "Whenever we spent several months here at a time and Papa was busy writing, we would have one of the specialty shops in New York send us down a couple of cases of delicacies to tide us over the monotonous periods and add a little spark to our lives. What a perfect treasure trove! We couldn't have found it at a more opportune time."

We must have been the best-fed pair in Cuba that summer. Each dinner was a gourmet meal with splendid wine. What a pity there weren't any friends to share it with us. Roberto stayed for lunch on the days he came to help, and his brother, José Luis, came by whenever he could get away from his important job as chief medical officer of Castro's army. On a couple of occasions Ernest's old friend from his first days in Cuba, Mayito Menocal, and his cousin Elicio Argüelles, came over and stayed to eat with us.

Meals were the focal part of the day, particularly dinner. It was often the only time we had a chance to relax and converse. We would dress for dinner casually, as opposed to carelessly, and whet our appetites with a Campari and soda and some Fats Waller or Frank Sinatra, unwinding from our chores over a leisurely, candle-lit meal. Soft-spoken, kind-eyed René, never intruding, was always on hand to fill the glasses or pass out the next course. The cat Stobbs never failed to appear, as much a part of the table decor as the silver candelabra, Steuben glass, and Dutch porcelain figurines. Traditionally, he had sat on his master's right, eyes closed as he purred contentedly. When the aroma became too much for him to bear, he sat up straight and stared till some diner was hypnotized into forking over a tasty morsel, very much against will and principle.

As we neared the end of our second week and our to-go pile was growing, Mary began to think seriously about how we would be able to exit the island and bring our cache with us. Pan Am told us that hand baggage only was allowed on their flights—a rule enforced with no exceptions. We explored the various means of sea transportation and found that absolutely nothing was leaving Cuba for the United States. One person half jokingly said we would have no trouble routing our belongings via China. With passing time, the idea became less absurd. Mary put in several calls to the minister of external affairs, Dr. Olivares, but she never got farther than his secretary, and her requests for a response were ignored. Frustrated, she appealed to José Luis, El Feo, to approach Fidel and ask him if he would come to the *finca* as he had promised.

"*Señora,* the premier's secretary telephoned this morning," I heard René tell Mary one afternoon as I came in for lunch. "Señor Castro will come here on Thursday in the afternoon."

"That's good news, René. Val, did you hear that? How are you doing with the papers? We must find out from Castro how we are going to move those damn things out of here."

"Yes, I heard. Thursday, why, that's tomorrow. We'll have been here exactly two weeks. To tell you the truth, I could use a few more days."

"We'll see if he can get us on a flight sometime next week, I don't have to worry what they charge for excess baggage since they won't take any. The more I look around the more I want to bring with me. He'll find us a way."

At two o'clock, while we were still at the luncheon table, there was a telephone call confirming Castro's intention to arrive that day *por la tarde*—that is, anytime between then and midnight, or, judging by the speed and accuracy of the officials we had been dealing with, anytime within the next week.

"He'll come this afternoon," Mary told Roberto and me when she returned from the phone. "No siesta for us. Let the servants stick around. They must be here to meet him. We'll continue working as usual."

Cushions were straightened, flowers freshened, everyone put on alert. Tense and restless though we were, we continued our work with poor concentration and frequent nervous glances at the clock. Time crawled.

At six o'clock I ventured, "What can be keeping him, Mary?"

"He always sleeps in the afternoon. He'll surely come about eight-thirty. Heavens, it's after six already, let's eat now." No one had given any thought to an evening meal. Mary called to the kitchen and asked that the luncheon leftovers be reheated with a little seasoning added. "We'll get our eating over with before El Jefe arrives."

The sound of every passing car on the main road heightened our expectation. At seven, we sat down to supper of Russian crab chow mein accompanied by Cuban rice and a bottle of rioja. Before the last mouthful, they arrived, three cars full. Someone quickly removed the food, someone else the wine. We jumped to our feet and, as rehearsed, the entire household lined up outside on the steps to greet Castro as he approached. An imposing figure, tall, full-bearded, cordial, and alert, the thirty-five-year-old premier, in his familiar fatigues, gave a smile and a nod to each individual as he passed. He seemed a trifle shy as he entered the house. He proceeded humbly, as if treading on hallowed ground, for he deeply admired Hemingway the man and the writer. The sorrow showing in his face was sincere. He clasped Mary's hand warmly and offered his condolences.

Fidel introduced us to his adjutant, whose eyes closely followed the premier's movements, and then to his *guardaespaldas* (bodyguard), a short swarthy young man, standing conspicuously by his side. A couple of uniformed men entered behind him but lurked in the background. Several security officers remained outside at attention. There were about ten in the group altogether. The servants, neatly clothed and shod and clearly awestruck, returned to the kitchen quarters, from which they peered whenever the door swung open, one or another of them slipping into the room to perform their duties. Mary immediately drew Fidel's attention to the spectacular night view of Havana from the dining room terrace, lights faintly twinkling in the twilight. He, anxious to get down to business, said, "They told me you wanted to talk to me?"

"Yes. Let's sit down inside. Will you take coffee?" Then, changing her mind, Mary continued, "But first I'd like to show you the house."

We went into Papa's bedroom, where the writer had worked each day standing up at his tall slant-topped desk facing the wall. The Royal typewriter sat there with paper inserted in the roller, waiting. Fidel's attention was elsewhere. "Which one shot the lion?" he asked, pointing with interest to the stretched-out skin of a beast with glass eyes, bared teeth, pink tongue, tawny mane, and long whiskers.

"That's my husband's lion," Mary said. "He shot it in Africa."

"What kind of gun did he use?" Fidel asked. He was clearly fascinated with the variety of animal heads and skins visible in every room. "Are all these animals from Africa?" He was keenly interested and eager as a boy as we walked from the guest room and into the dining room, where again he wanted to know the origin of each animal head. Were the animals related? he asked. Might some of them be imported into Cuba to help supplement the waning meat supply? What about the eland? He had picked up quickly on Mary's remark that the eland was Africa's best meat producer. "Why could we not import them to Cuba and set up eland farms to produce meat for ourselves?" His eyes widened when he stood beneath the American elk's great horns—a trophy Ernest had bagged in the late thirties in Wyoming and which was a record at the time. What kind of animal would have such antlers? He leaned back against the table to get a better view of it. "*¡Hombre!*" he exclaimed.

Mary showed him her room, decorated with her own trophies, both American and African.

"Look at him, where did you shoot him?"

"Right there in the shoulder with one shot."

"Just like this?" He demonstrated.

Mary nodded, smiling.

Suddenly he seemed to remember that there was business to attend to. "There was some small problem you had?"

"Yes. Roberto here will explain it." We moved to the sitting room. Coffee was passed around. We later learned that it should have been whiskey. Mary reiterated her intention to give the *finca* to the people—the *pueblo*, she emphasized, not the government of Cuba. She was unsubtly circumventing the government's policy of grabbing and nationalizing all private property. If she had to lose her home, at least she would designate how she wanted the property put to use, as a memorial to her husband and a gift to the people he loved.

Fidel acquiesced. He was direct in his speech, to the point. He came across as a man of his word, understanding, patient with difficulties. Mary said that she wanted nothing to be moved. People can read in the dining room or in the tower, she added. Tower? Castro's ears pricked. Could he see the tower? Once again we went outside. It was quite dark now. Mary led the way, with Fidel at her side. His men followed. Before they could ascend the concrete stairs, the bodyguards had pushed ahead of Mary, but Castro still went first, earning Mary's lasting admiration for bravery. Anyone could have been waiting there to ambush him. He was fearless, she marveled later. She would repeat the phrase over and over.

The tower was my least favorite spot at the *finca*. Four dozen cats— some with names but mostly anonymous—stalked the grounds. Their home was the bottom floor of the tower, a three-story building on the far end of the house. Mary had designed it in 1947 as a special surprise for Ernest's birthday. It was clear that Castro liked the tower. It was his type of place. Our first stop was the third floor, Papa's room, a whitewashed square, with desk and books and congenial clutter. Which books did he write here? was Fidel's first question. The answer was disappointing: none. We then climbed to the roof. It couldn't have been a clearer night. A canopy of stars twinkled down on us. Castro took his cap off and twirled it in the air lightheartedly. Then he lit up a cigar and listened carefully to everything Mary said before speaking. He agreed that the tower was built like a fortress but, in his opinion, it would prove poor for defense. He waved his hand in front of us. Any enemy could hide in the *matas*, the bushes below, or up on the hill. Puffing away on his cigar, frequently he called out *"Fósforo"* to his *guardaespaldas*, who promptly struck a match and rekindled the embers. As we descended, we stopped at the trunk room, a storage area taking up the entire second floor. He fondled the African spear there and poised it for a throw. Could you kill a lion with this? he asked. Yes, decidedly. His eye fell upon a piece of Cuban gold unearthed by a French archaeologist, and this held his attention for a few seconds.

Just as quickly his interest waned, and he was anxious once more to leave. We returned briskly to the house. On our way down he started to discuss who would take care of the museum, as he now called it. Roberto, who had been quite silent, immediately offered his services. He would be honored to be the caretaker of the Finca Vigía. As we approached the sitting room Castro said the caretaker's job would be a daily one; he would use guard dogs at night. He seemed anxious to depart.

"Can you spare just two more minutes?" Mary pressed him. He followed her to the library, where she had laid out a collection of photographs. "Maybe we can put some of these on the walls. Look at this," Mary continued. "These are hand-corrected galley proofs. They're very valuable."

"Are any more books going to be published?" he asked, his attention engaged again. "I'm told that there are unfinished manuscripts and that you will bring them out if there are instructions to that effect."

"Yes, there are manuscripts," Mary said, "but I haven't found any instructions concerning them yet. There was a note about his letters."

"Could you really burn them?" he asked.

"Certainly, if Ernest wanted me to do so," Mary answered with assurance.

Fidel seemed pleased at the vigor of her speech. "Is there anything else you want done?"

"I would like all of the staff to be kept on here at the *finca*. They have given many years of good service, and I consider them my friends. Papa would have wanted them to be taken care of. I would also like you to keep the *casita* for me to stay in when I return to Cuba," she said. "Finally, I must bring the unpublished manuscripts, our personal papers, and a few possessions back to the States with me, including a couple of the paintings. I'm having great difficulty finding a way to take them out of the country."

"Yes, that presents a problem." Castro nodded thoughtfully. Then a smile crept over his face. "You have my permission, but there's a little law we'll have to break." He laughed, and we laughed uneasily with him. "My office will draw up the papers for the establishment of the museum. I will see what I can do to help you with your departure. Let me know if you need anything. I am at your service."

We moved to the front step. Goodbyes and handshakes were extended all around. We waved as the cars disappeared down the driveway. We might have been seeing off old friends.

Our spirits were buoyed by the premier's visit. He had agreed to everything. It seemed that all our problems were solved. The house would remain intact and become a museum. The servants would be kept on in their jobs. Roberto was an excellent choice for curator. Few people knew the place as well as he did or had enjoyed such a long-standing friendship with the family. Mary would always have the little house to stay in when she returned to Cuba, and now that she had Castro's permission to remove the important papers and her own personal possessions, she became emboldened as she looked around the house.

"I shall take all the Venetian crystal and the china, of course. It would be foolish to leave the silver behind. But what about the paintings? Who's to say that all of these paintings are not my personal possessions?" she asked rhetorically. "Papa often forgot my birthday and impulsively would point to some cherished object of his and say it was mine, to make amends." She called for Cecilio, the carpenter, and asked him to measure the paintings and start building crates for the items that were to be shipped. There was a spring to Mary's step now as she walked around the house. I even heard her humming.

Midmorning a few days later, a black sedan pulled up in front of the house. It appeared to be an official car with an official driver. We watched a neatly dressed woman, probably in her early forties, emerge. She carried a briefcase and had a businesslike air about her. René opened the door. Our visitor was from the Ministry of Culture; the name René gave us was Russian. Mary greeted her pleasantly. The woman curtly shook her hand. She told us she was on loan from the Russian government to Cuba. Her expertise was art, and she had worked for several years at the Hermitage. She was training the Cubans in the art of appropriation, the confiscation and nationalization of all valuables. She found her Latin subordinates most inept and was serious in her mission to demonstrate how a job should be thoroughly accomplished. The Hemingway artifacts were an excellent example of a private collection that could be put to public use, and she intended to make this her model. After the cursory greeting and explanation, she fairly brushed Mary aside and said she must be about her work. She would catalog all the art items in the house, she noted as she reached into her bag for a legal pad and pen. She put on her glasses.

I could see Mary bristling, but she continued to be cordial. "To aid you in your efficiency," Mary said, "I shall point out the paintings we will be taking with us to the United States. You will not need to include them in your catalog."

The dark-haired, faintly attractive woman turned to Mary. There was an edge to her voice. "Everything in this house belongs to the Cuban government," she said icily. "Nothing will be leaving the country."

Cool as a cucumber, Mary played her trump card with a Cheshire smile. "Pardon me, but you are mistaken. Señor Castro visited this house only the other day, and he gave me his permission to bring whatever personal posessions I wish back to my home in the United States."

Without looking up, the ice maiden replied with equal satisfaction, "This is a communist country. Personal possessions do not exist. Señor Castro knows this better than anyone. He has neither the authority nor the power to change the law. Cuba's paintings will stay in Cuba."

Mary pursed her lips but did not reply. She nodded to me, and we both left the room. René was asked to stand by, observe the intruder, and see her to the door when she was ready to depart.

Mary had arrived in Cuba a grieving widow filled with idealism. She genuinely wanted to see her husband's memory endure by creating a shrine of the home he loved and dedicating it to the Cuban people, among whom he had lived for more than a third of his life. Here he had written some of his finest work. The bureaucratic, unrelenting attitude of the disagreeable Russian woman was a deep blow and did not bode well for the future of her scheme, but in an odd way, instead of defeating Mary, the encounter filled her with renewed determination. This time she would consider her own position more carefully. She now intended to take her possessions, and she would find a means of transporting them to the United States even if she had to go to Shanghai to do so. She walked around each room looking at the pictures, saying out loud in front of the Klee, "Yes, Papa gave me that for my birthday. I'm sure I could recall which year it was if I put my mind to it. And," she went on, standing before *The Guitarist,* "on one wedding anniversary—he never remembered any of them—he said the Gris was mine." And so as she passed each painting she asserted her right to ownership, vowing that not now nor ever would they be the property of the Cuban government.

"Val," she called to me, "do you remember the Braque that Papa kept on the shelves behind his desk? Have you seen it?" I did remember it, a Cubist still life in earthtone hues. I had seen Braque's work at the Jeu de Paume in Paris, and it amused me that Ernest kept the unframed canvas carefree among the clutter. He had acquired it from the artist in the twenties, and it had blended in so well we did not notice its absence until now. It was definitely not there. René was called in, but he had no explanation. "Has anyone at all been in the house since we were here?" Mary questioned him. He told us that after Don Ernesto's death a couple of men who identified themselves as government officials had come to inspect the house and property. He did not imagine that one of them would . . .

"Thank you, René," Mary said, and when he left the room she turned to me. "It's pointless to make a complaint." She was more determined than ever to finish packing and leave Cuba and the revolution behind her.

From then on, all our efforts were engaged in planning the getaway—not for ourselves, which we knew would be no challenge, but in finding some means of transportation for the wooden crates that were stealthily being packed, sealed, and stored in the garage, awaiting departure. The paintings would be removed from the walls at the very last minute. Mary had already picked out posters, photographs, and lesser works to hang in their stead so that there would be no telltale markings on the walls; the switch would not be apparent to those unfamiliar with the house.

It had to be ocean transportation because Cuba is an island and that was the only route available to us. No cargo ships were bound for the United States. No ships of any kind were bound for the States except the tiny rafts and fishing boats filled with desperate refugees clandestinely steering for the Florida coast. Everyone was scrambling. Life was the only possession they traveled with, and even that was a cargo in jeopardy. We decided we would go down to the harbor and see for ourselves what kind of vessels were putting in there. Perhaps we could avail ourselves of something bound for South America. Our minds were open. We were prepared for any eventuality.

As we sat on the pier, Mary puffed on a Camel cigarette. She had brought a carton with her and was now starting to ration them carefully. I noticed some children playing a short way off. *"Cuba sí! Yanqui no,"* they chanted, mimicking the grown-ups, as they laughed and pushed each other around. They became silent when they saw me watching them. One little girl, plucking up courage, came over to me. "Are you Russian?" she asked.

"No," I said.

"You're not a Yankee imperialist?" she prodded.

"Certainly not," I told her. "I come from Ireland."

"Holland," she said, frowning.

"No, Ireland," I repeated. "It's a small island like Cuba but in northern Europe. We had a revolution there too," I told her. "When I was your age, we would chant, 'Ireland *sí*, England *no*.' " I was improvising a little. She looked at me dubiously, not sure if I was making fun of her. Then she sidled away.

Three or four mornings passed like this, and each day our anxiety grew. I had taken to daydreaming, forgetting that I should be concentrating on the activity in the docks. "Val, Val," Mary called to me urgently one day. "Do you see what I see?" I strained my eyes, but nothing out of the ordinary came to my attention. Then I saw it: stars and stripes, an American flag. We made our way as fast as we could to the spot. She was a grubby-looking trawler, bigger than the fishing boats we were used to, but much smaller than a regular cargo boat. She was a little bit of both, we learned. A sailor was swabbing down the deck, with another sorting out ropes. "Ahoy there," Mary called out. "Are you from the United States?" We had seen the word *Tampa* and guessed it was the boat's home port.

"Yes, we're from Florida."

"What are you doing here?"

"We're on our way back from Venezuela with a cargo of lobster tails and shrimp, but our refrigeration has broken down and we've put in to see if we can have it fixed."

"Let me speak to your captain," Mary asked.

The rugged seafarer was disinclined to be social. He had a problem on his hands and wanted to solve it as quickly as possible; he had no time for idle chitchat. "If we can't fix the refrigeration, we'll sell the shellfish here and return to Tampa as soon as possible."

"Would you have room for four crates of household goods?" Mary asked. "I'll make it worth your while."

"Sorry, ma'am. No way we can take anything extra on board. We don't have the room and we don't have the documents."

"I have the Cuban government's permission. I'll provide you with the documents."

"No, I can't do it." He was adamant.

Mary refused to give up. "You'll never find the parts you need here to repair your icebox. You can sell the fish and I'll pay you well to take my belongings. You could store them in the refrigeration area. You will not take a loss, I promise you."

"What sort of price are you talking about?" he asked, and Mary knew she had won. They worked out a figure, half then and half upon delivery of the crates on U.S. soil.

"Be here with the boxes at eight tomorrow morning."

"You bet." Mary shook his weathered hand. We could hardly contain our excitement as we headed for the car.

Mary telephoned the premier's office at once and told his secretary that she had found a way to ship her belongings to the States but needed Castro's help. Could she discuss the matter with him? Castro's aide called back immediately. El Jefe had instructed him to facilitate the departure in any way possible. They would make sure there was no interference from the harbor police or customs. The exact contents were not discussed. Roberto came with us the next morning, and the loading went smoothly. We waved cheerily as the boat put out, our main mission accomplished.

Back at the *finca* the next goal was to leave the house in pristine order so that it could function as a museum as soon as possible. We looked through a mountain of magazines and newspapers, yellowing with age, spotted with mildew and laced with wormholes. The only remedy was to make a bonfire and burn the entire lot. Mary and I gathered the mountain of paper, and René and Puchilo arrived with wheelbarrows to cart the debris to the burn area, below the tennis court. Roberto, Mayito, and Elicio came to join in the antics, and by way of a farewell party Mary took out the last of the codfish from the deep freeze and asked the cook to prepare *bacalao* from her special recipe. The Basque dish was always served on Christmas Eve at the *finca*. When the fire was roaring Mary went back to the library and took the small packet of letters out of the file cabinet with Ernest's instructions attached. As we watched the flames curl around the little bundle Mary first hummed and then sang one of their old songs:

Soy como soy,
Y no como Papa quiere
Qué culpa tengo yo
De ser así?

I am as I am
And not as Papa wishes
Is it my fault
That I am so?

We all joined in the second verse. At that moment I felt no sadness seeing those letters go. I knew how desperately Ernest liked to guard his privacy. To disobey his last wishes would have been a sacrilege.

When Mary and I first arrived we had spent much time debating how we would determine which of the papers we would ship and which to leave behind. Mary's first idea was that the *finca* would become a learning center, and to that end she wanted to leave there as complete a record of her husband's life and most especially of his work as was prudent. It was a given that all original unpublished manuscripts would return to the United States with us, along with letters of a personal nature that related to the immediate family, particularly to Hemingway's three sons. Also we intended to take any material of literary and historical value that Mary felt would be important for the official biographer. Mary had little interest in removing the letters of Martha Gellhorn, her predecessor as Ernest's wife, nor those of Adriana Ivancich, the young Italian woman Hemingway became infatuated with in the late nineteen forties.

Original typescripts, hand-corrected galley proofs, some manuscripts of published works, a multitude of letters, and hand-penned notes of every description, from story ideas to shopping lists, were left behind. A massive collection of photographs—about three thousand, including several Robert Capa originals—remained at the *finca,* as did the entire library of books, many of which have Ernest's comments, notes, and ideas penned inside. All of the trophies stayed in place, along with virtually all the possessions he had accumulated in his lifetime. His Royal typewriter sits waiting. In the bathroom beside the scales, one can read the penciled dates and his weights recorded on the plaster wall for each day of the last years he was in residence. Every inch of the house still reveberated with the memory of the writer, like a moment not frozen in time but still breathing. Mary looked at what she was leaving behind and was satisfied.

On August 25, two days before we departed, Mary handed each member of the staff a check, in some cases amounting to a year's wages, as a parting gift from Papa, she said. She told them that the *finca* would become a museum and El Jefe had promised that their jobs would be secure. She would never forget them. They were her family, and nothing could change that. We had hardly seen Gregorio, captain of the *Pilar,* Ernest's faithful companion on the water for twenty years, but now he came from Cojímar, the little fishing village where he lived with his wife and three daughters, with his hat in his hand, his eyes clouded over. Mary spent extra time with Gregorio. "I want you to have the *Pilar,* Gregorio," she said. They both knew that this was not possible in reality, but the symbolic gesture bonded them and diminished the pain of loss they both felt so acutely. I had my own memories of Gregorio. He had offered me my first cigar, and we would smoke one together forty years later at his house in Cojímar, when he was 102. He had helped me reel in the first ocean fish I ever caught, a thirty-nine-pound sailfish that felt as if the weight of the world were in it. He had taught me the secret of his *salsa verde,* which never tasted as good as it did when he served it over freshly caught fish in the galley of the *Pilar.*

"Val," Mary said to me on our last day, "you should take whatever you want, whatever can fit in your bag, as a souvenir."

"You really mean it, Mary?" She didn't have to ask me twice. I went directly to the library. Books were all I wanted. I had my memories of the *finca* and of Ernest and Mary and our time together there. Nothing was needed to remind me of that, but books were different. I had never taken a book off the library shelf. That was Ernest's domain. Now my eyes scanned the shelves. I knew immediately what I wanted. I pulled out a dozen or so books, each with a very definite purpose. I started with Major Frederick Russell Burnham's *Scouting on Two Continents,* published by Doubleday in 1926. Then came *A Farewell to Arms* (1929), a first edition, his favorite among his own novels. I could not pass up Joyce's *Ulysses,* which we had discussed the first time we met. The 1924 edition was published in Paris by Sylvia Beach's Shakespeare and Company. Pound's *Pavannes and Divisions* (1918) was on my list, and a volume by Gertrude Stein with the inscription "To Ernest Hemingway whom I like young and whom I shall like better older." She was wrong about that. I also took George Borrow's *The Gypsies of Spain,* John O'Hara's *Butterfield 8,* and Cyril Connolly's *The Unquiet Grave.* Some time later I was surprised to find a note in the Connolly in Ernest's familiar rounded script: "Put in about Kipling and wonderful writing and then the friend who saw him (Swope) and the wife. Then about the flyers—Bishop the fishing—ribbon clerk—others—the long tirade." My souvenir package was completed with *The Hamlet of Archibald MacLeish,* T. E. Lawrence's *Seven Pillars of Wisdom,* a late-nineteenth-century book in Spanish on Goya's *The Disasters of War,* another book on the rules of bullfighting, and an early edition of *The Torrents of Spring,* published in Paris by Caresse Crosby in 1931.

We said goodbye to the *finca,* hugging every one of the staff before we left. They were to take care of the house, which was now theirs, we told them. At least in theory it belonged to the Cuban people. Juan drove us to the airport. Our attention was diverted by the chaos, the sheer number of people waiting standby, hoping to be able to leave, verging on hysteria when it became clear that many would be left behind. Every inch of the plane was filled, with children up to the age of ten sitting on their parents' laps. For the successful ones, tears at parting mingled with relief as they embarked on a new life.

A new life was starting for Mary too. As she contemplated what was ahead of her it occurred to both of us at about the same time that the valuable cargo we had sent in the shrimp and lobster boat was not insured. The paintings alone were worth more than a quarter of a million dollars—several million in today's currency—but the papers were priceless. Mary had been careful not to emphasize the value of the cargo lest the sailors be tempted. Nevertheless, we worked ourselves into a state of sheer anxiety, which subsided only when we reached Tampa and found all four crates intact. Everything was there exactly as we had delivered it.

In fact, more than everything, as I was to learn when I unpacked the papers six months later. Ernest's publisher, Charlie Scribner, had given me the use of a little office on the tenth floor of the Scribner Building on Fifth Avenue at Forty-eighth Street. To my dismay, a little army of Cuban termites had stowed away and were happily making inroads on the precious papers with a lacy fretwork. I was to spend four years in that room, reading through and sorting the rescued booty along with all the papers accumulated during Hemingway's lifetime.

CHAPTER SEVENTEEN

Picking Up the Pieces, Ketchum, Fall 1961:
"Best of All He Loved the Fall"

W E DID NOT DALLY in Florida but flew to Chicago, where we boarded the train for Shoshone, Idaho. Dave Roberts, sportswriter for the Cincinnati *Enquirer,* joined us, for the next item on our agenda was the opening of dove season, September 1. It was an event the Hemingways had hoped to participate in each year, but circumstances had never permitted it, starting with Mary's very first visit to Ketchum as a bride in 1946. Back then the journey had been interrupted in Casper, Wyoming, where she was hospitalized with an ectopic pregnancy. Not arriving in time for the opening of dove season became a standard family joke. However, Mary was determined to be in Ketchum on September 1, 1961. While we were still in Cuba she had asked me if I would travel out west with her and stay a couple of months before returning to New York.

We had developed an easy camaraderie in the weeks since Ernest's death. Mary dreaded returning alone to the Ketchum house, indelibly haunted by the tragedy. She took great pains to subdue the memory of Ernest's awful final moment, fully knowing it would be impossible to erase. To hide her grief, she assumed an air of gaiety. I understood her need for company and agreed to come. Outwardly I reasoned that my only experience of the American West was the fleeting visit to attend the funeral. On a deeper level, my true hope was that a time of quiet reflection in the place where Ernest had chosen to end his misery and where he now was laid to rest would give my own grief a chance to heal.

We drove the fifty-six miles from the Shoshone train station to Ketchum with Dave Roberts in his rented car. At the bottom of Timmerman Hill, snow-capped mountains rose majestically in the distance, and a brace of mourning doves winged their way across our vista; this was thought to be a very good omen. We were at an elevation of six thousand feet, with high mountains ahead, dense pine forests on one side, and a river meandering close by. Three miles from our destination we drove over the narrow steel-arched bridge that spans the Big Wood River before it flows on through the Hemingway property to the north of Ketchum. Mary became quite animated when she described to me the delights of autumn in Idaho. Dave chimed in with nuggets from his vast knowledge of local bird hunting. He had first come to Ketchum in 1947 and had barely missed a year hunting since then. They told me that '47 had been a splendid season. The Hemingways had stayed for Christmas that year, and the Coopers had come for New Year's along with Ingrid Bergman. It was the only time that both the stars of the movie of *For Whom the Bell Tolls* and the author had ever gotten together. That was the last really good year for the Hemingways and Coopers. Mary and Ernest stayed a short while in 1948—no Coops that year, no Hemingway children, who excelled at hunting and loved the area, and very few birds. Ernest and Mary did not return to Idaho for ten years, until 1958.

When Mary told me I could use one of her Winchester 20-gauge shotguns, a pair that Ernest had given her, I realized I would have the opportunity to put into practice my training on the hill at the *finca* that spring day, which now seemed so long ago. I would also get to know the good friends I had heard so much about: Pappy and Tilly Arnold, Clara Spiegel, Don Anderson, Chuck and Flos Atkinson, Ruth and Bud Purdy. To my Irish ears even the names had the ring of a cast of characters from a cowboy novel.

Dr. George Saviers and his wife, Pat, I already knew. I remembered Ernest's exasperation as he told of hunting with the couple. As George was set to aim at his prey, invariably Pat would shout, "George, George, look, look," and point out the deer, pheasant, or whatever, at which the animal would scuttle out of range. Pat, it seemed, never learned, and Ernest urged George not to bring her along. I can still hear his falsetto mimicking her voice, half bemused mockery, half suppressed anger. I don't believe George heeded the advice.

The Purdys had a ranch at Picabo (pronounced "Peekaboo") on the Silver Creek—one of the finest dry-fly trout streams in the West. Youthful, dark, and slight, Bud was a dedicated farmer who took pride in his work and his surroundings. There was no prettier ranch in the area. We were invited to shoot doves in a rough, fallow field of golden sunflowers. Later we walked through the stubble after pheasants, and later still crept stealthily along the irrigation ditches and the feeder springs in pursuit of mallard ducks. Neither Mary nor I could drive a car, so, determined to learn, we both took lessons and earned our licenses after passing a cursory test given by the sheriff himself. We were equally inept, and numerous arguments ensued after close calls, or suspected close calls, in each case the passenger accusing and the driver defending some near miss. Fortunately, as months passed no damage was done. We also acquired a dog, a liver-and-white short-haired puppy, affectionate, clumsy, and untrained for fieldwork. We named him Sage. Mary called the house the Block House because it was made out of a square slab of concrete, two stories with a hip roof, as strong as a prison and as charmless. In April 1959, as they were preparing to leave Cuba for Spain, she and Ernest had bought it from Henry J. "Bob" Topping, millionaire playboy and erstwhile husband of Lana Turner. They had visited the house once and learned it was for sale, and on the heels of the revolution that blew in with the new year they were uneasy about the mounting political tension in Cuba. Ernest was lukewarm at first look but wanted a quiet place where he could work without disturbance. It fit the bill. When we left Cuba in July 1960 he had already packed and shipped two trunks of papers and manuscripts to Ketchum. Now I found myself sorting through them at Mary's behest.

At first Mary had had little affection for the house, but over the years she customized it to suit her taste. One distinct virtue of Block House was the large southward-facing sundeck wrapped around the forty-foot living room. Picture windows offered a splendid view of the Big Wood River valley with its meandering trout stream. Fragrant sagebrush hills stretched behind the house to the north. Birdsong harmonized with the ripplesong of the little rapids in the wide, shallow river, flowing audibly and unceasingly. There was not another house in sight. Open and wild, it was about as distinct from the *finca* as any terrain could be. Ketchum lay a scant mile and a half away. Once a mining town, it was now the center of the high country sheep ranging industry and a major origin point for shipment to market by rail. Many Basques had moved there, drawn to the sheep country. For Ernest, it was reminiscent of his beloved Pamplona. Saloons were still called joints, and although gambling had been banned in the mid-fifties, there was an air of the casino about them. I seem to remember poker playing and a roulette wheel at the Alpine, where the patrons placed high stacks of silver dollars in front of them on the bar counter. The stacks diminished each time a new round of drinks was poured. The nearby resort of Sun Valley nestled in the mountains, a village dotted with chalets of rustic logs, some bedecked with antlers, surrounded by merry wildflower meadows that turned starkly white when the winter snows appeared. Its dry, powdery, abundant snow was the hallmark of great Western skiing. A dozen miles away lay the small town of Hailey, the 1885 birthplace of Ezra Pound—by accident, the natives used to say, since his father came out from Pennsylvania for the mining but did not stay long. Pound rates only a small corner in the little mining museum. Seat of Blaine County, Hailey was also the site of the nearest airport, where Larry Johnson, of Johnson's Flying Service, kept his planes. It was in Larry's Piper Apache that Ernest flew to Minnesota's Mayo Clinic for those two periods of treatment during the last sad months of his life.

Mary was settling into a routine, trying to forge a single life for herself. She delighted in showing me around the area, introducing me to the folks and the haunts she had enjoyed with Ernest. We weren't short of company. After Dave Roberts left, Alfred Rice appeared briefly to discuss the business of the estate and the future of the literary properties. Until her death Alfred remained Mary's confidant, mentor, and financial advisor as well as lawyer, agent, and trustee. Most years his fees amounted to close to 30 percent of the estate's annual income, 10 percent in each of the last three mentioned capacities. He became indispensible to Mary; for any purchase over two hundred dollars, he had to be consulted. I could never see Alfred without recalling Ernest's wry comment: "Al Rice grows leaner and meaner and more like Cassius with each passing year." Being the widow of the legend and busying herself with the details of the literary properties brought Mary some consolation during those difficult first days on her own.

During those months Mary and I developed a deep friendship that lasted until her death. Mary had great spirit. She was imaginative and inventive, a tough old bird, spunky but not boastful. She sometimes signed her letters to me "Your old bird." She was ambitious and had great staying power. She spoke her mind, never mincing words, never sparing feelings. Yet she was neither mean nor petty. She took a childlike joy in everything around her. With equal enthusiasm she listened to a solitary bird sing, inhaled the aroma of a freshly picked herb, caught a snowflake on her tongue, or beamed at receiving unexpected greetings. Many things delighted her, and her exuberance was catching. Mary taught me to cook, but more important, I learned from her the pleasures of the palate. When Mary and Ernest were married in 1946 she gave up her career as a successful journalist to become a full-time wife. It was a difficult marriage, and to her credit, she made it last. An only child, she was mindful too of her parents' needs as they reached old age and became infirm. For several years she successfully balanced her wifely and filial duties—a considerable feat since her parents were rigidly conservative Christian Scientists and her mother strongly opposed to liquor and swearing. They were obviously not suitable candidates for the Finca Vigía guest list.

Over the years Mary wrote me many sprightly letters or postcards whenever she traveled. A few days after I left New York for Paris in August 1960 she wrote me:

Val sweetheart—You can't imagine how dull it is around here without Somebody slipping in and immediately kicking off its shoes, without Somebody sitting on the yellow stool chitter-chattering while I do the salad, without Somebody going Ummm-mmm—glub glub while eating it, or likewise disliking it, making that disgusting Uaaaghaaaa sound. Nobody to steam around the shops with—nobody to help me, and give moral support against all the terrible T.V.—So I've almost given it up. Which is to say, all of us here miss you—I mean the black cat on the wall, the fingernails on the cupboard door, Greta, the elevator boys—especially the Irish boy—and especially me.

A surprise visit from Mary's old friend Alan Moorehead in November cheered her up. Alan had met Mary in 1938 when they both worked in the city room of the London *Daily Express*. Alan's wife, Lucy Milner, was a fashion writer and later women's page editor for the *Express*. She and Mary had immediately struck up a friendship. As Mary wrote in her autobiography, Alan became the most famous of that little group of journalists who worked together in London in the late thirties. Author of two novels and several highly praised works of nonfiction including *Gallipoli,* Alan's trip to the United States in 1961 brought him to see his New York publisher to discuss the American edition of *The Blue Nile.* It was to be a companion volume to *The White Nile,* which I remembered Ernest reading with pleasure. Both Mary's second husband, Noel Monks (to whom she was married before Ernest), and Alan were Australians from Melbourne. Noel had worked on a leading Melbourne newspaper before coming to London to join the *Daily Mail* just in time to cover the Spanish Civil War. Noel and Mary had been close friends with Alan and Lucy, and Mary's friendship with the Mooreheads continued through her marriage to Ernest and until her death. Genial and excellent company, Alan had blue eyes that twinkled as he caught us up on his recent adventures in Africa, tales spoken with a soft Down Under inflection. The stimulating weekend passed quickly as we hiked, picnicked, and talked well into the evenings.

For a short period, autumn cloaked the landscape, an artist's palette in a fleeting flurry of colors: bright golden aspen, the rich burgundy of sumac, coppery green willows standing sentinel by the river. Our favorite lunch was hot dogs charred on the open fire we lit during a pause on our walks, followed by toasted marshmallows skewered on a willow stick. When the first snows fell, we took out the wooden snowshoes Mary had purchased the winter before for herself and Ernest to exercise on between his trips to the Mayo Clinic. In the afternoons we plodded over the same hills north of the house in the shadow of the Boulder Mountain, deciphering pawprints and other telltale signs of secretive lives. Once we were lucky enough to see a great horned owl.

My favorites among Ernest's old hunting cronies were the Arnolds and Clara Spiegel. When he first arrived in Sun Valley, Ernest was completely surprised to find that Freddie Spiegel, who had been in the same Red Cross ambulance unit with him in World War I, had a summer place just across the road from the Arnolds. The Spiegels divorced, and it wasn't until 1947 that Clara stayed in Ketchum through the fall.

Lloyd (Pappy) Arnold was Sun Valley Resort's first official photographer. Union Pacific, the owner of the resort, wanted to lure as many celebrities as possible to enjoy a vacation in the mountains, since the publicity would guarantee that a clientele of uppercrust sportsmen and their women would follow. They knew Ernest Hemingway had been spending the hunting season in Montana near the Wyoming border, and they felt that with incentives, they might have a good chance to nudge him farther west, to Sun Valley. It took a couple of years to make contact, but on September 6, 1939, Ernest arrived in Sun Valley with Martha Gellhorn, soon to be his third wife. Pappy was assigned to Ernest, who called himself a "publicity property," and Ernest happily accommodated the photographer, who accompanied him fishing and hunting. Pappy had a deep affection for Ernest and never recovered from the writer's death. In his later years, I'm told, he developed a rare mania in which he imagined that he was Ernest Hemingway, and he retreated slowly and irrevocably into a fine and lasting madness.

Pappy's wife, Tilly—or Sir Till, as Ernest called her after he had "knighted" her in a mock ceremony—was a hearty cook and a welcoming hostess who was full of good sense. She was a true friend to Mary, sensing exactly when to approach and when to withdraw. All the Ketchum friends were loyal to the end, ordinary folks and good sporting companions. Mary felt this was a place in which she could settle.

In the daytime that fall we enjoyed all the outdoor activities: hiking, picnicking, bird hunting. Once or twice a week we ate out in the evening, at the Atkinsons' Christiania restaurant, at the Challenger Inn or the Ram in the Sun Valley resort, or on special occasions at Trail Creek Cabin, where Ernest had given a farewell dinner for Martha Gellhorn when she left to cover the Russo-Finnish war for *Collier*'s magazine in 1939.

When there was a lull in the activities, we would try to fathom what had gone so wrong with Ernest. Why had he taken such a drastic measure? There was a constant reminder in the presence of intruders. That fall a steady stream of curious tourists first went to the cemetery and then came to the house to look and take photographs. Mary could see them from her bedroom window. The initial annoyance turned to fury, and she would grab her shotgun from the rack in the living room, load it outside, and shoot at the tires as the cars approached. Seeing a slight blond woman in a red plaid shirt and blue jeans appear at the door with gun poised caused surprise and dismay. A warning shot would raise a little gravel and stir up dust in front of their windshields, and if they did not take heed, the tire would be the next target. I admired her spunk and no-nonsense approach. The word got around, and then we were mostly left in peace.

As time passed, Mary's heartache seemed to be easing, but she did not want me to leave. As each week went by she urged me to stay on a little longer. One day she felt a sharp chest pain and convinced herself she was having a heart attack. George Saviers was called and diagnosed an ulcer, which X-rays soon confirmed. Mary spent a couple of weeks in the local hospital, and I extended my stay again, as I could not allow her to convalesce alone. Thanksgiving came, my second in America. The first I had spent in Bucks County with the cast of *The Hostage* at the home of one of the producers. Now I was in Idaho feasting on wild duck and baked butternut squash. In spite of her delicate health, Mary cooked the wild birds, and we had a jolly celebration. We were still in Ketchum for Christmas, when Don Anderson, who headed the sports desk activities at Sun Valley and was a longtime Hemingway hunting friend, brought us a sagebrush, which Mary sprayed with silver paint and we hung ornaments on. We put together a wassail bowl and some hors d'oeuvres and hosted a gathering on Christmas Eve, Mary's first real social event since Ernest's death. By now the village was alive with tourists, Baldy Mountain astir with activity. The downhill skiing season was under way. Mary had long ago given up on the sport after various injuries, but she urged me to give it a try. A holiday mood prevailed, and we both could not help but get caught up in the revelry. Mary showed sheer joy when we bundled up to watch the Christmas candlelight procession of skiers schussing down the slopes to sip hot mulled wine afterward.

Not long after we arrived in Ketchum, Malcolm Cowley wrote Mary regarding Ernest's unpublished papers. He suggested that she might find the responsibility of being executrix too weighty and that it would be perfectly reasonable for her to turn over the remaining unpublished manuscripts to a committee of professionals for evaluation and decision on what should be published. Mary was adamant that Ernest had known what he was doing when he appointed her as his sole literary executrix. She intended to do the job on her own, but she would appreciate Cowley's advice occasionally, as well as that of Charles Scribner and a couple of other literary friends whose opinion she valued. Still, all decisions would be hers and hers alone. She was firm about wanting to fulfill the duties that go with the title of literary executrix. She told Cowley that once she returned to New York she would take care of things.

Now that the New Year had come, Mary planned for the enormous task. She asked me if I would be willing to continue to work with her, specifically taking care of Ernest's papers, his letters, and extraneous bits and pieces so that she would be free to concentrate on the literary properties. Alfred, consulted every step of the way, fully agreed to my new position. Carlos Baker had been designated the official biographer and had already set to work. Mary wanted all the papers cataloged and certain sensitive items removed before Carlos saw them. I was familiar enough with the Hemingways' affairs to know which items these were. I agreed to take on the task.

CHAPTER EIGHTEEN

New York, New Life, 1962

I HAD MY OWN reasons for wanting to get back to New York. By January 1962 I was convinced that I was expecting Brendan Behan's child. Brendan and I had been good friends for a number of years. I had met him in Enniskerry the summer I turned sixteen. He was already married to Beatrice then, and I always thought of them as a couple. Brendan was not a philanderer as far as I know, but he was a tremendous tease and loved to shock. I had often heard him say to pretty young women (and older women too), "I would love to take you to bed with me," or if he thought he could get away with it, "Wouldn't it be fun to fuck?"—sometimes with his wife close by. I thought it was all bravado, but I was careful not to put it to the test.

As we worked together in the late fall of 1960 and again in the spring of 1961, I saw a great deal of Brendan. I had left the Algonquin and moved to the Upper West Side. Brendan, who was an early riser, would often come and ring my doorbell about six o'clock in the morning and we would go out for breakfast. He had started working on *Richard's Cork Leg* at the time, and I typed it up as he went along. We also worked together on the book for Walter Minton, for which I traveled to Washington, D.C., to do some research and to select a number of photographs that I eventually borrowed from the Bettmann Archives. At this time, Brendan and Beatrice had been married for seven years. They dearly hoped to have children but so far had been unsuccessful.

In the months after our night together, distracted by Ernest's death and my travels, I ignored the signs, would not acknowledge to myself that I was pregnant. I told no one. As long as I stayed in Ketchum, I gave no thought to my predicament. When I returned to New York I saw a doctor, and my fears were confirmed. I gave serious thought to my future. I could not imagine Brendan and myself bringing up a child together, so I decided it was best to leave him out of it. Well-meaning mutual friends in New York were dismayed that I would contemplate such a course. How could I deprive the child of a father, or a father of his child? the arguments ran. This could be a turning point for Brendan: having parental responsibility might save his life, they speculated. It was common knowledge that Brendan had started drinking again. My friends threatened to tell Brendan if I didn't. So one day in late January I took up the phone and dialed Dublin. The moment I broke the news to Brendan he was elated. "I'm coming over," he said without hesitation. "I'll be there as soon as I can." Over the next few days, he telephoned me a dozen times. He said he had talked to Beatrice, and if I would agree, they wanted to bring up the child together in Ireland. Surely I could see this was the best thing? After grave thought and consideration, I gave him the answer he wanted. It seemed that might be the only way this strange quadrangle could work out in everyone's best interests.

Brendan arrived in New York in time for the birth of his son, whom we named after him. His euphoria continued and he tried to stay on the wagon, but he was bursting to share the news, and the pub was his proverbial grandstand. There he was plied with liquor by well-meaning friends and strangers. He fought his hangovers and renewed his promise to stay away from the booze. Soon after I came home from the hospital with baby Brendan, we had a grand baptism party with Lar and Helen Dunne standing as godparents. Now Brendan broke it to me gently: Beatrice had changed her mind. In fact, once she had had a chance to think about what had happened, she was very angry. However, Brendan said consolingly, he had talked to his mother. She was thrilled at having another grandson and would willingly bring him up as her own. Kathleen Behan was an old lady at the time, albeit a feisty and a magnificent one, but she neither had the youth nor enjoyed the circumstance that I envisioned for my son. I told Brendan equally gently that I had decided it was in our child's best interest to stay with me.

Over the next two years, Brendan was torn between his family in Dublin and his family in New York. There seemed no solution to the problem, nothing for him to do but to drink and forget. When he was in Ireland Brendan wrote heartbreaking letters about the pain of separation and missing his little son. He frequently flew back to New York, but that did not satisfy either, causing him to drink more heavily and exacerbate the problem. And in May 1963 Beatrice told him she was pregnant. I rejoiced for them. Blanaid Behan was born on November 24. She was named for her great-grandmother, the poet and playwright Blanaid Salkeld, who had translated Pushkin's poems into English. Brendan telephoned me on the day of his daughter's baptism. When I asked what they had named her, all he replied was, "I would like to call her Valerie." I had hoped that having a child would heal the marriage for both of them, that Brendan would truly take on the responsibility of being a father and that maybe sometime in the future the children would know each other. Listening to his voice across the Atlantic, I realized it was too late. I could tell from the belligerent tone that he was drinking. Four months later, on March 20, 1964, Brendan died from complications of diabetes and alcohol.

I threw myself into the work of sorting out Ernest's papers. I started to put together the pieces of the stories Ernest had told me about his family and incidents documented in the letters, notes, manuscripts, and papers accumulated over his lifetime. It was now my duty to decipher fifty years of correspondence spanning three generations of Hemingways and penned by some of the most interesting figures of the twentieth century. It took me some time to determine who was who. The closer the tie, the less information presented itself—often no address, maybe no date, only a nickname to clue me in to the identity of the writer. As I waded through the material and became more familiar with the content and chronology, I pieced together the triumphs and failures, aspirations, anxieties, strengths, vulnerabilities, and idiosyncrasies of Hemingway and those closest to him. Then I had to determine which of this material should be handed over to his biographer.

My little room was stacked with cardboard boxes and three Vuitton trunks. Mold, must, and mildew pervaded the air. There was scarcely room among the trunks and boxes for my desk and a chair in the cramped space, slightly offset by high ceilings and bare walls. Besides the papers we had brought from Cuba, the trunks were salvaged from places as disparate as Paris, Key West, and Idaho—a Hemingway geography.

The chronicle of Ernest's life and the emergence of Hemingway the character—surpassing any fictional character he could invent—held me enthralled day after day. A sample page from my inventory list reads:

Five scrapbooks documenting EH's childhood, the first from "birth to twenty-three months old," the final one "fifteen years five months to eighteen years old."

Notes, letters, manuscripts, including manuscripts not identifiable as those of EH, clippings from WW I, Italy 1918–1919, including photographs, postcards and a medal.

Galley proofs, manuscripts, press copy of Ulysses *by J. Joyce. French, German and Spanish newspapers, bills, tickets, programs, licenses, lists saved by EH. Bank statements, check books, theater and sports programs saved by EH. Maps. Printers notices, advertisements and jackets of books by EH.*

Old leather belt.

Unidentifiable tooth.

Decrepit stuffed bird in many pieces.

Assorted leather wallets.

Visitors to Forty-eighth Street were rare. They had to make themselves comfortable sitting on the boxes or trunks. After Mary's initial inspection and approval of the quarters, she never came again, but Hotch frequently knocked on the door, and I was happy to see him. I did not note anything sinister in his visits, nor was I alerted by the frequent inquiries, often of a specific nature, to read letters, notes, or even manuscripts. I let him see whatever material he requested. I had no idea that he was planning his own book, the popular *Papa Hemingway,* published in 1966. Mary sued him unsuccessfully to prevent publication of the memoir. I would venture to say it was not the content as much as the disloyalty of one of Ernest's closest friends that prompted Mary's action.

As I went through each piece of paper, I came to know a great deal about Ernest, more than I have ever gleaned about another human being. As a boy, he had learned to express himself with the written word, and this became a lifelong, ingrained, unshakable habit. It made my job both tedious and immensely challenging and interesting. Nothing could be disregarded. I had to peruse every word. On a rare occasion, what appeared to be an unimportant scribbling later became a vital clue to some incident, the kernel of the idea for a piece, or perhaps the only means of dating a particular happening. The manuscripts—endless pages, often written in that rounded longhand I knew so well—ranged from riveting material to excruciatingly self-indulgent prose. Few papers were labeled or in any semblance of order. Added to this, my inexperience made my job one of trial and error.

The pieces of paper together held the jigsaw of Hemingway's life. As I linked each piece, I began to have a clear picture of the sequence of events and the development of Hemingway's character. I saw that his habit of chronicling—with written notes, newspaper clippings, and other data—all the points of interest in his life from his teen years on naturally had led him into the field of journalism. I had heard him say that in his youth journalism was a stopgap between starvation and creative writing. He returned to reporting many times in later years as a means of participating in wars and engaging in sports epics and adventurous travel, as well as developing a financial cushion. The experiences also provided him with backdrops for his novels.

Ernest told me that journalism was a great teacher for a novelist. While practicing it he learned to observe accurately, to state "the true gen" and express it with the shortest, most direct sentence. In his early days as a foreign correspondent, this last was an absolute necessity for sending dispatches by cable, where every word must count and ambivalence was detrimental to the sense and accuracy of the story. In reading through his papers, I saw that he followed these same principles all his life.

Ernest's lifelong interest in war became apparent to me as I pieced together his history. His paternal grandfather, who presented him with his first gun on his tenth birthday, had fought in a volunteer Illinois infantry regiment in the Civil War. He loved to tell his grandson about getting hit in the head by a cannonball. It had been an accidentally self-inflicted wound sustained while taking his souvenir cannon shard down from a high shelf. The young Ernest had delighted in hearing of his grandfather's wartime exploits. Every phase of his own life became punctuated by war, although he never served as a soldier. After he graduated from high school in June 1917, Ernest's greatest desire was to go to war. His father opposed this, so instead he did a brief stint as a police reporter for the *Kansas City Star*. Within a year he was accepted by the American Red Cross Field Service, and he set off for Europe before his nineteenth birthday.

Ernest arrived in Italy at the end of April 1918. There he spent several weeks of inactivity near but behind the front line. On July 9, while on an errand to the front, he was wounded and earned a medal for rescuing a fellow soldier, whom he carried to safety before collapsing himself. I found that medal among his papers. His World War I experience, mainly from the hospital bed where he spent three months, was to have a profound influence on him for the rest of his life. It provided the material for his brilliant 1929 novel, *A Farewell to Arms*.

It was at that same Italian hospital that Ernest experienced his first adult love affair. The object of his affection was a young nurse, Agnes von Kurowsky, who dismissed him as the "kid"—a teenager too immature to match her twenty-seven years. In January 1919 he returned to his hometown of Oak Park, a hero. Beneath the surface he was a changed young

man: more mature, worldly wise, toughened by the horrors of war, forever
marked mentally and physically. His leg had been badly wounded, and he
would live the rest of his days with a metal kneecap and fragments of shrap-
nel embedded from thigh to toe. It was impossible for Ernest to settle into
the drab, monotonous middle-class American life expected of him by his
parents. Then in March Agnes blithely wrote that she had met a young Italian officer whom she planned to marry and that she wished Ernest well.
This news concluded two complete folders of letters from Agnes to Ernest
dated 1918 to 1919.

He distilled into fiction the beauty of their affair and the pain and horror of failed love and betrayal. From that point onward Ernest knew that
there was only one thing in his life he could rely on: his writing. Friends and
wives would come and go, but writing was a constant. It was the single most
important, most reliable, most compelling element in his life. It was what
propelled him to great heights, and when it failed him at the end, he
plunged into the depths of despair and nothingness, that "*nada y pues nada
y pues nada*" he wrote of so astutely in "A Clean Well-Lighted Place."

Ernest loved to have the last word. He was able to write one final time to
Agnes in 1922, after his marriage to Hadley Richardson. Now it was his
turn to tell her how happy he was and to wish her well. From that point onward Agnes became fiction—literally.

The story of Agnes was only one of the many tales I pieced together. It
was new to me, for I had never heard her name mentioned. What was no
surprise were the generous sprinkling of hooks and weights, spent cartridges and shells I found among the trunks' contents. I knew that hunting
was an important pastime during Ernest's childhood, and this sport recurs
with predictable frequency in all his works. I knew too that he had a mystical side to his character. He believed in external powers: the power of
prayer, the power of magic. He was superstitious in a lighthearted way. His
pockets always held a keepsake, something to bring him the luck he
needed. Among the papers nestled smoothed touchstones, yellowed elks'
teeth and worn rabbits' feet. Luck was vital to his life—the luck to write

well, the luck of the weather, the luck of fishing or of drawing good bulls for the corrida.

I was also aware of Ernest's ability to entertain those around him. He created many games and fantasies for the amusement of his sons and friends. He loved to invent names. He rechristened at least once almost everyone he knew, and trying to match up the names with the people presented a challenge for me. He used not only himself in his writings but often his friends as well.

At the time of my research, quite accidentally I met Harold Loeb. It was no secret that Loeb was a model for Robert Cohn in *The Sun Also Rises*. Thirty-five years after the novel was published, Loeb was still hurt and puzzled at how he could have inspired such mean-spiritedness in his friend Ernest. As the French say, *"Cherchez la femme!"* Loeb rivaled Hemingway for the affections of Lady Duff Twysden, and for that he was rewarded with a cruel fictional immortality. When we lunched together every conversation I had with Loeb inevitably returned to one piteous question: "Why did Ernest do this to me?"

In that little office I had plenty of time to mull over that fine line separating fact from fiction, especially when reading the manuscripts I found among Hemingway's papers—most of which have now been published posthumously in creatively edited forms. *A Moveable Feast* and *The Dangerous Summer* were intended for publication by the author, but *Islands in the Stream, The Garden of Eden,* and *True at First Light* were not even close to meeting Ernest's exacting publishing standards. They were, to a certain extent, reconstructed by editors specially chosen to shape the working drafts into coherent, saleable novels of reasonable length.

I read the rambling, sometimes incoherent pages detailing the adventures of Thomas Hudson and his three sons on the island of Bimini. There was no doubt in my mind that this was autobiographical. Ernest often said he would have been an artist if he'd had the talent for it. Maybe it was as a consolation that in real life he befriended artists and amassed a fine collection of paintings. Hudson's sons resembled the three Hemingway boys both physically and in temperament. Gigi was so fond of the description of himself as Andrew in *Islands in the Stream* that he used it as the epigraph to his own book, *Papa: A Personal Memoir.*

When the African diary, as I called it, came out to mark the centennial of Ernest's birth in July 1999, it was billed as "a fictional memoir," a hybrid that has gained recent popularity. I still wonder what Ernest would have thought of that. His *Green Hills of Africa* was of a similar ilk. It confirms that Hemingway was ahead of his time, always keen to innovate, to try what had never been attempted before.

Whenever his sons Jack (Bumby) or Gigi—who now preferred to be called Greg—came to New York they looked me up and we had lunch or a drink together. Both were keenly interested in probing me to find out if I knew Mary's intentions regarding the disposition of their father's estate and what portion they were likely to share. On March 16, 1962, Mary set up the foreign rights trust to encompass all foreign royalties, with Mary and Ernest's three sons as beneficiaries and Alfred Rice as trustee. It took a while before the first payment was disbursed, and both men were anxious to receive some money. They had hoped that there might be a more equitable settlement, but Mary was influenced by Rice, who saw to it that she retained complete control of the properties. I was cautious in my response but as encouraging as I could be. Mary had given Jack the gun Ernest had shot himself with, but as far as I know no other memento of their father was passed on to his sons.

A number of letters found by me in that cluttered office were of a very personal nature, and once I had ascertained sender and date, I often skipped over the content, feeling that I had no business intruding. The most grievous of these were from Greg to his father. In some cases, Ernest's unsent replies were attached. I knew that they had quarreled, but the root of their estrangement remained unclear to me. The letters were wildly accusatory on both sides. I felt strongly that this was not material Carlos Baker nor anyone else should see—then, fifty years from then, or ever. After careful consideration, I sent the entire correspondence to Greg by registered mail, noting that it was up to him to decide its fate. I don't remember if he acknowledged the packet, but many years later he told me I had done him a great disservice. He was at medical school in Miami, and the shock of suddenly being confronted with a past that was pure nightmare sent him spiraling into a deep depression and almost derailed his medical ambitions. The past comes back to haunt one at the most inconvenient moments. It was the most difficult decision I made that year, but I would do it again, in spite of Greg's reaction. It was his right to dispose of those letters as he wished.

I had been working for some months when Mary told me she had received a disturbing letter from Hadley, Ernest's first wife and Jack's mother. Hadley asked that Miró's *The Farm* be returned to her. She intended that Bumby would inherit it. The painting, she said, along with the royalties of *The Sun Also Rises* for her lifetime, was the essence of her divorce settlement in 1926. Ernest had written her in 1934 asking to borrow the painting. She sent it to him and he never returned it. This news had taken Mary completely by surprise. The painting was the single most valuable item she had inherited, and she was not inclined to let it go without evidence. She asked me if I had ever heard Ernest say that the painting belonged to Hadley or that he had borrowed it from her. I had not. He always referred affectionately to it as his painting. Mary was skeptical of Hadley's story. She told me to look very carefully through Hadley's letters to Ernest in 1934 to see if there was any mention of the loan. Once I had filed the letters in chronological order I easily found the letter in which Hadley replied to Ernest's request to lend him the Miró for a few months. I handed it over to Mary. Shortly afterward she told me she had settled with Hadley for twenty-five thousand dollars—one-tenth of the insured value of the painting at that time. The Miró was then hanging at the National Gallery in Washington, D.C. Mary was considering leaving Ernest's entire art collection to the gallery, taking advantage of a hefty tax deduction during her lifetime. She felt strongly that the paintings should be kept together in one spot and available for public viewing.

I never met Hadley, but I had occasion to correspond and talk with her in 1965, when Jack asked me if I would write an article for *Ski* magazine. Mary had passed the assignment on to Jack, who then passed it on to me; I called it "The Short Happy Ski Life of Ernest Hemingway." I found Hadley to be quite formal but friendly and informative. She was generous with her time, and in talking to her I began to form a distinct image of the "Hash" and "Wicky" in Ernest's stories and in *A Moveable Feast.* She was perhaps the only woman besides his sister, Ura, for whom he retained affection all his life. His deep sense of guilt for having deserted her and his young son never left him.

Carlos Baker came up from Princeton, where he was Woodrow Wilson professor of literature, to see Mary, and I met him on a number of occasions. He had the air of a scholar, serious, respectful of Mary, meticulous and matter-of-fact about Ernest, genial but not jovial. Mary rightly felt he would do the job conscientiously, neither causing ripples nor unearthing scandals. She expected him to produce a thoughtful, thorough, unimaginative biography. He struck me as a quiet, bookish, professorial type, moderate and even-tempered, a listener rather than a talker—the antithesis of his subject, I would say. He'd asked me to write him about two thousand words detailing my time in the Hemingway household. I could not do so with honesty, so I ignored this request, although I made every effort to aid him with other information and facilitate his research for the official biography. Two people I enjoyed seeing at that time were Harvey Breit of the *New York Times,* who had shared an intense correspondence with Ernest, and Philip Young, a Hemingway scholar and professor at Penn State University, whose work Ernest had deemed of dubious value.

Mary often invited me over for dinner. She was surrounded by a group of young people, mostly men, closer to my age than hers. There was young Winston S. Churchill, son of her friend Pammy Churchill, later Harriman. Peter Beard had graduated from Yale, written his *The End of the Game* and interviewed Isak Dinesen, and was then headed for Africa. Mary and Clara Spiegel had recently been on safari to Kenya and Tanzania, where Patrick was their professional hunter. Mary sent me many cards of their progress and presented me with a beautiful red silk sari upon her return. Almost the first person Mary met at the New Stanley Hotel in Nairobi was Peter Beard. Maria Cooper had seen a photograph of him in *Vogue* and had jokingly asked Mary to find him for her. Maria was young, beautiful, and single, and Peter was touted as one of the world's most eligible bachelors. I don't know whether Maria Cooper did meet Peter, but Mary and he became lifelong friends. When I first knew him, he was photographing for *Vogue* magazine and escorting a young Irish model. Others of the inner circle were Mary's godson, Peter Vanderwicken, who was a journalist, and Peter Buckley, a childhood friend of Bumby's in Paris, a fine photographer, aficionado of the corrida, and writer of children's books. Mary thought of us all as her family, and she clucked around like a mother hen. It was as close as she ever got to exercising her maternal instincts.

In January 1963 I found accommodation on the top floor of a brownstone on the West Side, and as soon as the garden apartment became available, I moved into it, staying four years. I had an excellent arrangement to board my son with a young couple who lived in New Jersey and were the parents of a toddler. Joe was a fireman, tall and thin with a craggy Irish face and curly hair. His beautiful Lebanese wife, Rosemary, petite and dark, was warm and loving and the perfect surrogate mother. Brendan often stayed with them during the work week and for longer periods when I traveled or spent time in Idaho with Mary.

I decided to seek a job in publishing, where the hours would be more regular than at a newspaper or magazine, but when I heard from a contact at the Irish consulate that *The Catholic Digest* was looking for a writer, I applied and was granted an interview. I sat in the conference room opposite the editor, giving her all the reasons I could think of why she should hire me. She listened attentively and when I had finished she said, "I have to admit that I had already filled the position when you telephoned but I really wanted to meet you. To be honest, based on your interview and curriculum vitae, I would never have hired you. I know of a position that is open, in the publicity department at Hawthorn Books. Ken Giniger, the president, is a friend, and if I recommend you, I think you have an excellent chance of landing the job. However, if you are interested, we need to completely rewrite your resumé, and I will give you a few pointers as to how to conduct a successful employment interview in the United States."

I thanked her, but was unsure whether I wanted to work in publicity instead of writing and editing. "Publishing as an industry pays very poorly, but within publishing, advertising and publicity people earn by far the best salaries. If you have a child to support, I strongly advise you to search in that area. Now, let's take a look at your credentials. First of all, you'll never get a decent job if you don't have a university degree."

"I don't," I said, but added, "An Irish high school diploma is equivalent to two years of college in the United States, if that's worth anything, and I have had five years' working experience." I was twenty-two. By the time I left this kind woman, I had acquired a college degree. My typing went from fair to fast, my smattering of French and Spanish became fluent, and my hodgepodge of experience was coherently classified and looked impressive. I was on my way to meet Ken Giniger and to start a new career.

It was pure luck that I turned up at Hawthorn Books when I did. Giniger, who played down his Jewish origins, was a true Anglophile who had a keen interest in Catholicism, which was at the height of its strength and influence in the United States. Hawthorn's list had a heavily Catholic aspect to it, and Bishop Fulton J. Sheen was its star author. Celebrating the publication of the bishop's most recent volume, Hawthorn had served an elegant Champagne brunch on a Friday, a day in the pre–Vatican II era when Catholics were forbidden to eat meat. All the prelates attending the event had to abstain from the main course, ham omelettes, leaving Giniger frustrated and his staff with red faces. When I came along, it was my Irish Catholic background, not my outstanding credentials, that won me the job. With me onboard Giniger knew that the faux pas would not be repeated.

The staff at Hawthorn was a singular bunch. The two or so years I worked there were an education and a pleasure. Giniger was a born teacher who often quizzed us at the weekly staff meetings: What were the first two full-page ads in the previous Sunday's *New York Times Book Review*? How did ad space and book reviews correspond in different publications? Hawthorn at the time was a subsidiary of Prentice Hall and governed by all the PH rules and regulations, which were myriad. It was run by the clock—the time clock, that is, a nasty beast that invariably ticked over to the next minute as soon as I entered, printing my card in red instead of black. My first six months there showed that I often arrived between 9:01 and 9:03. As a result, I was denied the customary midyear raise due to unpunctuality, Giniger told me regretfully. Within the company, starting at the top, we were a group of talented and some of us eccentric individuals, with a fierce loyalty to our leader and the literary cause.

About four months after I joined Hawthorn, Thurston McCawley, the publicity director, took off on vacation. He was excited to be going back to Spain for the first time since 1939. He talked with me about his trip, and I gave him my impressions of Madrid, Málaga, and other places. McCawley never returned. In fact, he was never heard from again. We waited a couple of months. There was no word or trace of Thurston. Giniger decided McCawley should be replaced. He promoted me, even though I was the newcomer and youngest in the department. I had just turned twenty-three.

With the title came an expense account and a good deal of leeway for creativity. I inherited a desk with the files of McCawley's predecessor, Maia Rodman. Maia had left Hawthorn to devote her time to writing children's books, at which she was successful. She published under her maiden name, Wojciechowska, probably because she did not want to be in the shadow of her ex-husband, art critic Selden Rodman. She won at least one Newbery Medal. Maia left extensive files detailing her duties as publicity director and projects she had worked on during her tenure. Her English—flawless, as a foreigner's can sometimes be—was quite colorful in her notes, which had been written for her eyes only. It was fascinating reading, highly amusing, and I also learned a great deal about both the job and my predecessor, whose Eastern European candor showed that she did not suffer from shyness or understatement—by-products of my Anglo-Irish upbringing. Maia maintained a friendship with the Ginigers. She surprised us now and then by popping unexpectedly into the office, which was on Fifth Avenue at Eleventh Street, always giving me excellent pointers on how to deal with difficult authors or tips for getting reviewers' attention.

If I had been asked what qualities were needed for a publicity director at that time, I would have to say that a great stamina for eating and drinking was essential and a facility for literary prattle was useful, along with a subtle rendering of the art of persuasion. Certainly my time with the Hemingways had prepared me for the task. I became a member of the Advertising Club on lower Park Avenue, the Press Club, and the Salmagundi Club, which was almost across the street from the office. I was having lunch at the Salmagundi Club one day in November when my companion, a young Englishman, the book review editor for *The Christian Science Monitor,* was called to the phone. He had to rush back to the office, he informed me. President Kennedy had been shot. I returned to Hawthorn with the news, tidied my desk, then left to spend the afternoon and evening at the *New Yorker.* A number of us squeezed into Brendan Gill's office, where, along with Susan Black and several writers, we waited for more news. We were in a state of shock.

James Thurber was a *New Yorker* contributor I had met as soon as I arrived in the United States. He had a show on Broadway, *A Thurber Carnival,* I think it was, at the same time as *The Hostage.* Jim was pretty frail then, confined to a wheelchair and with failing eyesight. Still, nothing seemed to affect his drinking. The Behans and I might have a drink or two with him before the show, and thus fortified he would wheel his way to the theater and cause some mayhem (or at least apprehension) before the curtain went up. I got the feeling that Thurber and Behan were regarded with similar distrust by the theater managements. The cry of "Author!" was one they dreaded, not welcomed. I was also surprised to find that Thurber was not a popular figure around the magazine offices. There was still resentment stemming from his memoir, *The Years with Ross.* As an outsider, I had thoroughly enjoyed the book, but it had rankled his coworkers. Brendan Gill was particularly indignant. His own turn came later after the publication of *Here at the New Yorker.* Brendan then found out that he was resented every bit as much as Thurber had been.

In the spring of 1963 the actress Beverly Bentley, whom I had met in Spain years ago, telephoned me in the middle of the night to tell me I must come over right away. She had just met the greatest person in the world, Norman Mailer. Beverly had a wide circle of friends and lovers and she was definitely a night owl, so this struck me neither as a momentous announcement nor as a reason to bestir myself. Soon afterward Beverly moved into Norman's Brooklyn Heights apartment, and from there she went to spend the summer with him and his various children in Provincetown. I saw a lot of Norman and Beverly on weekends in the fall and was watching television with them in their living room when the startling vision of Jack Ruby shooting Lee Harvey Oswald darted across the screen. Norman knew at once what had happened, while I was still trying to figure out what was going on. Norman had a fascination with the Kennedys and was particularly intrigued by the assassination and its sinister implications. For years he thought and puzzled over it, and later wrote about it. Norman was also taken with my little son. He had met and befriended his father, who had once helped him out of a jam. Beverly was now pregnant and they planned a December wedding. Norman had four girls, and he and Beverly were hoping for a boy, especially, they both said, a boy like my young Brendan. On St. Patrick's Day in 1964 their wish came true when Michael Burks Mailer was born.

Since I was working full time, Beverly suggested they take my son with them to Provincetown for the summer. He spent three months on the water with the Mailer family, and I flew up from New York every weekend. Beverly and Norman were deeply in love. Norman was enchanted with little Brendan. He taught him swimming, boxing, and the rudiments of tightrope walking. He had set up a tightrope on the deck about a foot or so high and he was trying to master it himself. His daughters Betsy and Dandy spent the summer there too, and with baby Michael in his bassinet, they were one big happy family. Provincetown was a haven for artists, and Norman and Beverly knew them all. On one night we attended a dinner party at Bob Motherwell's and on another occasion we visited Hans Hofmann's studio.

When Prentice Hall wanted to divest itself of Hawthorn Books, it was announced that Fred Kerner would buy the company. Many of us decided to leave in support of Ken Giniger, who we felt was given a raw deal. He had made Hawthorn what it was. When Norman learned that I was on the lookout for a job, he telephoned from Miami, where he was covering the Patterson fight. He told me that his publisher, Putnam, was looking for a publicity director. He had talked to Walter Minton, and I should arrange for an interview right away.

I had several offers based on my performance at Hawthorn, and I decided to take the position of publicity and promotion director at Walker and Company. They were on Fifth Avenue at Fifty-sixth Street. Walker was a small, privately owned firm, founded by Sam Walker and co-run with his wife, Beth, who was the children's book editor. Mysteries and current affairs were their bread and butter, but they also had a respectable stable of writers and a strong children's book section. John Kirk, whose father was president of Columbia University at the time, was the editor in chief. Many of the current-affairs writers were Columbia professors. When I arrived, they had just lost John le Carré, whose first two books had received a mediocre reception. Then came *The Spy Who Came In from the Cold,* which was a tremendous success—with another publisher. Walker was irritated that they had not perceived le Carré's value as a writer and held on to him. They determined to make up for the loss by putting all their weight behind a new thriller, Desmond Cory's fifth novel, *Deadfall.* Its silver jacket, accented by black text with a falling cat and Anthony Boucher's declaration that Cory is "suggestive of Ian Fleming with far better writing and plotting," launched *Deadfall,* and my career at Walker began with a major publicity campaign. The book, though good in its own way, did not meet expectations. "Dreadful," we privately tagged it after a while, and soon enough it faded into obscurity. Contrarily, my job flourished.

One day while lunching with Barbara Bannon, the fiction editor of *Publishers Weekly,* she told me that James Laughlin at New Directions was looking for a publicity director and she had recommended me. I was happy at Walker and Company and did not contemplate a change. Barbara thought I would be perfect for New Directions since it was such a literary house and, through my association with Hemingway, I already had connections with a number of their authors, such as Ezra Pound and Tennessee Williams. Working in publishing was like a game of musical chairs. It was quite usual to receive one or two job offers a year. This was the first time I was tempted to make a change.

I telephoned James Laughlin for an appointment. He and Brendan Gill were neighbors in Norfolk, Connecticut. Brendan put in a word on my behalf. We had a drink together at the Algonquin, during which with mock seriousness he schooled me in the art of the employment interview. First and foremost you must ask: What is the remuneration? he advised. Of course, I already knew what the remuneration would be. Laughlin was a notorious skinflint when it came to spending money, but generous in many other ways. I would be taking a reduction in pay in exchange for prestige. When I told Sam Walker I had been offered the position of publicity, promotion, and advertising director at New Directions, he heartily congratulated me and said he could not stand in the way of such an advancement in my career. I was slightly chagrined that he did not beg me to stay and offer me an increase in salary to emphasize his sincerity. Instead, Walker gave me a splendid sendoff and seemed genuinely pleased at my success.

Toward the end of 1965 I felt I had done as much as I could to put the Hemingway papers in order. I still had my office in the Scribner building, and Mary was disinclined to let me exit her life altogether, so she contrived another task for me. It was now clear that the Hemingway papers would be soon deposited in the Kennedy Library in Boston. How would it be, she asked me, if I would write to all the people who had corresponded at any length with Ernest over the years and request Xerox copies of their letters so that the two-way correspondence would be complete when the papers were presented to the library? I already had classified all the letters Ernest had received and had a complete list on hand of the people we wanted to reach. Some were dead, but a great number were not. I thought it was a brilliant idea and immediately wrote a sample form letter, which Mary approved. Then I ferreted out the present addresses of all the people on my list. I already knew a number of them personally. On December 10, 1965, the letter was mailed out to ninety-eight people, including eleven family members. I made a note to myself that this list had been culled from more than a thousand names. Twenty-nine people replied immediately. Among these were Mrs. Sherwood Anderson, John Gunther, Sara Murphy, George Plimpton, Thornton Wilder, Edmund Wilson, and Martha Gellhorn. It was a jolly assignment, and I amassed a large correspondence, some of it lively. Donald Gallup, of the Beinecke Rare Book and Manuscript Library at Yale University, had been referred to me by both Wilder and Wilson. Gallup now suggested we might do a little bartering: photocopies of Hemingway letters in exchange for copies of Gertrude Stein's correspondence with Ernest. He also suggested a similar arrangement with Edmund Wilson's letters. Martha Gellhorn said Ernest had requested her to return his letters when they separated, which she did, but she wondered where her letters to Ernest were, since he had also promised to return them. I could have told her that many of the letters remained in Cuba, but her last sentence was "You can take it that all the letters are destroyed," so I left it at that. Greg wrote to say that his letters from his father had been sold to his uncle Leicester. Patrick had given his to the Princeton Library, as had General Buck Lanham. The replies trickled in, some adding little asides, as from Grant Mason, whose ex-wife, Jane, had had an affair with Hemingway during the thirties. Mason wrote that he would be delighted to give or lend any correspondence between Ernest and himself, including various brief and allegedly amusing notes they wrote each other from time to time in longhand, if he could locate them. He wryly added that during the twenty years of his present marriage, neither his wife, Martha, nor he had come upon any memorabilia of Ernest. This confirmed his best memory that after he and Jane divorced, Jane (now married to her fourth husband, Arnold Gingrich) made off with anything and everything that had to do with Ernest, including some informal and very amateur photographs.

In contrast to the plush modern offices of Walker and Company on Manhattan's most elegant street, New Directions was housed downtown in a triangular wedge of a nineteenth-century building at 333 Sixth Avenue. An extraordinary architectural feat for the time, despite wear and tear, it was still very servicable. These offices were dusty, cluttered, and brimming with books, magazines, and other printed matter.

James Laughlin, an heir to the Pittsburgh steel fortune, had always wanted to be a poet. As an undergraduate at Harvard he had sent some of his poems to Ezra Pound. Pound replied that Laughlin should become a publisher of poets—advice the young student took to heart. Pound became one of his most prominent authors. Later in life, Laughlin returned to his first love and had a number of his poems published. New Directions had an excellent stable of writers, both American and foreign. Beat poetry had recently emerged, and the New Directions offices were not far from Greenwich Village. Every now and then there was a visit from a down-at-heel author hoping for a small advance. Laughlin dealt with those matters himself. Allen Ginsberg came by, and Gregory Corso popped in when he returned from Paris. I got a glimpse of Denise Levertov, who lived in the Village when not at her farm in Maine. Lawrence Ferlinghetti and Kenneth Patchen telephoned from the West Coast, and Thomas Merton communicated from Gethsemani Abbey in Kentucky. We published Lincoln Kirstein's *Rhymes of a PFC* that year, George Oppen's *This in Which,* Ezra Pound's *The Cantos* and a special edition of *A Lume Spento,* Yukio Mishima's *Death in Midsummer,* and *New Directions 19,* an anthology of current literature culled from our authors. Herman Hesse's *Siddhartha* was our bestseller, mainly because almost every college student was required to buy a copy.

CHAPTER NINETEEN

For Better, for Worse, in Sickness and in Health

*B*Y THE SPRING OF 1966 I was seriously thinking of returning to
Europe. I had never intended to settle in America. The end of my Hemingway work was in sight, and although my job at New Directions was a step
up in prestige from Hawthorn and Walker, the work was much less challenging. New Directions had an amazing roster of authors and one of the
best backlists in the business, but James Laughlin, the founder, kept tight
control on all areas of the company. He tended to write the advertising copy
and deal with the more interesting aspects of publicity himself. I enjoyed
reading the superb backlist and met some very interesting authors, but I felt
it was time to move on.

Over the years since I had met him, Greg Hemingway kept in touch
with me by phone and letter, and we saw each other whenever he was in
Manhattan. He was the first person to telephone me when news of Brendan
Behan's death came over the wires. He offered to come and take care of my
two-year-old if I wanted to fly back to Dublin to attend the funeral. And he
invited me to his graduation from medical school on June 7, 1964, at the
University of Miami.

That spring Greg started a six-month fellowship in orthopedics at
Boston City Hospital. He began coming down to New York on his days off.

He often looked me up and sometimes stayed overnight. We had been close friends since his father's funeral, always having good fun with lots of laughter. I found him a diversion and thought of him as family, like a cousin. After he casually said that he and his second wife, Alice, were in the process of divorcing, he asked me if I would go out with him. I was unsure. My sights were upon Europe. Intending to leave during the summer, I had not renewed my lease for the garden apartment on West Seventy-first Street. I was torn by what I wanted to do and where. With Greg a continuing presence in my life, I agreed to stay the summer, temporarily subletting an apartment in Hell's Kitchen from an actor friend, Kelly Fitzpatrick. Maybe my ambiguity and impending departure were what brought an urgency to Greg's courtship. He was wonderfully funny and had a flair for romance. It still amuses me when I recall his arrival early Easter Sunday morning, hidden behind an enormous lily he had carried all the way from Boston on the airplane and in taxis.

He was well liked by my friends, particularly Norman Mailer. We spent a fair part of that summer in Provincetown, where he and Norman and Dr. Ted Hager landed a 735-pound tuna, close to a record at the time. We flew to Bimini for weekends, where we stayed at the Compleat Angler and hobnobbed with Leicester Hemingway, who at that time wrote and edited the local newspaper, the *Bimini Bugle*. Greg became intent upon us getting married. He was fond of young Brendan, and I rightly intuited that life with Greg would never be dull. However, he had already been married twice and was the father of four children, just as Norman had been when he and Beverly married. I saw how well Beverly managed with Norman's four girls and their own boy, not hesitating to include my toddler in the fold for the summer months as well, so I did not find the prospect of inheriting a ready-made family daunting. I also noted the amicable terms Norman maintained with his ex-wives, not realizing that this was a unique situation. Still, I held off on the decision. In late summer I flew to England to attend my brother Peter's wedding. When I landed at JFK on the return trip Greg met me with a wedding ring and tickets for another flight to Mexico City, where we were married the next day without fanfare. That evening we flew to Acapulco for our honeymoon. As we dined on our wedding night in the hotel restaurant overlooking the beach, Greg briefly left the table. He had a large grin on his face when he returned. "I just telephoned Mary collect to give her the good news," he said, to my horror. It had not occurred to me what Mary would think of our union, but I knew that at best she would take it badly. She had always had a tenuous relationship with Greg. At least now I need not worry about breaking the news to her. Our married life was off to a rollicking start.

"What could it mean?" I asked Helen Dunne a short while after Greg and I were settled in New York. There were lipstick and cosmetics in Greg's car, which I was sure had not been there earlier. When he caught me looking, he casually remarked it was stuff his ex-wife had left behind, and with a shrug he deposited the bundle in a garbage bin. But later when I searched for a missing glove, I found more cosmetics and nylons tucked underneath the seat.

"Do you love him?" Helen asked. "Do you want your marriage to work?"

"Of course I do," I answered truthfully.

"Some men are wanderers," she told me. "Marriage is based on much more than casual sex. Perhaps you are not fulfilling his needs. Think about it. My advice is, if you want your marriage to last, keep your eyes open and your mouth closed."

Greg had plans; foremost was to work as a doctor in an underdeveloped area, specifically East Africa. He had spent a year and a half in Tanzania as a professional hunter before he applied to medical school. He was keen to return. After graduating from Harvard his brother Patrick had moved to Tanzania, where he now ran his own safari company. The prospect of life in Africa suited me admirably. That dark continent had and still has a strong pull for me. For many years my first cousin Raymond, who was an Anglican missionary, and his wife, Audrey, had lived in Kenya, where three of their five children were born.

I was keen to fall in with Greg's plans and aided and abetted him in whatever way I could. First, he felt that he needed more training. He applied to Jackson Memorial Hospital in Miami for a residency in anaesthesiology.

There was a wait of several months before the program was scheduled to start. He began a protracted custody battle with his second wife, Alice, who, he said, was mentally unstable. She lived in Miami, and he decided it would be better if we moved closer to his children, the reason he desired a residency in Florida. In the meantime, we had found a cheery apartment on East Sixty-eighth Street, not far from the armory. I continued to work at New Directions. Greg was a keen tennis player, and to keep him amused while I worked, I introduced him to my predecessor at Hawthorn Books, Maia Rodman, who excelled at tennis. By coincidence Maia, a few years older than Greg, had been his tennis coach in Key West the summer he was seventeen. Maia had also met Ernest on a number of occasions.

Introducing Maia to Greg took care of the immediate problem of keeping him occupied in an unfamiliar city while I worked, but it created another one. Maia fell madly in love with Greg and made no secret of it. Maia was to be a fairly constant presence during the first ten years of our marriage. On the feast of St. Gregory that first year she presented him with an expensive, specially strung tennis racquet. In 1972 she dedicated her book, *The Life and Death of a Brave Bull,* illustrated by John Groth, to Gregory.

In midsummer 1967 we left for Miami with Brendan and our infant son, Seán. Barbara Bannon asked me if I would read fiction for *Publishers Weekly,* and as soon as I was settled in Florida she sent me three galleys every week or ten days. I read them and then duly dispatched my précis and evaluation. We had rented a three-bedroom ranch-style house in a subdivision in south Miami, where a close friend of Greg's lived with his wife and two little girls, an infant and a toddler. Being a suburban housewife was an entirely new and disagreeable experience. Greg had an arduous schedule at the hospital, where he spent long hours, returning home exhausted. We were fortunate in having an excellent Guatemalan woman, Lydia, to help care for the boys.

Not long after we arrived in Miami, quite inadvertently I found out that Greg's divorce from Alice had not been finalized at the time of our marriage in Mexico City the previous year. I was stunned. When I put it to him, Greg was unconcerned. He was sure that it had, but maybe he had been misinformed, he said. To put my mind at ease, why not remarry in Florida? We celebrated our second wedding with a family party of Champagne and good cheer at Leicester and Doris Hemingway's Spanish colonial house on the edge of the bay overlooking Miami Beach.

One day I pulled out a pair of pantyhose from underneath the bathroom sink. "Strange," I said out loud, holding them up. "What can these be doing here?"

Greg was close by and looked up. "Lydia must have left them," he said casually. But it was clear to me that they were far too large for our nanny's small, wiry frame. I was puzzled.

One night I awoke abruptly. Greg was deeply asleep. As I gently touched him I felt a smooth silk rustle against my hand. I drew away at the unexpected sensation. I reached out again to reassure myself. Then I sat up and in the half dark peered at the sleeping figure beside me. My favorite nightgown was draped over his body. I turned away from him and forced myself to sleep, hoping that the dawn would bring an explanation of this bizarre image. I must have slept soundly, for when I woke, Greg was awake and in unusually good form. I wondered if my nocturnal discovery had been nothing but a nightmare.

Life in Miami was not dull. We were keen on sailing, and when Greg was free we rented a sloop and set sail in Biscayne Bay. When he had more time off, we boarded a small seaplane to the island of Bimini, where we sailed, fished, and snorkeled. For relaxation in the evenings while sipping rum, we listened to the interminable tales of Hemingway's escapades there in the thirties. Everyone over a certain age seemed to have known Papa, to have lifted a pint with him or have challenged him to arm-wrestle in the bar on the wharf. Every Sunday, we dined at Leicester Hemingway's bayside house on the causeway to Miami Beach. His wife, Doris, was an expansive hostess, providing loads of food and drink for as many people as could fit around their large dining room table. There was never an empty place. Leicester would always entertain us with his latest scheme. One was inventing his own island on a raft anchored in international waters and calling it New Atlantis. He planned to issue stamps, mint coinage, and apply to the

World Bank for a grant. He went to great lengths to realize his plans. All his schemes were imaginative and provided lively conversation but by their very impracticality were doomed to failure. Ever buoyant, ever optimistic, Leicester followed his adventurous bent, anticipating the moment when he would strike it rich, while Doris's steady, responsible job in the publications department at the University of Miami kept the family afloat. Leicester must have been a magical father, and I suspect his two daughters would not have wished their dad to have been any other way.

Norman Mailer's friend Buzz Farbar visited us. We had recently been in New York for a visit and seen Norman, George Plimpton, Buzz, and a number of other friends. While we were in town Mary Hemingway took us out to dinner at La Caravelle. Greg's brother Jack was there, and Pat might have come too. As we were having dessert Mary made an announcement. Bearing in mind that when Ernest had left her everything in his will he had added he "knew she would take care of his sons," she wanted each of the boys to receive some portion of their father's property. To Jack, the eldest, she said she would bequeath the house in Ketchum. Jack had moved with his family from San Francisco to Idaho. I no longer remember what she had in mind for Pat, who lived in Tanzania. Greg would get land in Bimini because Mary knew we enjoyed spending time there. She planned that we should have it as soon as the title could be changed.

The next morning I said to Greg, "Let's write Mary thanking her for the gift."

"Absolutely not," he retorted indignantly. "That property was bought by my mother and father. It belongs far more to me than to Mary. I have no intention of thanking her for giving me what is already mine."

I let it pass. Each time we went to Bimini after that, we walked up the hill to the Hemingway lot, a fine spread on the pinnacle that afforded the very best 360-degree view of the island. We mused about what kind of house we would build there and of the fun we would have in years to come as we vacationed on the island with our children. A year later we were smacked with a cold blast of reality. Upon climbing the hill to the lot we were confronted by a high chain-link fence topped with barbed wire. A white wooden sign with black letters stated: *Keep Out. Property of the Museum of Natural History. Gift of the Ernest Hemingway Estate.* Greg fumed. I wanted to say, "We should have written that letter," but I kept silent.

On that same visit to New York, Buzz introduced us to his friend Jerry Lieber, author of a song Elvis Presley made famous, "Hound Dog." We visited Lieber at his Central Park West apartment, quite impressed by the chauffeur-driven Rolls Royce that afterward took him away to his next appointment. Jerry said something to Greg that set Greg thinking. He told us he would like to buy the rights to one of Hemingway's short stories because he had an innovative idea about how he would use it. Greg told him to get in touch with Mary, who was executrix of the estate. "I have nothing to do with my father's works. You'll have to talk to Mary," he said.

"But you do," Lieber insisted. "You are an heir to the estate."

"On the contrary," replied Greg. "My two brothers and I were left nothing."

"Check it out," Lieber told him. "You will find otherwise. By American copyright law, children of writers cannot be disinherited." Jerry cited the case of a songwriter who had disinherited his widow and children. The court awarded them a portion of his royalties, and the precedent was set. At the time, Greg dismissed this as just wishful thinking on Lieber's part because the songwriter was keen to get the rights. The case probably only referred to music royalties.

But once we returned to Miami, Greg could not get the idea out of his mind. What if Jerry was right? He telephoned Buzz and asked him to visit. Before he did so, he was to talk to Lieber and find out all the details regarding the copyright case. As soon as Buzz left, Greg went down to the law library at the University of Miami, his alma mater. Sure enough, he found the description of the case Lieber had cited, and its verdict. Greg became extremely excited. It still was unclear whether this law would apply to the three Hemingway sons. He got in touch with both his brothers, Jack in Idaho and Patrick in Tanzania. He said he intended to find the best copyright lawyers in America to advise him on the implications of the case. Would they each pay a third of the costs? He would do all the contact work.

They agreed, probably imagining this to be another of the harebrained schemes for which Greg was notorious. Greg hired the respected Boston firm of Ropes and Gray. It took them months to ascertain that Jerry Lieber's statement was correct: the three Hemingway sons could not be disinherited. They were entitled to a portion of the renewal rights of the royalties. Greg was elated. He calculated his next move. He would approach Alfred Rice. Obviously Rice must not have been aware of the law or they would have been receiving the money. Greg would state the facts and then ask Rice outright to honor the obligation. He would tell Alfred that with the expertise of Ropes and Gray behind them, the three brothers would sue the Ernest Hemingway estate if a settlement was not made promptly.

Greg called New York. "Do you know about the case, Al?"

"Yes, of course I do."

"Doesn't that mean that Jack, Pat, and I should be receiving royalties?"

"It could mean that."

"Then why aren't we?" Greg asked.

"It was never determined how the royalties should be split," Alfred replied, elaborating, "That is, what portion should go each to the widow and children."

"We can easily determine that among ourselves," Greg offered.

"Besides," Alfred continued, "you are already receiving part of the royalties through the Hemingway foreign rights trust. That's why Mary and I set it up. Because we could not determine how the renewal rights should be divided, we set up the trust instead."

"I don't recall that you ever mentioned that before," Greg said thoughtfully.

"Check it out," Alfred went on. "You boys accepted the foreign rights money in lieu of the renewal rights. It's as simple as that. Is there anything else I can help you with?" With that, Alfred hung up.

At first Greg felt he had wasted his time and money pursuing the issue. He took out his foreign rights trust file, but there was nothing there to indicate that the distribution of foreign royalties took the place of the renewal rights. After further consultation with Ropes and Gray, Rice was approached again, this time with an ultimatum: pay up or we sue. In short course, Alfred arranged that the renewal rights would be split four ways, 25 percent to Mary and each of the sons. There was a token amount given to cover the seven years of missed royalties, which helped take care of the legal fees. Greg had triumphed. His brothers were pleased with the outcome. Thereafter, the annual royalty income they each received was doubled.

While all this was going on, one day I discovered that my camera was missing. I searched everywhere but couldn't find it. My glance fell on the bathroom's wastepaper basket. There were a number of discarded Polaroid photos there. I took them out, thinking they might lead me to my absent gift. They were blurry, and each image looked the same. All I could make out was a pair of men's legs. Why would anyone want to photograph that?

In the summer of 1968, Lorian, Greg's sixteen-year-old daughter from his first marriage, came down to visit us. Greg had not seen her since she was four. He was excited and full of plans. It was a good reunion. It was also my first close-up contact with the American teenager. Lorian arrived beautifully coiffed and outfitted. When her parents had divorced, her mother remarried right away and in due course gave birth to two more girls. Lorian complained about the treatment she received, particularly from her stepfather. She was outraged that her parents expected her to babysit her sisters. She decided to live with us. At the time, we had one car, a Volkswagen Bug, already four years old. The children christened it Byebyes, and it was to give us good service for many years to come. It was the single possession Greg brought to the marriage. I was soon to learn that he had a loathing for belongings and divested himself of them at the earliest possible moment. Greg supplemented our transportation with a motorcycle, which he used to get to and from work, and for amusing the children when he was home. With the pittance Greg made as a medical resident, the ten dollars I received from *Publishers Weekly* per galley, and a modest income from the Hemingway foreign rights trust, a second car was out of the question. By contrast, Lorian told us her mother and stepfather had given her a small convertible for her birthday six months before.

I could not have afforded the quality of clothes my step sported nor the visits to the beauty parlor to which she seeme tomed. It was hard to imagine that she would find life with us part good. And in fact, after a couple of weeks Lorian returned home to North Carolina. She had a fairly rocky life at the outset, battling alcohol and other addictions. I am proud to report that she weaned herself from the substances and has been clean for sixteen years. She parlayed her experiences into a novel, a memoir, and other writing. We have become good friends over the years, and I look forward to her visits.

As his residency wore on, Greg became less enchanted with his work. The grueling hours—twenty-four on and twelve off—began to take their toll. He became irritable and had difficulty sleeping. I came to really know Greg for the first time during that Florida period. In New York I had been consumed by my work and bewitched by love; our time together had been for entertainment and diversion. Now, without a regular job and with full-time help, I observed Greg's moods closely. He filled me in more fully on his medical history, though there were major gaps. He spoke of months in a mental institution after a breakdown when he was in the army. During a six-month period he had received about thirty electric shock treatments. This breakdown had followed his first divorce. At the time he was living in Africa. Once the U.S. government became aware that he was single again, he was immediately drafted into the army and ordered to training camp. It was there that he met his lifelong friend and mentor, Dr. Edward (Ted) Hager. Here was the one person throughout the years Greg could count upon, and the person most responsible for his emergence from a mental institution to take up his medical studies, sticking with it until he received his medical degree. Our second son, Edward, was named for Ted Hager.

I knew that in spite of his rugged exterior, his pronounced masculinity, his confidence in his medical acumen, Greg had a fragile component. But nothing could have prepared me for the strange news I was about to receive. I came across more articles of clothing tucked in unexpected corners, and sometimes my own clothes vanished. I asked Greg if he could explain what was going on. I was perplexed when he burst into tears. He made me promise to continue to love him if he told me. He made me swear that I would never leave him. I could not imagine anything that would stop me loving him. I have never been a quitter and I had not expected marriage to Greg to be an easy road. I wiped his tears and reassured him. There was nothing to fear. Had I not promised twice to stay with him for better or for worse, in sickness and in health? I had no intention of going back on my word.

He brightened. You see, for as long as he could remember, he said, he had a habit that he just could not shake. No matter how hard he tried, he failed. It was the underlying cause of all the unhappiness in his life, of his break with his father, of his mental breakdowns. I was mystified. I could not imagine what he would say next. It was almost a relief to hear him continue: whenever he was under stress, he put on a pair of nylon stockings, and it acted like a tranquilizer to soothe his nerves or allay his fears. It gave him comfort and strength, and as far as he could see, there was no harm to it. Still, people who didn't understand would ridicule him. It must be our solemn secret. No one, absolutely no one, was to know. I nodded in agreement. It seemed absurd to me, trivial. I don't know what I had imagined he would say; what I heard puzzled me but did not cause undue alarm.

He continued. It had all started the day he was born, maybe even before. His father, with two sons, dearly wanted a daughter. His mother, having suffered two Cesareans, was warned by the doctor that after Greg she should have no more children. She feared this second boy child would destroy her marriage. As he grew Greg felt the tension between his parents. His mother blamed him for the rift that gradually pried them apart. A few days after his second birthday, Ernest and Pauline took off for Africa, a much-anticipated safari paid for in part by Pauline's rich uncle Gus. Pauline dearly hoped that the new adventures would bring the couple closer together. The trip inspired Ernest's *Green Hills of Africa*. They were away seven months.

While his parents were gallivanting in the bush, poor little Gigi was being terrorized by Ada, the nurse in whose charge he was left in Key West.

She ruled by fear, threatening to leave him, as his parents had done, whenever he was bad. She would put on her hat and coat and walk out slamming the door and not return until his screams and imploring reached an unbearable pitch. She tyrannized him, telling him she was the only one in the world who cared for him and that if he did not behave, she would leave him too. It was during this time, he told me, that he first went to his mother's chest of drawers and took out her stockings and rubbed them against his cheek. Ada did not wear hosiery in the Florida heat. He associated stockings only with his mother, who was gone. He had remembered clinging to her leg and liking the silky feeling and the closeness it brought him to his mother, who was not an affectionate person. Now that she was far away, he clung to the stockings, which gave him security and a secret joy. That is how it started. That was all there was to it. He emphasized, "I am not a transvestite. I do not want to dress up as a woman. It is the stockings, only the stockings. They are my security blanket and I cannot give them up. Do you still love me?"

Greg was such a masculine figure to me and to all of those who knew him that—improbable as his confession seemed—I believed him without understanding. Totally ignorant of the psyche and its intricacies, I relied upon my good old convent upbringing. The nuns had pounded into our heads, "You can make anything you want of yourselves; the world is yours for the taking. There is no handicap so great that it cannot be overcome. All you need is willpower." I determined that if Greg could not give up this crutch on his own, I would help him. We would do more things together, play more tennis, scuba-dive, do crossword puzzles, play poker, whatever was necessary. I would amuse him. Everything would be all right. There was no need to worry. He relaxed a little, and began to minimize the problem. Now that the crisis had passed, he almost enjoyed talking about it. He was doubtful that his condition could be cured. All his life he had tried and failed. It was just a small human weakness, a flaw in an otherwise noble character. I was perhaps the only person in the universe who would be able to understand. I loved him, and this was an essential part of him. He had tried to rid himself of the cancer, but in the end he knew no matter how hard he tried it would never be eradicated. Although I didn't voice it, I was equally of the opinion that the problem could be solved and that I would help him do it. Furthermore, I was relieved that he did not have other women, as I had suspected. The revelation temporarily brought us closer together.

It was hard to know what to make of my newfound knowledge. Our sex life was perfectly normal. He was a devoted father to the children. Unless there were telltale signs I did not search for, I put it out of my mind. Greg dressed conservatively, preferring suits, button-down shirts with ties, and leather dress shoes to casual clothes. He wore grays mostly, or khakis with a navy blazer. In Florida he favored blue pinstripe seersucker suits or white duck pants and a jacket with loafers. He never wore jewelry. He had no interest in the theater and opera, but he loved a good action movie like *The Godfather*. Everything he did, he did with gusto: he was an avid jogger long before it became fashionable, he played tennis like a pro, he was a crack shot and had excelled as a big game hunter in Africa. He was intrepid; he had the courage of a lion and drove a car as if he were competing in the Indy 500. Although he was short, he was muscular, with the strength of an ox. He had a sharp intellect coupled with a sense of compassion and a wish to put his talents to good use in helping humanity. He was sincere and believable, and his actions appeared in sync with his aspirations. Everything about him exuded masculinity. I was easily able to forget our secret.

Just as he had cut short his orthopedic fellowship in Boston, Greg now tired of anaesthesiology after completing about fifteen months of the two-year program. I'm not so sure that it was tiredness as much as fear. Throughout his life, I was to find that he rarely completed any project or assignment. Fear of failure or inadequacy, or maybe more accurately fear of not being first or best, forced him to quit before the project ended. He was highly competitive. Besides, now we were starting to receive the extra royalties, or at least they were promised. I would learn, but did not know it then, that as long as Greg had or could borrow any money, he saw no need to work. He was still embroiled in a custody battle with Alice, but he had seen a lot less of his children than I expected. He was far more interested in quarreling with his second wife. I did not care for Florida as a place to live. We agreed we were both ready to head back to New York, where we arrived in time for Christmas 1968 with our three sons. Greg had adopted Brendan, now six; Seán was a year and a half, and Edward was an infant. We settled into a fifteenth-floor apartment on Lexington and Eighty-seventh Street, our home for the next eight years. Greg continued to think about working in a third-world country. I had my hands full with the children and settling back into city life.

When our belongings arrived from Florida, I noted that two boxes of my personal items were missing. Greg had been present when I had told the movers these boxes were of particular value to me and that I wanted them to be given special treatment. There was, in fact, little of value in them, but they contained the entire record of my childhood: letters, photos, books, some watercolors and mementos. My mother a few months before had given up her flat on Seapoint Avenue and had sent me everything I had left behind when I went to Spain. These boxes' contents would hardly be of interest to anyone but myself. To my horror, the boxes failed to arrive. The movers suggested I fill out a lost-articles form and said that they would be traced. Three weeks went by before the manager of the moving company telephoned. I was mistaken, she told me; there were no missing boxes. But, I objected, I had distinctly marked those two boxes to be given special care. Yes, she said, but after I left, my husband had removed the boxes, telling the movers he would bring them with him in the car to New York. I was astounded. When Greg came home I asked him about it. He sheepishly admitted that he had taken the boxes. He said someone broke into the car on his way from Florida and stole them. I asked him where and when and if he had reported it to the police. He said, no, he hadn't. He hadn't noticed they were gone until he arrived in New York, so he did not know where or when they were taken. He said he was too scared to tell me about it because he knew I would be angry. He had been present when our shipment was delivered and heard me reporting the missing boxes and had said nothing. I was disgusted. To this day, I don't understand what happened, but I would be willing to bet that the car was not broken into, and for whatever twisted reasons, Greg disposed of those things because they were important to me. It was an attempt to dominate my life by eliminating the past.

The myth Greg had presented to me in Miami of his not being a transvestite had been quickly dispelled. Before he had given up his residency at Jackson Memorial Hospital that year, he had arrived home one day with a nurse's uniform, including white stockings. He said he had picked it up accidentally, thinking it was his white coat. In New York, as our income from the royalties grew, Greg carelessly left receipts around, showing that he had purchased clothes, jewelry, wigs, and cosmetics from Saks Fifth Avenue. He was always careful not to let the children or me see him "relaxing," so I tried to put his habit out of mind, concentrating on the household and my job. He often stayed at home while I worked. He loved to take the children on outings and buy them expensive toys. He also taught them baseball in Central Park, took them to the children's zoo, and watched as they sailed model boats in the pond. Little Egypt, next to the Metropolitan Museum, was a favorite playground, and other parents remarked to me that he was an admirable father and we were so lucky. Our children adored him.

After a few months as a housewife I had become restless and needed outside stimulation. Kay O'Sullivan, who had visited us in Miami, asked me to write a newsletter for the Guinness-Harp Corporation, an overseas division of the Irish brewery. Kay declared I could plan my own hours and would be completely autonomous. I had no corporate experience, so it represented a challenge. I agreed. I could not help seeing the irony of being employed by the very company I had escaped from Ireland to avoid working for ten years before. I continued working part time with Guinness for the next eleven years, and when we left New York for Montana in July 1980, it was with farewell gifts of a Tiffany carriage clock and a dozen Waterford crystal glasses tucked in my suitcase in appreciation for my decade of work.

Greg said he still intended to take a job overseas for a nonprofit organization, but when it came to the point of applying, he felt he could not move before the custody suit was settled. He also began to talk about having more electric shock treatments. He said that the electric shock really cleared his brain of all the cobwebs. It was the one thing that would make him reach his full potential as a doctor. Greg had received his medical degree in 1964. From the outset he had intended to use his medical skills in the service of the poor, preferably in an underdeveloped country. To that end he started (but never completed) a number of residencies so that he would have a well-rounded background to handle any emergency. He never acquired a specialty; instead he accumulated a smattering of medical knowledge and experience. He maintained that shock treatments made him see things clearly; difficult medical problems became simple to solve. Throughout his life he had needed the shocks to keep his brain in shape as well as to destroy the bad memories that crippled him and caused depression. I had no knowledge of the efficacy or otherwise of electric shock therapy, so I could only listen. I knew that while he was a resident at Jackson Memorial Hospital in Miami he had seen a psychiatrist there, a David Pinosky, but I was not aware of what they discussed. In January 1970, when I was already pregnant with our daughter, Vanessa, Greg made an appointment to go up to Boston to see Dr. Robert Arnot, who had previously treated him with electric shock therapy. In Ireland when I was growing up, a visit to a psychiatrist was something to be ashamed of, a deep secret, but when I came to the States, it seemed that almost everyone I met went to a therapist of some sort. It was a matter of pride, a status symbol, and very often a topic for social conversation. I was not concerned that Greg was discussing his difficulties with a doctor. It seemed a sensible thing to do. I flew with him to Boston, where we stayed at the Copley Plaza Hotel.

He became agitated the night before treatment. He told me that he was really scared because on the last occasion while he was under the anesthetic, his heart had stopped, and he feared it might happen again. But he also felt he must have the treatment if he was to make anything of his life. I talked to him thoughout the night. He did not have to submit to the treatment, but on the other hand, if he was determined to go through with it, the doctors would not put him in any danger. It was at this same hospital that his heart had stopped three years before. I was sure they would not take an unnecessary risk. I went with him to the hospital and watched them set up the heart monitor before they put him out. When they placed the suction cups on his head, I could stand it no longer and went to the waiting room. While he was in recovery, Dr. Arnot took the time to talk with me. He said that the treatment was successful. He was a great advocate of electric shock therapy, he told me; everyone would benefit from it. In his opinion, it would be a better world if every person submitted to the treatment once a year.

We spoke a little bit about Greg's disposition. I told him how obsessed Greg was with his ex-wife, thinking up ways he could upset Alice, fantasizing her death, even plotting how he would kill her if only he could get away with it. We had watched some Hitchcock movies that had set his imagination spinning. This behavior occurred at night when he could not sleep. Some nights he dialed her number and then hung up thirty and forty times, until she took the phone off the hook. I almost resented it when Arnot said to me: "Don't worry about it until you become his target. Be happy he has someone else to bear the brunt of his anger."

Finally, we talked about the history of suicide in the Hemingway family. That canny doctor predicted that Greg would never commit suicide. He classified Greg as a transvestite, someone with a compulsion to wear clothes of the opposite sex. "He has his alternate persona," Arnot told me. "In assuming a female identity, Greg in effect kills himself. I predict *that* will be his only form of suicide." I was not overly concerned by what I heard, probably because I had no clear understanding. I thought all our troubles would be over if the custody battle was settled and our family moved to a place where Greg could put his skills as a doctor to use. I still held out the hope of living in Africa.

In the spring of 1972, on the recommendation of Ted Hager, we brought the children to Cabo San Lucas in Baja California for a short vacation. It was to be the first of many pleasant trips to Mexico. When Greg wrote his memoir, he dedicated it to the owner of the resort, Bud Parr. We had to fly in from La Paz because there was no passable road. The resort was exclusive, breathtakingly beautiful, perched on a cliff overlooking the Sea of Cortez, where seals basked in the sun and happily spouting whales passed by on their migratory travels. We played tennis, snorkeled, rented scuba equipment, went deep-sea fishing, did some horseback riding, and visited the little town at the edge of the cape. Greg thought Mexico might not be a bad place to settle, so he inquired about the possibility of practicing medicine there. When he approached the powers that be with this suggestion, he was told indignantly, "Practice? We have no need for people coming here to practice. We accept only fully qualified physicians."

CHAPTER TWENTY

The Donkey, the Mule, and the Pony

IN LATE 1971 ALICE had a schizophrenic breakdown and Greg was awarded custody of John, Maria, and Patrick. The children came to live with us in our two-bedroom New York apartment. Greg continued to think of working in Africa but did little to realize his ambition. Sometimes I thought it was a cover for not finding any regular employment. We had corresponded with his brother Patrick, who was becoming more and more pessimistic about the political atmosphere of East Africa and the precarious future for whites there. Pat recommended that we look into other countries. With his new custodial responsibility, and at my urging, in 1972 Greg finally made a move to obtain employment. He had hardly worked in two years. In midsummer he applied to CARE and was offered a position in Nicaragua. We were both interviewed and passed by the personnel department in New York. In September we landed in Managua on a speculative trip. They would look us over in situ and we would look them over before signing a two-year contract. I set out with high hopes that a new phase of our lives was beginning. However, when we had a chance to look at the city, I had never seen an uglier capital than drab, smoggy Managua.

We were staying at the Hilton. Greg, who had a sure sense for news, quickly learned that Howard Hughes was living on the seventh floor of the hotel. The entire floor was taken up with his entourage and was sealed off from public access. One day Greg dared me to walk down the stairs from our eleventh-floor room to see if I could meet Hughes. I gamely took up the bet but was turned away by an armed security guard.

From Managua, we flew due east in a small Air Force plane to a distant rain forest. We were accompanied by a couple of government officers (one a member of the Somoza family), a pair of Australian volunteer nurses, the pilot and copilot, several live chickens, and two cylinders of calor gas. Before taking off, the copilot shook his head and said the plane was badly overloaded. He quarrelled with the Australian nurses, asking them to offload some of their supplies. They were adamant that everything was coming with them. If they were lucky, they got to Managua once a month, and life, they reckoned, would be unbearable without these basic necessities. The copilot said doubtfully, "We'll give it a try." As the plane taxied down the runway I grimly noted the remains of two wrecked planes shoved to one side. Luckily, we took off without incident, right over Lake Nicaragua—a large lake that boasts of the deadly freshwater cub shark, *Carcharhinus leucas*—and headed due east into the mountains. If the plane faltered now, we would be fodder for these sharp-toothed fish.

Somoza, the minister for social services, pointed out the farmland beneath us, describing various programs they were introducing to help the peasants become self-sufficient. A huge percentage of the population was illiterate. Mostly the peasants were laborers on ranches, which produced some of the finest beef eaten in the United States. The workers were paid a pittance. The government wanted to change this, Somoza told us. We would be able to judge for ourselves from the project we were going to see. With the money they had received from international aid, something like $6 million, they had cleared an area in the rain forest and built one central village and four satellites. The best peasant workers were offered free land in this rain forest clearing. There was no road yet, but that would come. The people were flown in. Equipment too was brought in by the government and leased to the people to till and cultivate the land. As we approached the little airstrip, the pilot let out a curse. The plane ascended sharply and circled the field. We looked down and saw a number of people lined up along the side of the airstrip. On the strip itself there were a donkey, a mule, and a pony in what appeared to be a race. Samosa explained to us that the planes arrived so infrequently that the landing strip was sometimes used as a racetrack. The donkey, mule, and pony were the only beasts in the area, so they had to place handicaps to make the race remotely even. Nobody had any money, so the bets were made in lemons, sugarcane, beans, or whatever other commodity was available.

As we swooped over them in one more circle, the runway was cleared and we were able to land. The entire population was there to meet us, including the beasts of burden. The people were not shy in looking us over, but of greater interest was the cargo. We walked through the puddles of a dirt lane to the wooden shack that would be our home for the next two years if we signed the contract. Next to our shack was the clinic, and across the path opposite us was the *comandante*'s wooden dwelling. The *comandante* was the governor of the settlement. He was father figure, legislator, judge and jury: a mini-dictator. All local power rested in him. The *comandante,* dressed in military uniform, had met us at the plane and walked us the few yards to our hut. He invited us to breakfast the next morning.

As we sat at the rough-hewn breakfast table eating chicken and rice and drinking lemon juice and water sweetened with sugar cane, we were given an overview of the project and the people involved. The comandante was a short, jocular man with dark wavy hair and an impressive moustache. A small unsheathed revolver was tucked into his belt. It was easy to keep law and order, he told us, tapping the revolver. Any infraction of the law would be dealt with swiftly. No need for judges or jails. He then cited a couple of cases where justice had been meted out on the spot. He owned the only source of communication with the outside world in the area: a small but powerful transistor radio, which sat on his windowsill. There was no glass in the village, only square openings for windows. A young lad had come along one day and snatched the *comandante*'s radio. Within minutes he was dead. "One bullet," the *comandante* said with satisfaction as he stood up to demonstrate his prowess. I avoided catching Greg's eye.

Across the table was the clinic director. A German doctor, about to complete his two-year stint, he spoke to Greg about the medicines available and the types of patients he would be seeing. "The people are so stupid. They are just like animals," he said disdainfully. "Look at them now." Twenty or more were lined up outside the clinic door, several with children obviously dying from malnutrition and intestinal infections. "There is a sign that clearly states the clinic hours are on Monday, Wednesday, and Friday from nine until two. This is Tuesday. None of them can read, so they will be waiting there until tomorrow morning. They simply don't learn." I noted Greg's eyes narrowing. The doctor had absolutely nothing else to do and could have opened the clinic on those other days, but it gave him pleasure to watch the distress of his patients, whom he heartily despised. We later learned that this doctor had become an incurable rummy as a result of his fondness for the homemade local brew.

By the end of the week, for want of any communication with the outside world, I had lost all sense of time. I could not have told one day from the next, nor even had I any strict sense of how long we had been away. We had every variation of chicken and rice for our meals. As time passed, there was less and less chicken until it became just a memory, jogged by the tiniest piece of skin or sliver of bone. Lemon water with sugar cane juice was our only beverage. We walked to the other villages and spent some time with the Australian nurses who were the real medical caregivers.

Prospects for farming in the area were dismal. It was unlikely that crops would grow sufficiently to keep the population above starvation level, and their chances of ever paying the rental cost on the equipment was negligible. The people were slowly starving to death and becoming more and more in debt to the government. An apathy and helplessness pervaded that were both appalling and relentless. It would be almost impossible for a Westerner to spend two years in this atmosphere without going crazy, the nurses told us. They had already witnessed workers being carried to the plane under restraints. It reminded me of the hapless, trapped explorer in Evelyn Waugh's *A Handful of Dust*. The nurses did not care for the doctor, but they said his callous behavior followed a pattern. The job was so hopeless and frustrating that the inevitable failure brought out the worst in some people. Months would go by with no news from the outside world, no planes coming in with supplies, nothing to relieve the monotony. The more they told us, the more I could see that Greg was determined to take over the situation and make it work. I wondered how we could bring our children to this place for two years. I imagined Greg having a disagreement with the *comandante*. With one bullet, he could be obliterated. We would be a disappeared family, never to be heard from again.

I had brought a camera along with me and taken a number of photographs. As we boarded the plane to leave, the same copilot who had brought us took my camera bag as he helped me onto the plane. He did not return the bag to me, so as we disembarked at Managua I asked for it. "Camera bag? You didn't have any camera bag with you," he said emphatically. I suspected that it was more for the film than for the cheap automatic camera that the bag had been confiscated. Six million dollars of international money had been received and badly misused for this Nicaraguan project. It was likely that much of the money had lined politicians' pockets. My photographs would present a different picture from what was painted by the Nicaraguan government. I felt greatly relieved when we were back on U.S. soil. Greg, however, was all fired up. He was determined that he would accept the job and really make a success of it. But fate stepped in. The devastating earthquake that shook Managua soon afterward put an end to the CARE project in the rain forest. All funding went to help restore the capital city and aid its inhabitants. We received a letter of apology and regret from CARE.

By spring 1973, disappointed that the Nicaraguan appointment had not worked out, and recovering from a bout of depression, Greg started thinking about other possibilities. A letter from Patrick urged us to come and visit him in Tanzania before it was too late. He found the situation there untenable and intended to leave at the latest by mid-1975. We planned a trip the following August. We would take Brendan and Seán, leaving Edward and our daughter, Vanessa, now three, in New York. Greg asked Uncle Leicester if he would give John, Maria, and Patrick a temporary home until he had made a decision regarding his career and we settled upon a place to live. Les and Doris were happy to have the children and welcomed the money that Greg offered to help with their keep.

Africa was everything I imagined it to be and more. We were purely on vacation, not suffering any of the annoyances Patrick had complained about and which were goading him to leave, so it was an unimaginable thrill. Pat took us hunting high in the mountains, and we soaked in the beauty and exotic strangeness of it all. Greg's brother was a widower who lived with his young daughter and a number of servants in a charming colonial house on a coffee plantation in full view of Mount Kilimanjaro. Patrick had planned a short safari with Greg and me while we left the boys with their cousin. It was a beautiful, magical trip, and I was sad to leave. More than ever I wanted to come back and spend time in East Africa.

However, we had planned to visit Ireland immediately afterward. Greg had never been there, and my family was anxious to meet him. Ireland per se had not appealed to him as a place to visit, so to entice him there, I had arranged through Guinness for the use of one of their boats, on which we would cruise the Shannon. Greg had been keen to man the boat and navigate the river. To my surprise, he had even invited my mother to join us. But at the point of departure from Africa, Greg changed his mind, deciding to stay on in Arusha and forget about Ireland. From the little we had seen, the political climate in Tanzania was benign. It might be the place for us to move after all. I was really torn between my obligation to my family in Ireland and to Guinness, which was providing the boat, and my desire to support Greg's wishes. Somehow I managed to persuade him to carry out the journey as originally planned. He came unwillingly, arriving in Ireland in very bad humor, determined to hate every moment of it. In Dublin he refused to meet any of my relatives or friends, and I was beginning to regret my decision to persuade him. We were staying at the Gresham Hotel in central Dublin, but he hardly emerged from the room. Once we left for Carrick-on-Shannon, where we were to pick up the boat, however, his spirits lightened, and on the river Greg was back to being his gallant, ebullient self. My mother was completely charmed. Greg was so taken with Ireland that now he decided *this* was the place where we would settle. He put all his energy into finding out how he could get a license to practice medicine there.

Imagining the family in some third-world village by the time the children reached school age, and not forgetting my promise to Brendan's father that his son would have an Irish education, I had put the boys down to attend a Jesuit boarding school in Ireland, Clongowes Wood College, where James Joyce had done a short stint (which he recaptured in *A Portrait of the Artist as a Young Man*). In the spring of 1974 it was time for Brendan to sit for the Clongowes entrance examination. Greg and I accompanied him to County Kildare. By this time Greg was thoroughly immersed in studying for the Irish medical boards. He had returned to Ireland twice since the previous summer and on both occasions stayed at Summerhill with Ciss and Nan Dunne, who thought he was the greatest thing since sliced pan (bread), as they say in that part of the country. I have several letters written by Nan, who was thrilled at the idea of our living in Ireland and was conspiring with Greg to find just the right house for us.

By March 1974 he had set his heart on the house he intended to be our home and was keen to show it to me. We rented a car and drove all over the country, stopping to pay homage at Yeats's grave in County Sligo and making a special trip to Lifford, County Donegal, where Greg's dream house, Port Hall, was situated. It was described in the brochure as "a Georgian residence on 456 acres. Excellent arable and stock farm which includes the lands of Corkan Isle, Island More, Wood Island and Port Hall." He had already had some correspondence with the owners, and they were as keen as he that I should like it.

The house and grounds fulfilled their promise, a veritable Eden. There was only one drawback. The River Foyle, which divides County Donegal from County Down, ran right along the property line. This was at the height of the revival of the "troubles." The river was an unmarked border between the North and the South, and Port Hall provided an ideal hideout for IRA men on the run. With Greg's propensity for helping the underdog and sticking his neck out, with the usefulness of his medical skills to aid the wounded, I could see that this situation was little better than the one in

Nicaragua as far as living in a danger zone was concerned. Also, it was pointed out that since Port Hall had long had an absentee landlord, the poor farmers on the other side of the river, in the North, had become accustomed to shooing their cattle onto Port Hall land to graze when the river was low in the summer and recovering them in the spring before the waters swelled again. There would be fierce resistance, we were warned, to "Yankees" trying to abolish this custom. Only a madman would contemplate living on the land mine that Port Hall was in 1974.

On the wild Atlantic coast, we took in Yeats country and stayed in zany little bed-and-breakfasts, winds roaring and waves lashing in thunderous crescendos. Although he found the climate exceptionally chilly and damp, Greg insisted that this was where he wanted to live. In spite of my reservations, I did not discourage him. I felt if Greg were fully occupied, his mental health would become normal.

Upon our return to New York the nagging question was how could we afford to purchase Port Hall, never mind run it. Greg appealed to Alfred Rice. Always cautious and conservative, Alfred was not encouraging. Greg's portion of the royalties for the forseeable future would come nowhere near the figure needed, and because most of that money was tied up in a trust, no bank would provide a loan against it. On top of this, Greg did not have a record of regular employment, so his borrowing power was nil. Alfred was absolutely sure that Mary would not be prepared to offer any loan to purchase the Irish estate.

If Mary had been unhappy when she learned so abruptly eight years before that Greg and I were married, she had kept it to herself. Greg had been fifteen when she married Ernest, and from the beginning, beneath a veneer of friendship, they had been wary of each other. Five years before Mary's arrival, the three boys had accepted Martha Gellhorn as their stepmother and came to like her very much. By the time Mary settled into the Finca Vigía, however, Jack was already in his twenties and Patrick eighteen. Greg was the only one who might have come under her authority. Mary, for her part, was in her late thirties and had had no close contact with children or teenagers in her busy life as a journalist. She was an only child of parents who themselves were only children when she was born, so she had grown up without siblings or first cousins. She lacked any understanding of young people and distrusted them. She shied away from taking responsibility for them. After I married Greg, I learned of the unpleasant incident that had irrevocably driven a wedge between Mary and Greg.

During that first summer in Cuba several items of Mary's underwear were missing and her maid was accused of theft. Although the young girl swore through her tears that she was innocent, Mary disbelieved her. She was dismissed and sent home to her village in disgrace. After Greg had returned to boarding school in September, all the missing items were found under the mattress of his bed in the little house. This was possibly the first time that Greg's habit became known to his father. I'm not sure that the discovery was ever discussed between father and son, but from that time onward, a barrier of resentment and disillusionment built up on both sides. Greg told me that his parents had always ignored his problem, pretending it did not exist or would go away. He never received any of the help he so desperately needed. He resented his parents for this. Had they cared about him enough they might have sought a means of ridding him of the detestable habit that was to plague his existence. He also felt that his father, his mother, and Mary were more concerned about the embarrassment publicity would bring than in finding a cure for him.

The situation between Mary and Greg was further complicated when Ernest made Mary his sole heir. Greg then became resentful of her, wasting energy each day as he voiced his wish for her imminent demise, getting a mild thrill from plotting theoretical murders, as he had done for his ex-wife, Alice. My husband definitely had a morbid streak. He was riveted to the page when Truman Capote's *In Cold Blood* was serialized in the *New Yorker* that year. He bought the book as soon as it appeared in 1975, reading it over and over, analyzing each character, his motives and methods. It was chilling.

Mary invited Greg and myself fairly regularly to dinner parties at her penthouse on East Sixty-fifth Street, but there was always tension. She was ill at ease with him, and it showed, which I think pleased him. When our son

Seán was born we asked Martha Gellhorn to be his godmother. Marty was a journalist like Mary, but far more cultured and thoughtful. She had also written very presentable fiction. She was fearless and far too independent to make a good wife. Her marriage to Hemingway had been a failure, leaving both of them reeking with bitterness. Marty said to me in 1997, "I should have taken my mother's advice and never married him. The relationship was fine as long as we were lovers. Marriage was a disaster. My wise mother knew it and tried to warn me, but I would not listen to her." Marty declined to be Seán's godmother, telling us, "I can't be a godmother because I don't believe in God." But she did send him a sterling silver Tiffany mug with his name and date of birth on it. She followed his career with interest and was pleased to learn in our last communication that he had received his Ph.D. in classical archaeology from her alma mater, Bryn Mawr.

Failing with Marty, Greg had then suggested that we ask Mary to be godmother. Although she had no greater belief in God than Marty did, she accepted. Brendan Gill was godfather, although he was disappointed to find that the name was Seán, not Shawn to honor the editor of the "family weekly," the *New Yorker*. He accepted nonetheless, and his daughter Kate commemorated the occasion with a pen and ink congratulatory drawing. Mary's and Seán's birthdays were exactly a week apart in April, which prompted us in later years to have a dual celebration by attending the Ringling Brothers Barnum and Bailey Circus at Madison Square Garden. Johnny Ringling North had been a friend of the Hemingways over the years, which resulted in our being treated to the best seats in the house.

As Greg stewed about how he could find the money to buy Port Hall, his thoughts turned to Mary. For some years she had been writing her autobiography, which was to be published by Knopf as *How It Was*. Bob Gottlieb was her editor, and I met him a number of times at her apartment. He and his wife, Maria Tucci, sometimes attended Mary's dinners. Mary was totally obsessed with the project as it grew and grew. She began talking of a two- or even multivolume *oeuvre*. As Greg mulled this over, he thought that if Mary would not lend us the money, perhaps he could find a subtle way to let her taste his displeasure. Over the years Greg had been approached many times by publishers to write his memoirs but had never entertained the idea for a moment. His relationship with his father, adoring and loving as a child, had become precarious through his teenage years, with a final bitter break at the age of nineteen. I was now familiar with the full story.

Greg had been married at the time, and his wife, Jane, was almost seven months pregnant. They had been living in Los Angeles, where Greg was enrolled at UCLA in an undergraduate program. Immediately after high school he had spent his freshman year at St. John's College in Annapolis, but he had done so poorly he left at the end of the year, pretending it had never happened. He completely erased the experience from his curriculum vitae. That year he had met L. Ron Hubbard and become enamored with Scientology. He also met Jane, and they were married shortly afterward.

Under stress, Greg reverted to his cross-dressing childhood habit, but this time he went out in drag. After entering a public bathroom he was arrested and brought to the police station. He telephoned his aunt Jinny, his mother's sister in San Francisco. Pauline was visiting Jinny at the time. She immediately flew to L.A. to see her son. She also took care to make whatever arrangements were necessary so that there would be no press coverage of the incident. After she had arrived and saw Greg, she telephoned Ernest in Havana. Apparently, from Greg's account, his father exploded with rage and blamed Pauline for their son's problems. At 4 a.m. the next morning Pauline died suddenly of a tumor of the adrenal medulla. She was fifty-six years old. Father and son each blamed the other for Pauline's death. Later, when he was a medical doctor, Greg knew that both had been wrong. The condition that Pauline had would have killed her no matter what the circumstances. Unfortunately, by that time, 1964, his father was already dead.

During our marriage, Greg never discussed his father and was generally short or disparaging with people who brought up his name. Our children learned nothing about their grandfather at home. Instead they were taught to develop their own identities. Greg resented personal possessions. He especially resented anything that had belonged to his father. Early in our marriage I had several such items. When redecorating, Mary had given me five skins of zebra that Ernest had shot in East Africa in 1954. Impulsively, Greg gave these to a couple he brought home for dinner one night. They admired the skins, and as they were leaving he rolled all five up into a bundle and thrust them into the man's arms without as much as a by-your-leave to me. We never saw or heard from the people again. They probably were afraid we might ask them to return the skins.

Greg threw himself headlong into his writing project, never letting his goal out of sight. He talked with writers and editors and learned exactly how to go about writing a memoir. Greg enlisted the help of a number of people, starting with Uncle Leicester. Leicester came to stay with us for a couple of weeks. He was sixteen years younger than Ernest and seventeen years older than Greg. When Greg was a youngster growing up in Key West, Leicester spent several months at a time living in the household. Greg had had so much electric shock therapy over the years that his childhood memories were faulty, and Leicester was able to supply some of the long-forgotten details. Norman Mailer was enthusiastic about the project and recommended his agent, Scott Meredith, who had no trouble selling the book to Simon and Schuster. It was assigned to editor Michael Korda. Norman agreed to write a preface.

Every flat surface available in our apartment was taken over by the book. I remained skeptical of the project, knowing how Greg felt about his father and his nefarious goal in producing the book, but kept as low a profile as possible. Among the people besides Leicester who actively helped Greg were Denis Brian, at the time a writer for the *National Enquirer,* who later wrote *The True Gen;* William Weatherby, a Farrar, Straus editor who had just finished editing the first Mishima biography in English, *The Life and Death of Yukio Mishima,* by Henry Scott-Stokes; and Ralph Fuentes, a medical colleague. Weatherby introduced us to Michael J. Arlen, son of Michael Arlen of *The Green Hat,* recommending that Greg read his *Exiles,* which was nominated for a National Book Award that year.

Greg accumulated a number of father-and-son memoirs, as well as the books that had been published on his own father. He studied them assiduously, underlining the pertinent parts and frequently making a note in the margin, often vigorously disagreeing with the author. Greg interviewed

George Brown, Ernest's friend, who had run a boxing gym in New York City in the thirties. George was godfather to our son Edward. He was always dapper, and though he never married, in later years his lady love was Georgette Cohan, daughter of George M. of "Yankee Doodle Dandy" fame. They were an inseparable twosome. George spent a good deal of time in 1974 filling Greg in on his memories of Ernest. Greg decided he could write better if he was high on marijuana, which Buzz Farbar was happy to supply. Buzz committed suicide in 1991 after he was released from jail where he served time on a drug-selling charge, but in those days the light stuff was plentiful and easy to come by.

Greg tried hard to pry some information out of me about his father's last couple of years, but I was adamant that I would not supply any details, trivial or otherwise. However, inadvertently through me he was to inherit a windfall. It was exactly during this time that Mary asked me if I would go over some of the papers we had secreted from Carlos Baker. She was on the verge of donating all the Hemingway papers to the Kennedy Library, then under construction in Boston. She wanted me to check through these files to see whether they could now be presented with the other papers which were housed at Scribners, or whether we should hold off for a future date. She suggested that I work on the papers in my apartment.

I brought the steel file cabinet home and kept it securely locked, determined to work on it when Greg was not around. Innocent fool that I was, one day in November 1974 I came home from my job at Guinness to find a note from Greg saying he had taken off for the resort of Cabo San Lucas, where he would have complete freedom and privacy to finish his book. (Although I did not learn about it until much later, with him was an attractive young Australian lady whom I had introduced to him.) I was secretly pleased and decided his absence would give me a chance to finish my work for Mary and return the papers to her, for I felt it was a grave responsibility having them in the house. Alas, I found the file cabinet jimmied open; the most important files had been removed. The papers were never recovered. I reported the loss to Alfred Rice, who said there was no point in upsetting

Mary, since there was nothing to be done. Greg had probably destroyed or sold the papers and we were unlikely to see them again.

When Greg returned after six weeks in Cabo he was still in the manic phase of his bipolar condition. I had learned that Greg was a classic manic-depressive. He had studied the disease extensively and medicated himself. He tried every new drug that came out, even lithium, although with that he was monitored by a fellow physician. In his extreme manic state, aggravated by the weed, Greg took to jogging around the Central Park reservoir in the early mornings. He noted that Simon and Schuster editor Michael Korda was in the habit of traveling the same route on horseback. When Greg was high his patience level was ultralow. He had telephoned Michael about something and had not reached him, nor had he received an immediate reply. He took off in his jogging suit all the way down to the Simon and Schuster offices. He jogged right past the editor's secretary, who attempted to intercept him, and burst into Korda's office. As Greg described it to me later that day, Korda was on the phone and at that very moment was saying something like, "Well, of course Greg Hemingway's a psychopath," and he looked up to find his subject peering over the desk angrily asking him, "So, I'm a psychopath, Michael?" Whatever the true nature of the encounter and actual words, the altercation was followed a short time later by Simon and Schuster dropping Greg's book. The contract was picked up by Houghton Mifflin. Rob Cowley, Malcolm's son, became his new editor. Cowley's even temperament and wise guidance were exactly what Greg needed, and although the book turned out to be a more slender volume than originally planned, it was a highly creditable piece of work that was praised both by critics and those who had known Ernest, especially Greg's two brothers.

When Greg had announced that he was going to write a book about his father and that it would be on the bookstore shelves before Mary's memoir, I had had my doubts. When he had added that he would write it so well he would get the front page of the *New York Times Book Review,* I thought, *Dream on.* But that is exactly what he did. His book was highly acclaimed by the critics, and it became a Book-of-the-Month Club alternate selection. Greg received a deluge of congratulatory correspondence.

A coda to the Korda episode, which I vividly remember: Greg became obsessed with Michael and his early morning canter in the park. Morning after morning, Greg timed his run exactly so that he could stalk the editor, jogging alongside him, taunting him and muttering menacingly. At the time *The Godfather* was playing at a movie theater on Eighty-sixth Street and Third Avenue. Greg loved movies, but I had never seen him so obsessed with a film. He went to see *The Godfather* almost every day. From our living room window on the fifteenth floor we could watch the crowds queueing all the way to Eighty-seventh and Lexington, and as soon as the tail of the queue disappeared, Greg would dash down to the theater and buy his ticket. His favorite scene was the one in which the head of a dead horse is placed in its owner's bed, in revenge and as a warning. Greg fantasized as to how he could treat Michael Korda to this scene in reality. He imagined that he would kill Korda's horse, and even ironed out all the technical difficulties of getting the horse's head into the editor's bed. Best of all, he pictured how it would be to watch the expression on Korda's face at the moment he encountered the grisly scene.

Another product of Greg's manic phase while writing the book was that to each successive assistant writer or advisor he promised 10 percent of the royalties, until I counted a total of 120 percent. In only one case was he held to his promise, and that was by Uncle Leicester. Against his uncle's protests Greg had formally made a contract with his uncle that Leicester was to receive 10 percent of all the book's royalties. At the time Leicester and Doris had been looking after Greg's three children for more than three years. When the book came out, Les asked when he would receive a royalty check. Greg, who had tossed out all of Les's contribution before the book was published, said, "You don't really think I meant it, do you?" Leicester was floored. When Greg dismissed a second request as nonsense, Leicester sued Greg, and they settled for 5 percent before it went to court. The rift was permanent. The two would never see each other again.

In spite of the break, Greg's children continued to live in Miami with their cousins and eccentric but loving uncle and pragmatic aunt. Doris, in addition to her regular job, brought in extra income writing romance novels under a pseudonym. As time went on the two younger children were placed with other family members. When Brendan went away to boarding school in Ireland, I arranged for John to attend the Canterbury School in Connecticut, as his father and his uncle Patrick had done before him.

About this time my own uncle Patrick spent some weeks in the United States on business. Subsuperior general of the Augustinian order, he was now stationed in Rome. The order was closing a number of its schools and colleges in the United States, and it was his mission to oversee the sales of the properties involved. He spent a couple of weeks in New York and looked us up. He was still fairly formidable, but less daunting than I had found him as a teenager. He appeared at our apartment several mornings for breakfast, bringing with him his trademark vintage Heidsieck. He and Greg got along splendidly. There's nothing like a fine Champagne for breakfast to get the day off to a flying start. Uncle Pat announced that his superior general, a French man, was coming in for a few days, and he expected us to give a dinner party of the highest caliber in his honor. Greg was delighted. He praised my cooking and qualities as a hostess. I took advantage of the occasion to buy a fine tablecloth and silverware and was quite intimidated at the thought of providing duck à l'orange for eight. I remember cutting my finger as I was preparing the food and hoping I would not leave a trail of blood. However, the evening was a success.

I had had no idea that Greg could speak French so well; certainly he had little trouble making himself understood. Somewhere from the depths he was able to retrieve his vast knowledge of Catholicism. From all appearances at our dinner party he seemed to be a staunch pillar of the congregation. Our guests were impressed. When they were leaving, Greg reached up to the top bookshelf and pulled out a specially bound French edition of Hemingway's works, which Ernest had given me when we were in Paris. Greg thrust it into the superior general's hand, saying, "My father's copy. He would be proud for you to have it."

I continued trying to overlook my husband's cross-dressing habit.

When I confided in my mother, she exclaimed that I had little to complain about. It would be a better world if more men were in touch with their feminine sides instead of getting drunk or creating violence. Greg's brother Pat brushed his habit off with the remark, "It's just one of those nasty things like picking one's nose. As long as it's done in private, it is no one else's business." I kept my eyes open but my mouth shut, as Helen Dunne had advised me. But as time went on, Greg became more careless in leaving items for me to find. When I ignored them, he started wearing my clothes and jewelry—always my favorites, or something he knew I had intended to wear for a particular occasion. He left them in a disgusting condition, reeking of perfume or stained with makeup around the neck and sleeves. I did not realize that he wanted a confrontation. My paying no attention was spurring him on to be more daring, stoking the fires of his anger. When I broke down and asked him to please leave my things alone, he defied me, seeming to relish my reaction and hoping for more discord. I responded by wearing a single outfit and keeping a few changes of clothes at my office.

Concurrently, there was the cycle of his bipolar condition. The manic phases always coincided with the trust checks and a flow of cash, which enabled the most extravagant behavior and negated my husband's need to hold a regular job. While Greg was engaged in some major project such as Nicaragua, Africa, Ireland, or the book, those were the best times we had together. I aided him in every scheme, no matter how improbable, because I truly believed that underneath the layers of instability Greg was a worthwhile person with much to contribute. But he was his own worst enemy. I felt if I tried hard enough, if I believed in his ability absolutely, he would be able to shake off his problems and fulfill the potential we were both certain he had. My knowledge of mental illness was minuscule. Living with it did not bring enlightenment. I fell back on the precepts of my childhood. You can become whatever you want; it is all a matter of willpower. It was many years before I came to the conclusion that Greg had no interest in changing. He had put on the mask, and now he had become the mask.

Money without a plan of action meant Greg was off to the boutiques. I never saw any of the items listed on the invoices. I imagine they went down the incinerator or into a garbage bin when he tired of them. He spent hundreds of dollars, used his playthings once, and then disposed of them. As he spent more money on his fetish, less was left for the household. He began to resent the expenditures needed for his family. The highs would be followed by depressions, which became more profound with each passing year. Many days he was unable to get out of bed. He was thoroughly ashamed of his habit in this phase. He cried and begged me to forgive him for his behavior, making me promise that I would never leave him.

In 1967 Christine Jorgensen's *A Personal Autobiography* was published. It recounted the tale of a twenty-five-year-old ex-GI from the Bronx who had gone to Denmark for a sex change operation in 1953—at that time a rare occurrence. George became the glamorous Christine, a ninety-pound blonde with a successful career as a nightclub entertainer. I did not read the book, a popular paperback in the late sixties. Greg bought a copy and studied it with the usual thoroughness he applied when a subject interested him. One day in the mid-seventies he told me that he had an appointment with a doctor called Renée Richards. I had never known him to consult a doctor other than a colleague or a psychiatrist, and certainly never a woman. I was curious. Then he casually mentioned that he had met her at a tennis party and, almost as an aside, that she was a transsexual. I kept a poker face and made no remark.

When we were about to go back to Ireland in the spring of 1974 I could not find my Irish passport and had to obtain a temporary one for the journey. About the same time Greg left a letter on top of the bureau in the bedroom. It was addressed to whom it may concern, and it was dated September 13, 1973, which was right after we had returned from our African and Irish trip, and signed by a Charles H. Ihlenfeld, M.D. It stated that Gregory Hemingway was a patient and under treatment at the office of Harry Benjamin, M.D. When I asked Greg what it meant, he said that Benjamin specialized in sex changes and that he was considering the operation but had not completely made up his mind about it. "I probably won't do it," he said as casually as if we were discussing him buying a new suit, "because I like to have it both ways. I can be a man or a woman whenever I want. This piece of paper means that if I'm picked up in drag, I'm covered because the doctor will vouch that I'm a patient in the preliminary stages of becoming a transsexual." He then boasted of how expert his cross-dressing had become. The reason I could not find my passport was because he had taken it and used it on both his trips to Ireland. He had traveled around the country impersonating me before throwing the passport away. I did not know how to react. This was absurd, so outrageous, and so improbable that I wondered if he was inventing it. But there was the piece of paper to prove that at least part of what he said was true.

After he had turned in the completed manuscript of his book in September 1975, Greg lost interest in it. He also suffered his accustomed depression, but a little deeper than usual. He badly wanted an escape. Thoughts of moving to Ireland or Africa had vanished. His brother Patrick had left Tanzania and settled in Montana with his teenage daughter. Patrick encouraged us to move there too. Montana needed competent doctors to work in the hinterland every bit as much as the third world countries. It could provide all the challenges without the inherent dangers. With the book behind him, Greg set his sights higher now. He had always felt intense competition with his father. If he could only win a Nobel Prize for medicine, that would even the score. If he could discover something of vital importance for mankind, it would set him ahead.

An article in the January 1973 issue of *National Geographic* had caught Greg's attention. It was Alexander Leaf's account of his research in three remote areas of the world where a disproportionate number of people live to astounding ages. Leaf called his article, "Every Day Is a Gift When You Are Over 100." Greg started a lively correspondence with the Harvard Medical School professor, who was also chief of medical services at Massachusetts General Hospital. Greg's first thought was that we would go to Abkhazia, an autonomous republic in the Georgian S.S.R., and Dr. Leaf offered both encouragement and introductions. Mary said we could draw upon the Hemingway Russian royalties while we were there. Determined to learn Russian, Greg purchased a set of records and a manual. Every day he turned on the record player and practiced the sentences aloud while we tiptoed around the apartment. After three months of careful study, he was pleased with his progress until, quite by accident one day, he noticed that all the time the player had been set at 78 rpm instead of 33⅓. When the record was played at the correct speed, the words sounded like gibberish to his ears. He was furious and did not have the patience or the will to start over. His desire to go to Russia diminished.

Still, in the late summer of 1975, Greg surmised that if he could find the key to longevity, he might establish his own immortality. His mood swung from low to high as he pursued the story and set about doing the research. Dr. Leaf's article described a little Ecuadorian village, high in the Andes just north of Peru, called Vilcabamba. Here there were people said to be 130 years old and older, sound of mind and limb. Because of its proximity and the fact that we both spoke Spanish, he decided we would go down there first and find out whatever it was—climate, diet, genes—that made these people unique. Greg hired a young Harvard medical student, Philip Roux-Lough, son of the Guinness-Harp Corporation president, to come with us in the fall. He and I set out together, and Philip joined us at the Christmas break. This team of three was serious and intent upon its mission. I brought a recorder, tapes, and a camera. I was the interviewer and note keeper, while Greg toted his electrocardiograph and other medical implements to administer examinations and gather medical data. Philip contributed his youthful, brilliant mind, open and eager, full of enthusiasm and not a little common sense.

It did not take us long to realize that there was no scientific basis for the phenomenon. In fact, the minimum amount of digging led us to believe that these people were probably in their eighties and that not one of them had lived a full century. There were neither birth nor baptismal certificates. The people, who were illiterate, had no recollection of historical events beyond thirty years, nor did they have any real clue as to their chronological ages. It was unusual to find a family of four generations, and we came across none that had five generations alive simultaneously. If what the oldest man, Miguel Carpio, who claimed he was 135 years old, said was true, his youngest child would have been born to his wife when she was in her eighties, some sixty years after they had married. This was not only unlikely, it was impossible.

I still have the notes, tapes, photographs, medical reports, cardiograms, and samples of hair, fingernails, soil, and water. Greg experimented a little with the local belladonna plant, a hallucinogen. Perhaps that had induced the aura of agelessness among the elderly Vilcabambans. Our assistant, Philip, who was six foot five, of sturdy build with wavy golden hair and a fair freckled complexion, appeared to the small, dark Indian villagers as a god. They followed him everywhere, touching him when they could get close enough and making him offerings of a single cigarette or an orange. At first he was dismayed, but we told him to enjoy his divinity; it might be short-lived. We returned to New York, enlightened but deflated. Greg suffered a deeper depression that winter and was hospitalized in Florida, once again receiving electric shock treatments.

Patrick felt that a move to Montana was imperative for his brother's mental health. He surmised that city life aggravated the depressions, whereas in the Big Sky country stress is at a minimum. Besides, it would be a far better life for the family. Greg looked into medical jobs. The children became excited. Imagine living in a real house instead of an apartment, with wide open spaces instead of concrete pavements. Imagine having a room of one's own, a horse apiece, a family dog, cats galore and chickens. I was doubtful. Each year I loved New York more. The three youngest children were doing well at home, and John and Brendan were away at boarding school. Maria had returned to live with her mother in California, and young Patrick was secure with Leicester's son Peter Hemingway and his family in Saskatchewan, across the Canadian border due north of Montana. We had friends in New York. My job was interesting. Greg never held a job for long, nor wished to stay in one place. What guarantee was there that he would do so now? We might well arrive in Montana and find a few months later that he wanted to move elsewhere. I set upon a compromise. If he kept a job in Montana for a year, the children and I would join him.

Paradoxically, at the same time he sought a job and stability for the family, he also began to talk more of having the sex-change operation. In the winters of preceding years, Greg had been hospitalized for severe depression and received electric shock treatments. After more than a decade of marriage, I realized that his world was one of fantasy, that he cultivated a continuing chaos around him so that his inadequacies would go unnoticed in the mayhem and disarray, allowing him to retreat undisturbed into his secret life. As fast as I would solve a problem, or at least tackle it in a sensible way, he set about creating another one. I was still determined not to be defeated, but I was reaching a point of saturation.

The papers were full of James Morris's sex change. The brilliant and successful British travel writer, husband and father of three, stunned his colleagues and readers by announcing that he had become Jan Morris. Greg followed the story closely, and I did too. One evening when the children were asleep, Greg said to me, "If I had a sex change, could we still be friends? Could we continue living together as girlfriends, going out to lunch, shopping and to the beauty parlor? Wouldn't it be fun?" Frankly, I could not think of anything I would enjoy less. I'd much rather read a book than go shopping, see a play than go to the beauty parlor. From the time I learned of Greg's transvestite tendencies, I had tried to show him by my example that clothes and cosmetics are gloss and glitter and not what people are made of. I had grown up in the convent without a mirror, always wearing a uniform. I never had been attached to frippery. I replied that I hoped we would always be friends, but not the kind he had just outlined. To me he was a husband, and if that role ended, our lives would diverge.

In the seventies, working for Guinness and with close ties to the Irish government, I became involved in the situation in Northern Ireland. Violence had broken out again, and there seemed no solution to "the troubles." John Hume, then deputy leader of the moderate Catholic political party, the Social Democratic Labor Party (SDLP), came over to the United States to gather funds and educate Americans as to the real situation in the North. John later became the Northern Irish representative to the EEC parliament in Brussels and subsequently was awarded a Nobel peace prize. John enlisted my help in the United States, and I set up the New Ireland Campaign for him in 1978, together with an American-Irish attorney, Joe Fallon. Later that year I visited the SDLP offices in Belfast. It was my first time in the North, and the situation was grim. There was a bomb scare on the train from Dublin. Most people shrugged and said it was a normal occurrence. When I walked to lunch with Dan MacGreavy across the war-torn city, we took a roundabout route because, Dan said, it would do me no good to be seen out on the streets with him. I had great admiration for that small group of people who would not give up hope, no matter what the odds, that peace could be achieved. "It will take a generation," Dan said. He spoke the truth. Another twenty years would pass before a peaceful solution was even in sight.

During our last couple of years in New York while Greg was trying to establish himself as a doctor in Montana, I saw Mary as often as I could. She and Greg had a falling-out at some point. He had threatened her. She told the doormen that under no circumstances was he to be allowed in the building. I took to visiting her once a week on my way home from work. She was drinking and no longer eating properly. I tried to find reasons to take her out, and one came along on the night of her seventieth birthday. Brian Friel's play *The Faith Healer* was opening that same night. I had been at the dress rehearsal but was keen to go to the opening and to the cast party afterward. Although I should have known better, I talked myself into rolling the two occasions into one and inviting Mary to the show. We would eat something light afterward, then I would take her home and go on to the cast party. We were given excellent seats, back row center in the orchestra. I was on the aisle, and next to Mary sat José Quintero, the director, with one of the producers seated next to him.

For a long time I had only seen Mary in her apartment. I had no idea how deeply alcoholic she had become. At home she always had the gin bottle at her fingertips. Now, as we sat in the darkened theater waiting for the show to begin, she began to get fidgety. When the play started, things were no better. *The Faith Healer* had originally been written for radio. James Mason walked onstage alone and immediately plunged into what seemed to be an interminable monologue. Mary had no clue what he was talking about, and even less interest. She was parched for want of a gin and tonic. She wriggled and writhed and started asking me how much longer we would have to endure this incomprehensible stuff. I tried to calm her, but only her Tanqueray could have done that. As her voice rose to a hoarse whisper, the people in front of us turned around and told her to shush. Only forty minutes into the show, one of the producers came to me and said, "Get her out of here." As quietly as I could, I steered Mary out of the darkened hall and onto Forty-fifth Street. "Well, thank God for that," she said. "Let's go and have a drink."

Out of the corner of my eye I saw the author pacing up and down outside the theater. Brian can never bear to sit through a first night of his own play. When he saw us leaving he rushed over. "Is there anything wrong, Valerie?" he asked.

"No," I said, "unfortunately Mary's not feeling too well, so I'm taking her home."

Mary, not knowing or caring whom I was talking to, butted in. "I'm feeling perfectly fine. But I've never seen a more boring play in my life." I hailed a cab and whisked her away, thoroughly mortified.

When Brendan came home for the holidays, I sent him to Mary's apartment with our Christmas gift. He must not have been smartly dressed, for the doorman motioned him to the service entrance, thinking he was a delivery boy. He went up in the freight elevator and rang the doorbell. Mary took the package and thrust a dollar bill into Brendan's hand. Tilly Arnold, visiting from Ketchum, said to Mary, "That's young Brendan." Mary looked at him again. "So it is," she replied, snatching the dollar back. "Merry Christmas to you and the family," she said without inviting him in.

The next year at the boys' school in New York it was my turn to be class mother, which entailed acting as a liaison between the parents and faculty. The shah of Iran, then dying of cancer, had fled to New York with his wife and three children after the Iranian revolution. His younger boy, Ali, was enrolled at St. David's through David Rockefeller, a friend of the Pahlavis. Ali was in Seán's class, and he was accompanied everywhere by a pair of bodyguards dressed as school coaches. They sat in on all the classes. As class mother, I received many anxious and some angry telephone calls from parents who threatened to remove their children if the young prince was not immediately withdrawn. They said their children were put in jeopardy by the boy's presence. I tried to calm them down. Ali was just a child. He had lost his home and his country, and his father would soon die of cancer. The school would never allow any pupils to be put in harm's way. A little tolerance and a positive attitude was what was needed, not anger and hysteria. I may not have been popular, but I got my point across. No children were withdrawn. No violence erupted, and sharing that year with a young exile was a positive experience for our children.

Ali was allowed to invite two classmates to his birthday party. He chose Seán and Corbett Powers. I bought a game of Chutes and Ladders, wrapped it up, and sent Seán off in the huge black limousine that came to collect him. Later, when I asked about the party, he said they drove for a long time. He had no idea where they were because the bulletproof windows were darkened. They went into an apartment building and took the elevator up to a high floor. The party was held in a large room filled with adults. They all sat at one long table and were served strange food. Ali's brother and sister and a few other children were there. After eating, each gift, sitting on a velvet cushion, was brought out by a manservant and presented with great pomp to the birthday boy. The gifts started out with a large bar of gold, followed by smaller bars, silver, jewels and many serious grown-up types of presents. Seán felt very odd seeing the humble game of Chutes and Ladders presented with a bow and treated as if it also were worth its weight in gold.

During the four years from mid-1976 to mid-1980 Greg spent his time between Montana and New York, never staying long in either place. We joined him for school vacations. In the summer of 1976, a month after his memoir was published, Greg had accepted a job as a general practitioner in Fort Benton, Montana. Once a military installation, Fort Benton, less than an hour north of Great Falls on the Missouri River, had served as a camping ground for Lewis and Clark in June 1805. It became known as "the birthplace of Montana" after the first steamboat arrived from St. Louis in 1859, and the town soon headed all western commercial navigation on the Missouri. It was also a thriving trading center for Indians and Canadian fur trappers in the early years before Montana became a state. By the 1970s the town had lost its commercial prominence, but still held a certain charm. I was doubtful that Greg would stick to the job for any length of time. In the previous twelve years he had worked only sporadically, taking temporary jobs of three hours daily as a general physician at, among other places, Standard Oil, General Motors, the International Ladies' Garment Workers Union, and McGraw-Hill. He had been successful and well liked and a couple of his colleagues became close friends, but as soon as his trust check came in he would quit. We spent a month with him that summer. He took us to Glacier National Park, and his brother Patrick arranged an African-safari-like vacation in the Bob Marshall Wilderness, where we camped in style on the edge of a lake in idyllic circumstances.

Greg was given temporary hospital privileges on July 1, which became permanent on October 1. In August he tried to persuade his son John to join him. He told me he said to John, "We are blood kin. I don't want to say father and son because *father* conjures up images in my mind of *my* father, and I certainly don't want to be that kind of father to you, subtly authoritarian and completely dominating with an overpowering personality. I want to teach you a few things *by example* and share some experiences with you before it's too late, before I lose you completely. I also want to start putting some money aside for your college education, and frankly this is easier to do when you're around than when you're just a nebulous obligation I have to send a check to once a month." John declined to join his father. I was not surprised to see Greg back in New York for Christmas followed by a brief hospitalization for depression early in the new year. However, he quickly bounced back and returned to Fort Benton until June 1, when he quit his job, deciding that he needed more medical training. He said he would apply for an internship in Bakersfield, California. Either this plan fell through or he abandoned the idea. In October 1977 he again checked into the hospital for treatment. He stayed in New York through Christmas.

When he had recovered, he set out for the West once more. This time he found a job with the Allied Chemical Company in Green River, Wyoming. It was early 1978. His letters were filled with enthusiasm. We were to join him immediately. He sent me all the papers involved with his hiring: pension plan, medical benefits, and so on. It was important to his image that his family be with him from the beginning. He wrote glowingly of the area and the people. I capitulated. I saw no option but to pack up and leave New York. Greg had really made the effort, demonstrating that he wanted to live out West and was capable of finding employment and settling down. With a heavy heart, I planned our move. Within three weeks Greg was in touch again. "Stay where you are," he told me. He did not say why, but the Green River job had fallen through. He returned to New York, yet the pull of the West was still strong. He flew to Montana to look for work. By midsummer 1978 he was appointed Garfield County medical officer with the provision that he could take some months off for medical training before working full time.

Garfield County has a population of fifteen hundred people, unchanged since the turn of the century. The seat of the county is Jordan, a town of approximately five hundred, who mostly live in trailer homes. Jordan was later to become famous as the site of the Freemen, who defied the FBI in the mid-1990s. News of the standoff was reported all over the world. One of the bleakest and most desolate places I have ever been in, situated in the flats of eastern Montana, Jordan is something of a desert in the summer: hot, flat, dry, and dusty. In the winter, it is unbearably cold. Barren of trees and mountains, it lacks the charm and the winter recreation facilities of the other parts of the state. Blind to the physical hardships and ugliness, Greg sang the praises of Garfield County. We joined him that summer, camping outside White Sulphur Springs in full view of the Checkerboard Mountains and then enjoying a week at a dude ranch north of Livingston. Before returning to New York, we traveled through Yellowstone National Park, staying in the Roosevelt Lodge in Wyoming. The children were enchanted and were keen to make the move. It was agreed that we would live in Bozeman, a charming university town in the mountains three hundred miles west of Jordan, where Pat and his daughter lived. Greg returned to New York for several months of training and made his way back to Montana in 1979.

I flew to Bozeman in August and we bought a house on Bridger Canyon

Road, high in the Rocky Mountains, five minutes away from the local ski hill, Bridger Bowl. I managed to eke out one more year of schooling in New York for the children and promised that we would join him in June of 1980. We arrived on July 4, shortly after the eruption of the Mount St. Helens volcano. The countryside was shrouded in ashes. Greg was still in Jordan, having competed his first year as the county medical officer, and by all accounts was highly regarded there. The children each had a horse as promised. They learned to hunt and fish and in the winter to ski both downhill and cross country. I mastered the automobile. After many false starts, our new life now began.

CHAPTER TWENTY-ONE

Decline and Fall

*I*N THE LATE SEVENTIES Mary still went out to Idaho for the summer and autumn, so she did not view our move to Montana as a separation. By 1981, however, she was in bad shape. Patrick, his daughter, and I went to Boston to celebrate the opening of the Kennedy Library in her place. Later that year, Alfred telephoned me to come quickly to New York to sign Mary into St. Luke's Hospital. I was her closest living relative, he told me, and the one who knew her best. She was at death's door and hallucinating. I stayed in her apartment at night and spent my days with her in the hospital. Alfred phoned, telling me to take the pistol from Mary's bedside table and put it in the safe-deposit box at the bank. I remember picking up the dainty pearl-handled gun and wondering whether it was loaded or not. It seemed to me that if one kept a pistol by the bedside, it would be loaded. I had my heart in my mouth all the way to Citibank, prepared for an explosion. About the third day in the hospital, when we were busy planning the details of her funeral, Mary took a sudden and decisive turn for the better. When I left New York to return to Montana, she was well on her way to recovery. She begged me to take her with me and I would gladly have done so, but I knew that as long as I was married to Greg it would be impossible.

Over the next five years, I visited Mary whenever I went back to New

York. She was well taken care of with nurses around the clock, but she feared that they were stealing her belongings. She may have been right. She became increasingly feeble, and her mind failed. She lost her short-term memory completely, and there was an Alice in Wonderland aura about her. I particularly remember one time when she told me in a conspiratorial whisper that Peter Buckley had visited her. Peter was a large man. "I don't know how he came in," she said. "It's a mystery. He's too big to fit in the door. He took up the whole room. He couldn't have come in the window, I don't think it opens." Mary lived in the penthouse on the twenty-sixth floor. To her, I was as when she had first met me. "Val, are you twenty-one yet?" she once asked. "It's time you thought about getting married." There was a picture of my children on her dressing table. "Who are those children?" she asked. I told her they were mine. I thought it better not to mention Greg. "Nonsense, Val," she said. "You're far too young to have children." I was over forty at the time.

As we settled into life in Montana, I knew Pat was right about it being a great place to bring up children. Greg seemed to thrive too. He was so excited about our arrival and had carefully organized everything so that we could start to take advantage of our new surroundings at once. He had bought camping equipment, fishing gear, an inflatable raft, guns, bows and arrows, two horses, a pony, and even skiing equipment and a snowmobile. Life would be one long holiday. He took quite a bit of time off that summer of 1980 to show us around. Friends, both children and adult, came from New York to visit. Our first guests were a psychiatrist and his companion who had lived in our New York building. Greg seemed to be coping well at his job, and on occasional weekends we went to visit him in Jordan, where the river is the Big Dry and the antelope roam freely. We drove up to the Fort Peck Reservoir and out to his friend Art Larson's ranch, where our daughter Vanessa was presented with a fluffy gray farm kitten she named Chessie.

The children joined 4-H. Vanessa's project was chickens, twenty-five of them, each with its own name. The rooster was called Godfrey. Edward chose dog obedience. Greg carefully picked out a Brittany spaniel, a pedigreed hunter, for his twelfth birthday. Edward named him Rin Tin Tin.

Dog he was, obedient not. None of us noticed when Seán went to the Orvis fly-fishing shop after school and learned the art of fly tying. He became an ardent and expert fly fisherman. I took up quilting. John came to visit us during his summer holidays from UCLA. Young Patrick came from Saskatchewan, where he was living with Leceister's son Peter and his family. And Maria visited us too. It appeared our life had finally taken a new and better turn.

That first winter we all learned to ski. The snow was late coming, so our first lessons were at Big Sky, the resort Chet Huntley helped build after he retired from newscasting. As the children were lined up in front of the instructor, who was priming them on ski etiquette and basics, all at once a figure appeared heading straight down the slope at high speed, sweeping by far too close for safety. Disgusted, the instructor pointed out, "That man's crazy and dangerous. That is exactly how you should not behave on skis."

"That's our dad," the boys shouted out in chorus, not sure whether they should be proud or ashamed.

That spring, Greg planned for us to go back to Mexico's Cabo San Lucas. We retained happy family memories of our three previous visits. It would be a lovely respite from the grim Montana winter, which finally came with a vengeance. By mid-March snow, cold, and eternal whiteness begins to pall on the spirit and we longed for warmth and the ocean. It was our first return since his memoir had been published.

Bud Parr, the owner of the resort to whom he had dedicated the book, greeted us warmly with oversized margaritas and Shirley Temples, which we sipped in the spacious open lobby to the catchy rhythm of the mariachi band. The first two days were everything we had hoped for: tennis, snorkeling, deep-sea fishing, and wonderful food in the large dining room looking out on the turquoise ocean, the brown seals sunning themselves on the rocky ledges right beneath us. This time Greg had rented a car, so we drove down to the small town at the cape's end and browsed in the boutiques and at the market. On the morning of the third day, Greg took the car. "I'm going into town," he said. "I'll be back shortly." When he did not return by lunchtime, I was faintly irked but not concerned.

The resort included full pension; tables and times of meals were designated and expected to be observed. We held out till the last possible moment, then went to eat. When dinner came and there was still no sign of my husband, I started to worry. All afternoon we had waited, canceling our activities while we strained our eyes watching the road for the navy blue rented car. When a full night went by, I was uneasy. Life had taught me that it was more likely to be a crisis of Greg's making than an automobile accident, which we would have heard about. Another day passed. We went through the gestures of enjoying ourselves, but underneath we worried and wondered. The hotel had no phones except in the office, where a call would not be private. They took no checks or credit cards, only cash. I had a new worry. How would I pay for our week's accommodation? It would amount to more than three thousand dollars, which Greg had brought in cash, but which had vanished with him. I had no more than a twenty-dollar bill, hardly enough to take a taxi to town and back. I had to consider my options when it became clear that Greg, wherever he was, had abandoned us.

We walked to the town a couple of miles away in the searing heat. Credit cards were useless there too. I changed my dollars into peso coins and found a pay phone. I had timed it so that I would reach Alfred Rice at his New York office. I told him of our predicament. He was not sympathetic, but he promised to wire the needed cash immediately so that we would be able to leave the resort and fly back to Montana at the end of the week as planned. I was grateful, not knowing where else I could have turned. With that hurdle jumped, we tried to make the most of the sunshine, but our hearts were not in it. I put forth all sorts of faintly plausible reasons as to why their dad had disappeared so abruptly, and since there was absolutely nothing we could do about it, we put on the best face we could until the time of our departure.

As we walked along the crazy paved pathway to the hotel, overgrown with ground cover and bordered by lush tropical plants, Edward reminded us of one enchanted moment on an earlier trip. Walking along this same path Greg had stopped and said, "What's that?" The children's eyes had followed his finger. There was a little gem box covered in Chinese silk peeking through the greenery. Edward had picked it up. Inside was a daz-zling diamond and ruby ring. Greg took the ring out and, turning to me, said, "It's for you."

"Somebody must have dropped it." I pushed it away. "We'd better hand it in at the desk."

"Finders keepers," Greg said.

"Keep it, keep it!" chorused the children. As I protested again, there had been something in Greg's expression that made me take the box with feigned delight. Later, when we were alone, Greg confessed that he had bought the ring for me and staged the find. It was some time before the chil-dren realized what had really happened. Now we laughed sadly as we re-membered. I still have the ring, which brings back the magical moments in my marriage that helped to make the painful times bearable.

I also remembered another incident at Cabo from our first time there. I'd met two men about Greg's age on the tennis courts. They told me they had both been on the UCLA tennis team. I said in that case they must know my husband, who had been an alternate, but the name did not ring a bell. When Greg learned of my conversation and that I had arranged for us to meet them, he was inordinately angry.

"Why did you tell them a stupid lie like that?" he angrily asked.

"But you've always said you were an alternate on the UCLA tennis team," I protested.

"That was just tennis party talk." All that week he avoided coming into contact with the two men, making sure that we did not dine or use the courts at the same time.

Returning to Montana, Seán found his acceptance letter from the Gro-ton School in the mailbox. His triumph was somewhat diminished because his father was not there to share it. I quickly learned that Greg was back at work in Jordan and that nothing untoward appeared to have happened. He did not come home the following weekend. Instead, we received a letter which began, "Dear Family, I'm terribly ashamed of the way I left without notice, and how I missed some of the best few days of the year we have to spend together. I love you all very much." I found it impossible to be angry at Greg for any length of time. He had a way of being abjectly miserable and sincerely apologetic about his behavior and responded so lovingly to my pardoning him that even though I could foresee the pattern, each time I caved in. I never gave up hope that he would change. When we saw him the following weekend he took us all out to dinner at Jack Cole's restaurant, a great treat, to celebrate Seán's success.

The seasons passed, one after another. Greg planted a garden and appeared to be a devoted husband and father. In November he celebrated his fiftieth birthday. I wanted to mark the occasion with a party, but he was adamant that there be no celebration. Seán returned from boarding school for Christmas. Our new custom was to drive up into the Bridgers, chop down a tree on Christmas Eve, bring it home, and decorate it together in front of the roaring fire while sipping from cups of eggnog and listening to Christmas carols. Greg was to come home on the twenty-third, but he did not show up, nor did he telephone. We feared that something had happened. We were right. He called midday Christmas Eve from about a hundred miles away: he had run off the road the night before, the car was totaled, would I come and get him? We were happy to have him home for Christmas, although there was no tree that year. In two and a half years, Greg totaled five cars. Each time he escaped without a scratch. On one occasion he totaled a bull along with the car. He paid for the bull, but the cars were a complete write-off. He did not bother to inform the insurance company in case his premium was increased. His eyesight was excellent and he had incredible reflexes. He was an absolute daredevil with a car, thrilling the children when they were younger by doing a "Clint Eastwood"—a 180-degree turn on the ice at the mouth of Bridger Canyon, one of the most dangerous spots on the road between our house and town. As they grew older and realized the sheer lunacy of the game, the children gained a healthy fear of this maneuver.

The next year went by with a number of ups and downs, but it wasn't until September that I received a real shock. In June 1982 Edward was accepted at Portsmouth Abbey and was scheduled to start in September. However, Greg claimed he could not afford the expense. He put on his self-

pitying act, complaining of the burden of family and how he gained no pleasure or reward from it.

Greg took the first week off work in August with the intention of traveling to Canada to pick up his son Patrick and bring him to Bozeman. Young
Patrick was looking forward to the holiday because, although he lived close
enough, he had not seen his father for a year. We planned to stay at home
and take advantage of the excellent spring creek fishing at the Call of the
Wild ranch in Livingston. We booked the fishing, and Greg enthusiastically
bought new equipment. He made meticulous plans to meet Patrick and
drive him back to Bozeman.

On the evening of Friday, August 6, Greg arrived home about six, looking ashen, and burst into tears. He said he had tried to drive to Canada but
had turned back three times. He could not pick up his son. He telephoned
Patrick, did not say where he was, cried into the phone, and hung up in the
middle of the conversation. Greg used the week to withdraw from a drug he
was taking for depression. The drug seemed to be doing some good, but
Greg said it impaired his memory to the point where he could not remember patients' names, even if the people were familiar to him. All week he was
depressed, sick, listless. He spoke of feeling so incompetent that he was
likely to kill a patient. He complained of not being able to cope, of lack of
money. At intervals he was hostile or unpleasant toward me. Both days fishing he showed little interest. One of the children developed a facial tic that
became more pronounced as the summer advanced. Edward and Vanessa
were at home as little as possible.

I urged Greg to take a leave of absence. We could get by without the
money. He obviously needed a rest away from his medical duties. I knew he
was seeing a psychiatrist in Billings. I called the doctor, asking him to persuade Greg to give up his work until his confidence returned and he regained some mental stability. Then and over the next six months that
doctor repeatedly told me that Greg was absolutely fine, better with each
visit, I was not to worry.

One weekend in September when Greg was home and the children
were in bed, he casually said to me that he had decided to go through with

the sex change operation after all. In fact, he was in the process of preparing for the transformation. I didn't believe him and told him so. He was just trying to taunt me, to provoke a reaction. He often claimed both his previous wives had been mentally unstable, and he blamed them for the chaos in his life that had prevented him from fulfilling his potential; their problems helped deflect attention from his shortcomings. I think when he was depressed he found my constancy and steadfastness irksome. Instead of falling apart and giving up, I never ceased hoping and trying to find a solution. Now he went to the car and brought back a file showing that under an assumed name, he was undergoing treatment in Great Falls preliminary to having a sex change. I made a mental note of the doctor's name and address. Greg told me that he had visited this doctor a number of times since he had come to Montana in 1976. While he was in Fort Benton, he had facial surgery to reduce the size of his nose. I had not noticed this, as Greg's appearance would change considerably from his thin, anxious manic periods to his bloated depressions. In spite of the many previous warnings, I was shocked, but I refused to be drawn into hysterics or an argument. I told him, "It's your life, do what you have to do, but make sure that you settle your affairs before you discard your present identity." With this incident, I at last came to a realization our marriage would never attain normalcy. Greg was drawn to a life that precluded marriage and fatherhood. What had once been his temporary escape had taken him over completely. Perhaps it was his desire, or maybe he was helpless to prevent it. Whichever the case, I had no power to change him.

On September 21 I wrote to Greg's plastic surgeon, detailing Greg's deceptive use of a pseudonym, fraudulent prescriptions, and numerous psychological problems. The doctor replied with a brief note saying that what I described in my letter was news to him. At the same time, he sent Greg a copy of my letter addressed to his office in Jordan, noting that someone claiming to be his wife had made the preposterous accusation that he was posing as one of his own patients. Greg telephoned me in a frightful rage. How dare I butt into his affairs and put his job in jeopardy? If his secretary had opened this letter, he would have been fired amid scandal. I had better watch it or my life wouldn't be worth two cents. From that point on until we parted, I was in a state of physical fear. I knew better than anyone that Greg was capable of following through on his threats. Over the years, I had witnessed his bouts of violence. Up until then, he had been more likely to damage property or himself than others. When he had been let go by one of the medical services he worked for in New York, he went back that night and brutally smashed their ground-floor plate-glass window. On another occasion when someone had annoyed him, he punched his fist into the elevator of our apartment building, breaking several fingers. I did not want to take any chance that future violence might be directed toward me. The boys were away at school or college. Vanessa and I were now alone in the house.

The weekends passed. Sometimes Greg came home, sometimes not. He always arrived late and it was clear he had stopped at a motel on the way to indulge in his habit. He became increasingly careless, arriving with obvious lipstick stains, eye makeup, ears bloody from self-piercing, traces of nail polish. During the weekends he was distant and quarrelsome or weepy and apologetic. He talked constantly of his fear of accidentally causing harm to his patients. I begged him to give up the job or take a leave of absence. I comforted him in whatever way I could. When he left I called one of Greg's psychiatrists with my fears. As usual, he reassured me that Greg was capable of working, that his mental health was improving and I was not to worry.

I found that whenever Greg came home I suffered a migraine either right before or immediately after he left. One Friday night I did not wait up for Greg's arrival because my headache was so penetrating. Vanessa was away for a long weekend. When Greg came in, I tried not to wake up, but he shook me, wanting to know what was the matter. He told me he had just the right pills to cure my headache. He brought a glass of water and guided my hand as I took four small tablets. When I next regained consciousness it was Monday morning. A good friend who got on well with Greg but who knew I was scared when he was home, told me later she had stopped by when she saw his car in the driveway. After greeting him, she asked where I was. Greg said I had gone shopping in town. She noticed that my car was in the garage. She returned later in the day. When Greg said I had not returned, she told him she knew I was in the house and she wanted to see me. Greg said I was suffering from a migraine and did not want to be disturbed, which was why he had lied to her earlier. She went into the bedroom and found me obviously drugged, completely groggy, but still able to answer the basic questions she put to me. She came back a couple of times over the weekend. When I awoke my mouth was dry, my tongue numb, and my movements spastic. The next Thursday I went skiing and my coordination had not completely returned. I took a tumble and injured my knee. From then on, I made a rule with Vanessa that neither of us should be in the house alone with Greg. We would protect each other.

On Good Friday that year, 1983, I received the call I dreaded. The hospital administrator from Jordan telephoned and he asked me to immediately drive down and pick up my husband "before there was a riot." I gathered that it had to do with his behavior while in drag, which had outraged some of the townspeople. I told him that I had no influence over Greg. I would ask John Bietenduefel—a huge, amiable friend of ours—if he would go instead. John was an admirable fisherman. He had taught us to fly–fish and the art of fly tying. He had even invented a fly, which he called the Duefenbeetle. He agreed to fetch Greg. He drove the six hours to Jordan but later reported that there was no trace of Greg in Garfield County. On Easter Sunday, Vanessa answered the phone. It was the sheriff. She handed the receiver to me. Did I know where my husband was? No, I didn't. What was the trouble? They had registered some complaints from Big Sky resort that a man in drag, using my identification, had gone into several boutiques and had tried on women's clothing, leaving it smeared with makeup and lipstick. The stores were demanding compensation. A couple of days later a call came from Sun Valley with a similar complaint.

Greg apparently came to his senses, covered his tracks, paid for the damage, and returned home a week later as though nothing had happened. In the meantime I had called his Billings psychiatrist and given him the bad news. I was surprised by his reaction. "Oh, Mrs. Hemingway," he said. "You have nothing to worry about. Dr. Hemingway was just here. He told me all about it. He has taken a leave of absence from his job so that he can train for the Boston Marathon. I think this is an excellent move. Don't hesitate to call me whenever you need to. Goodbye."

Greg now threw all his energy into training for the Boston Marathon. He was fifty-one and in his manic state he convinced himself he would make his name as the oldest winner. Every day he ran along Bridger Canyon Road, hiding bottles of Gatorade two miles apart, timing himself, building up endurance. He booked his hotel accomodation in Boston and got in touch with old friends to tell them of this new venture. A few days before the race, he held a press conference luncheon at the Grantree Inn in Bozeman. He told the reporters he had a scoop for them. He wanted the Montana press to be the first to print the news. I remember warning one of the reporters afterward, "Unless you want to be made a fool of, don't print anything until you have confirmed the news from another source." My disbelief in my husband was put down to poor sportsmanship; the reporters were completely convinced by Greg's performance. He vanished for the period of the marathon. I don't know where. I do know that he did not use the air ticket or his accommodations at the Copley Plaza in Boston, although both were charged to his credit card. A couple of days after the marathon, his psychiatrist telephoned me to share his congratulations to Greg with me. "You see," he told me. "I was right all along. Greg telephoned to say he ran the marathon and although he didn't win, he placed high. It's an incredible feat for someone of his age. You should be proud." This man, like most of the world, believed Greg. I threw up my hands in despair. It was a couple of weeks before Greg returned this time. He was still manic, belligerent, and taunting. I was glad the boys would soon return home for the summer.

I made one last desperate effort to get Greg medical help, which I was convinced he needed. I knew that his most precious possession was his medical license. Maybe if that was threatened he would seek help. I called Dr. Edward King, whom I knew to be the liaison between ailing or addictive doctors and the Montana Medical Association. I explained my predicament. He listened sympathetically and promised to come and see Greg. A date was fixed. I told Greg Dr. King was coming for lunch. I suspect he knew Dr. King's position vis-à-vis the MMA. Greg was immaculately dressed, articulate, and charming. After the meal, the two physicians went for a walk to talk privately. Dr. King reported back to me that he found Greg in excellent condition, I had nothing to worry about. Greg even discussed a couple of local job prospects he was considering.

Greg often dressed in the morning in a suit and tie and said he was going to work. I have no idea how he spent the day. When the summer holidays came, he was charming to the boys but increasingly menacing to me. He continually violated my clothes and possessions until my patience was too sorely tried. The children mostly saw the good side of Greg, his penchant for having fun with them. I was a killjoy. Finally, one day in late summer I called them outside, sat them down, and told them that their father was a transvestite. I explained what that meant. Our youngest, Vanessa, was fourteen. I said that in itself it was not necessarily a bad thing, but that their father was using his abnormality to drive me crazy. He had destroyed most of my clothes and stolen my jewelry, including a diamond and sapphire ring my mother had given me for my thirtieth birthday. I cherished this ring, knowing what a sacrifice it was to her to have saved up to buy it for me. They were flabbergasted. Not one of them had the slightest inkling, it was almost impossible for them to comprehend. Greg was such a father figure, masculine, brave, and kind. They must have thought I had taken leave of my senses.

My outburst severed the last link of Greg's trust I had retained. He was mortified for his children to learn the truth. There was no turning back. It probably took a long time before the revelation made any sense to them, but their world was shattered. The close bond Greg had with them was broken. Now he felt they would despise him, just as he imagined the rest of the world did. He was wrong. To this day all of his children for the most part have a great affection for him, remembering above all the good and magical times he conjured up for them.

I felt less secure when the boys returned to school, and I worried for Vanessa. We kept our rule that we were always to be at home together. I took a job at the local bookstore and did volunteer work at the church in order to fill the time while she was at school. Greg thought of new ways to intimidate me. He disconnected the phone when I came home, hid my car keys, and cornered me against the wall and screamed at me, his spit splattering my face. He followed me all over the house, and if I closed a door (including the bathroom), he kicked it in. I went to see a psychologist to find out if there were any options open to me to alleviate our plight. I will never forget her advice, reached after several sessions. "Carefully pack an overnight bag with the barest necessities. Pick Vanessa up at school. Get a ticket on the Greyhound bus to a place you've never heard of. Take a new name and start a new life." The more I mulled over this advice, the more absurd it seemed. Greg was sick. As a cure, I was to take one child, abandon the others, start my life over in a strange place with a new name. This was no cure for the problem. It avoided it. I had never run away, and I never would. I didn't see that psychologist again.

One day Greg physically attacked me in front of Vanessa. The two of us bolted from the house on foot. It was winter, and as we scrambled up the hill to our neighbor's house, I slipped on an icy patch and sprained my ankle. After that, I knew we could not return. Friends arranged a safe house in town. We had no phone and no furniture, and I was instructed to park several blocks away so that Greg would not find us. Every evening the makings of a meal was left on the doorstep. In two weeks, the boys would be home for Christmas. My lawyer asked for a restraining order, requiring Greg to leave the house for ninety days and let us back in. At the hearing, it was decided that Greg should receive psychiatric help. Another hearing was set for three months ahead.

Vanessa and I were still in our hideaway when the boys arrived home. They stayed with Greg at the house and after a few days reported that their dad was fine, that Vanessa and I should come out to see them. We had heavy snowfall that year. Shortly after I entered the house, Greg snatched my car keys and flung them outside while we watched helplessly. It would be May before the snow melted and they could be found. My family minus my husband hitchhiked into town. The boys stayed with us. On Christmas Eve, my lawyer notified me that we could return home; Greg had left. On the doorstep someone, I never found out who, put all the makings of a Christmas dinner with gifts for the children. We found the pipes had burst so there was no water, but we were happy to be together, and somehow we managed to make the holiday a memorable one.

Greg's lawyer had insisted to the judge that I also should be examined by the same psychiatrist that examined Greg. It was mid-March when I went for my appointment. I had expected my mental state to be questioned. In his office, the doctor motioned me to sit down. "I have seen your husband," he said thumbing through his notes, "and I am happy to say I find Dr. Hemingway to be an extremely astute and able man. I detect no trace of mental instability in him. I have enjoyed talking with him and am proud to be his colleague." Then he looked directly at me. "And I will tell you this: if my findings had been any different, my report to the judge would be the same. No one is going to order me to rat on a fellow physician. Good day to you." The psychiatrist clearly resented being called before the judge to testify in the case. As I passed the receptionist's desk she said, "That will be sixty dollars, please." I was crestfallen. There was absolutely no hope of Greg getting the medical attention he so desperately needed.

Greg stayed around Bozeman for a couple of months, then left for Missoula, a college town to the north. He settled at the Thunderbird Motel. In June, the sheriff knocked at my door and presented me with a divorce summons. It would take three and a half years before the decree became final. I heard of Greg from time to time during those years and saw him on two occasions. Twice there were notices in the Bozeman paper that he had been arrested for criminal mischief. Both times he was in drag and had become violent when asked to leave a public place. He told the court that he was writing a novel about a woman and his escapades were research. After several similar arrests, the judge sentenced him to five years in jail. He was not a week in the cell before he was transferred to the psychiatric wing of St. James Hospital in Butte. His new psychiatrist asked me to visit. I drove to Butte. We had a conversation similar to all the conversations I had with psychiatrists regarding Greg over the years. He found Greg to be extremely intelligent; perhaps he was bipolar, but he could not find any serious sign of insanity. Greg had explained to him that he was addicted to sleeping pills and other pills, which he self-prescribed, and sometimes this altered his behavior. Greg was now weaning himself off the pills. (He still had his Montana medical license, although he had not worked in three years.) He then persuaded his new doctor to ask the judge's permission for Greg's transfer to an Atlanta sanitorium for addicted physicians. It was a successful plea. I attended the hearing. Greg was put on a plane for Atlanta. I learned that once the plane touched down, he switched to a flight for Miami, where he lived for the next four years without any medical attention. Montana was glad to be rid of him. The case was dropped.

I attended several hearings to finalize the divorce. Greg never appeared, nor would he cooperate in replying to the judge's requests for information and participation. I was in limbo, neither married nor divorced. The proceedings dragged on. I decided to enroll at Montana State University in an undergraduate degree program to employ my mind in a positive way. It was an invigorating experience, and in five years I graduated with highest honors and a B.A. in modern languages.

During spring break, Vanessa came up to Montreal with me to visit her grandmother for the last time. My mother, Millicent, retained her deep admiration and affection for Greg. She died in April 1986. I will always remember her saying to Vanessa from her hospital bed, "I would give anything to see your father walk in that door right now."

Mary Hemingway died in November the same year. Eleven months later, Greg and I were divorced. More than twenty-eight years had passed since that fateful day when I had walked into the Suecia hotel in Madrid to interview Ernest Hemingway. From that day on, for better and for worse, my life was inextricably linked to the Hemingway family.

CHAPTER TWENTY-TWO

A Time to Speak

*T*HE PARADOXES AND INCONSISTENCIES of my childhood have followed me throughout my life. When I married Greg I acquired his name. Because it was less cumbersome than Danby-Smith, after our divorce I retained the Hemingway surname. At every mention it invites the question, are you related to the writer? That honor and that burden belong to my children, not me. Rather, I aspire to be my own person, to live as an independent-thinking woman.

Although I resisted coming to Montana in 1980 and imagined I would leave at the first opportunity, I have made Bozeman my home. In the years since Greg and I parted, I have traveled a great deal: to Europe, to the Middle East, and to North and East Africa. I have written a number of articles and collaborated on a book with a photographer friend. For that project, we interviewed fifty-three people in eight countries over a two-year period. Our encounter with Mary Leakey at the archaeologist's Kenya home, three months before her death, was the last interview she granted. I have spoken at literary conferences in the United States and Europe. On three occasions I have excavated ancient artifacts in the searing heat of the Golan Heights. I have visited archaeological sites in Turkey, Tunisia, Morocco, and Greece. Whenever adventure beckons, I willingly follow.

In 1999, on assignment for a French magazine, I returned to Cuba for the first time since 1961. It was the centenary year of Ernest's birth. I found Havana down at heel. The city buildings were laced with scaffolding. My brother Michael accompanied me. His head narrowly missed being pounded by a falling brick in the downtown area. If I had to name an essential item needed for a trip to Havana, I would advise, "Pack a hard hat in your suitcase."

Ernest Hemingway's spirit is imprinted all over Havana as if proclaiming Don Ernesto a modern-day patron saint. No tourist can visit the city without being aware of the American writer's presence. His name and image are everywhere; Hemingway tours abound. Buses of tourists stop at the Ambos Mundos Hotel, the Floridita, the Bodeguita del Medio, the Ernest Hemingway Marina.

The Finca Vigía is now the Museo Ernest Hemingway, the most visited museum on the island. The admission fees gathered, three American dollars per person, far exceed the takings at all other Cuban cultural spots.

I telephoned for a taxi. "Museo Ernest Hemingway," I told the operator.

"Certainly. Your name?" was the response.

"Hemingway," I said.

"Yes, I know, the Hemingway Museum. What is *your* name?"

"Hemingway," I repeated.

"No more joking." The voice was sharp. "Please give me your *real* name."

"Valerie," I said. "My real name is Valerie."

The young museum director, Danilo Arrate-Hernández, took me around. Compared to Havana, the Finca Vigía had aged well, due to a little care and a fresh coat of whitewash in place of the peeling paint I remembered. In deference to the quantity of visitors and to minimize wear and tear, tourists must peer through windows at the interior, which has been preserved just as it was in the writer's lifetime. Permits to enter the house are granted only in special cases. As I walked into the sitting room, time stood still. Eerily, I was transported back to evenings when Ernest, Mary, and I had sipped our cocktails in this room before dinner, to soothing strains of music. The record player, records, the ice bucket, glasses, and liquor bottles were all there; the overstuffed chairs with their chintz covers slightly more faded, exactly as we had left them. Momentarily disoriented, I expected Ernest to approach from the bedroom greeting me with his wide, toothy grin, or to hear René swishing through the swinging door between kitchen and dining room, bearing a bucket of ice. Danilo was asking me if I would talk to the staff that afternoon. I had to shake myself to understand what he was saying.

Pilar now sits where the tennis court used to be. Varnished, polished and landlocked, the old fishing vessel has acquired a deceptive elegance. Danilo told me her mate, Gregorio, was still alive at 101 years of age. He lived in the nearby fishing village of Cojímar, where the *Pilar* had been docked during her many years in service. Would I like to visit him? the director asked.

Thirty-eight years after our last meeting, I entered the small, ship-shape front room. The old man rocked slowly in a cane-seated wooden chair, savoring a cigar. He sported a fresh shirt; his navy cap perched atop a head of thick white hair. *El Capitán,* the cap proclaimed. His eyes alert, his hearing unimpaired, Gregorio gazed at me intently. A faint glimmer of recognition crossed his face. A plastic bucket beside the chair served as spitoon. A walking cane hung within his reach.

I spoke of our days on the Gulf Stream trolling for prized black marlin. I recalled the tasty fresh fish doused with *salsa verde* he had prepared in the galley, and the time he helped me land my first sailfish. Gregorio was silent, puffing on his cigar, occasionally spitting into the bucket at his side. His daughter Elvira, his grandson Rafael, my brother Michael, and I conversed as though he weren't there. When I glanced at him, tears were streaming down Gregorio's cheeks.

"I miss him," he explained, pointing to the portrait of Ernest above his head. "It makes me sad to hear people talk about those days. He was the friend of my heart. When I remember that he is gone, I am filled with tears."

"Can I take you to lunch at La Terraza?" I was referring to the harborside seafood restaurant Ernest had mentioned in *The Old Man and the Sea* and *Islands in the Stream.*

"*¿Como no?*" The old man brightened. "Let's go now."

We passed through the bar into the oblong dining room overlooking the ocean. Ernest's round table in the left-hand corner by the window was occupied. That was where we used to sit, to keep an eye on *Pilar* docked in the water below. Now a high-rise building partially blocked the view. Unhesitatingly, Gregorio led us to the back of the room, where he sat at the head of a table, strategically placed. A row of distinctive black and white photos, showing Ernest and his mate fishing, hung above the captain's head.

The tables quickly filled with tourists, French, German, South American. Most were there to celebrate the great American author. What luck they had chosen that day! The closest they could come to their hero was to meet his mate, Gregorio Fuentes. They approached unabashedly, to look, to shake hands, to ask for an autograph, to take a photo.

Gregorio, Ernest's contemporary, was fifty when *The Old Man and the Sea* was written. Now, he had not only outlived the author, he had survived to assume the identity of the fictional character, the old man Santiago. Gregorio's career as mate of *Pilar* had become indistinguishable from his incarnation as the protagonist of *The Old Man and the Sea.* Like his employer, Gregorio had become a legend. "This reminds me of the old days with Don Ernesto," I said. "Except now *you* are the one they seek."

"Not so," Gregorio replied sadly. "I am only the friend of the great one."

"Did you know there is a drink named after *abuelo* [Grandfather]?" Rafael asked me. "Look over there." He pointed to a waiter holding a circular tray laden with cocktail glasses filled with a Gulf Stream–blue liquid. "That's a Gregorio. You must try it." Off he went to fetch some samples.

The meal ended with fine Cuban cigars provided by Danilo. As I pressed mine between my lips, the centenarian leaned forward without missing a beat, struck a match, and held the flame close while I puffed. I remembered that day long ago when, much to Ernest's disgust and my amusement, Gregorio had offered me my first cigar.

"Today is a good day," I said.

I felt Gregorio's bony hand squeezing my knee underneath the table.

"It is not a good day unless it ends in bed." The old man looked into my eyes. I gripped his hand firmly to thwart its wandering. He sighed. "The worst thing about growing old is having to sleep alone."

I chuckled to myself as I waved goodbye to him. "There's life in the old devil yet."

Later, at the *finca*, I met with Danilo and the museum staff in their offices, housed in the former garage. Stairs ascend to the *casita*, the little house where I had lived.

"When are you going to write your story?" Danilo asked me. "You could stay in the *casita*, where you would be free to work and to come and go as you please. Remember, you are always welcome."

Danilo's query echoed that of many who, over the years, have urged me to write this book. I refused repeatedly. Some things are too painful to recall, too private to be shared. Yet time, as it heals it ameliorates, allowing experience to fall into perspective. In the words of Ecclesiastes: "To every thing there is a season, and a time to every purpose under the heavens: a time to be born, a time to die; . . . a time to keep silence, and a time to speak."

This is my time to speak.

*E*ARLY IN 1995 THE owner of the Thunderbird Motel telephoned me. Greg was staying there, she said. He had just returned from Trinidad, Colorado, where he had had a sex change operation. He had not stayed for the postoperative period and now was hemorrhaging badly. She did not know who to call or what to do. She had telephoned me a number of times in the 1980s with concerns about Greg, and on one occasion the children and I had visited her to thank her for her kindness and the genuine affection she had shown Greg. I reassured her that she was welcome to call upon me anytime. Although Greg and I were no longer married, his well-being would always be a priority for me.

I asked Edward, who was living in Bozeman, if he would go to Missoula and take care of his father, which he did. It was a difficult task for him, but he handled it well. I hoped that the change would give Greg—or Gloria, as he called himself—the peace and contentment he was looking for. I felt cowardly about having to break the news to the other children. They were grown-ups now, and I trusted they were sufficiently worldly wise that, though shocking and even hurtful, the information would not be detrimental to their lives.

I never had it in my heart to be angry with Greg, except momentarily, for he suffered far more than anyone I have ever known. So much of life passed him by because he was wallowing in despair, soaring with destructive mania, or discontented with the essence of his being. I remember back to that moment when he first left: the sadness, my feeling of abject failure, augmented by relief. Early one morning I was sitting with a cup of coffee looking through the picture window at the dark blue outline of the Bridger Mountains etched against the true blue of the sky, with the shadow of pine trees creeping upward. It was so beautiful, so peaceful. What an unbelievable luxury it was not to worry, not to fear, not to be threatened. In our final year together, life around Greg had become a prolonged nightmare. Now I could savor the simplest of pleasures. The ticking of a clock for comfort, the singing of a bird for joy, the taste of a raspberry fresh from the garden still bathed in dew. It was sheer happiness and it was infinite.

In 1998 I went to Boston's Kennedy Library to do some research. I entered the Hemingway Room and, for the first time, saw the papers I had worked with for so many years in their new setting. I was looking something up and for a moment my heart stopped. I thought I was hallucinating. When I organized the papers thirty-five years before, I had removed every trace of communication between Ernest and me. Now, as if it were a message from the spirit world, I was reading a letter from Ernest to me that I had never laid eyes on before. It was dated October 26, 1960. "Dearest Val," it began. He asked me to get in touch with him as soon as I received the letter, which was to be hand-delivered. The untrustworthy messenger had sold the correspondence to a collector who later donated it to the University of Virginia. When we parted in Spain, I told Ernest I would wait to hear from him, and he could depend upon an immediate response. It is a great sorrow to me to know that he had reached out and been unaware his letter was not delivered. Four weeks after he wrote that letter, he made his first suicide attempt. I honestly don't think my hearing from him would have made a difference in the outcome that morning of July 2, 1961, but I feel that the deception must have added to his final despair.

My son Edward telephoned me from New York on October 1, 2001. He told me his dad had died in a woman's prison that morning. I thought I must have heard wrong. He was speaking on a friend's cell phone and it was a bad connection, but indeed that was what he had said. I was soon to learn that Greg had been picked up in a disoriented state early one morning while walking home from a party. He was booked for "indecent exposure." He had been naked but carrying a dress and high-heeled shoes. They placed him in the women's jail. Although he was clearly mentally ill and not a danger to anyone, and a hundred dollars was all that was needed for his bail, he remained in the jail. Five days later, he was found dead of heart disease in his cell after an officer came to fetch him for a court appearance.

Memories are curious things, so selective and geared to the mood of the moment. On October 7, my children and I met in New York City to pay tribute to their father. That was where they had known him best. We walked along the streets of their childhood, past the apartment building, Sherry House, on East Eighty-seventh Street where we had spent ten years. Edward was an infant when we moved there, and it was the first home Vanessa knew. We followed the path past the schools to which Greg had often accompanied them or from which he picked them up. We passed Little Egypt, the Central Park playground within sight of Cleopatra's Needle, where he took them on Saturday mornings. We strolled through the baseball fields, where he had spared no pains in teaching them the finer points of the game. We couldn't omit the zoo, a passion of his when they were preschoolers; at one time the name of every animal, no matter how exotic or obscure, could be recited by each one of them. I can remember a three-year-old Seán in his bearskin coat pointing to the animals and saying, "Coati-mondi," "Paca," "Coon." That October day we lunched at the Stanhope Hotel, which was where we had celebrated special occasions or rewarded diligence as the children grew older. We concluded with an afternoon's rowing on the lake, the apex of fatherly outings on a sunny weekend during our New York City years. Our memories were tender and funny. We laughed a great deal and felt very grateful for the many magical moments we had experienced together. These formed the backbone of our lives and can never be erased.

Exactly a week before he died, Greg left a message on my telephone machine. I did something I had never done before, I taped it. He thanked me for the good years we had together and concluded with, "You did a wonderful job with our children."

Ernest knew his youngest and at one time favorite son better than anyone. He wrote of him in *Islands in the Stream,*

> The smallest boy was fair and was built like a pocket battle-ship. He was a copy of Thomas Hudson, physically, reduced in scale and widened and shortened. His skin was freckled when it tanned and he had a humorous face and was born being very old. He was a devil, too, and deviled both his older brothers, and he had a dark side to him that nobody except Thomas Hudson could ever understand. . . . He was a boy born to be quite wicked who was being very good and he carried his wickedness around with him transmuted into a sort of teasing gaiety. But he was a bad boy and the others knew it and he knew it. He was just being good while his badness grew inside him.

Greg was so proud of this passage that he used it as a frontispiece for his memoir. He loved to read it over and over, as his compulsive nature prompted him to, and he always marveled at how much in a certain way his father truly understood and loved him. It saddened my husband that they had been unable to communicate these feelings to each other while they were alive.

There is one change I would make: the wickedness and badness of the little boy were the seeds of sickness, not evil. All his life Greg fought a losing battle against a crippling illness. He lacked the critical early help because his parents were unable or unwilling to accept his condition, nor could he come to terms with it for a long time. He took up the study of medicine in the hope that he himself might find a cure, or at least a solace. Failing, he developed an alternate persona, a character into which he could retreat from the unbearable responsibilities of being—from, among other things, the impossible task of being his father's son, of never ever measuring up to what was expected of him or of what he expected of himself. He was successful at so many things he put his mind to: medicine, writing, athletics. He could achieve almost any objective except the one he desired most: to win his father's affection and approval, to become Andrew Hudson, the little boy who was so close to his father before the wickedness, that is, the sickness, took over.

The opening line to Ford Madox Ford's novel *The Good Soldier* I make my closing line: "This is the saddest story I have ever heard." It is the saddest story and it is, in part, my own.

SELECT BIBLIOGRAPHY

Arnold, Lloyd. *High on the Wild with Hemingway.* Caldwell, ID: Caxton, 1968.

Baker, Carlos. *Ernest Hemingway: A Life Story.* New York: Scribner's, 1969.

———, ed. *Ernest Hemingway: Selected Letters, 1917–1961.* New York: Scribner's, 1981.

Behan, Brendan. *Borstal Boy.* London: Hutchinson, 1958.

———. *Brendan Behan's Island.* New York: Geis, 1962.

———. *Brendan Behan's New York.* New York: Geis, 1964.

———. *Confessions of an Irish Rebel.* New York: Geis, 1965.

———. *The Complete Plays.* New York: Grove, 1978.

———. *The Scarperer.* New York: Doubleday, 1964.

Brenan, Gerald. *Personal Record (1920–1972).* New York: Knopf, 1975.

———. *The Face of Spain.* New York: Grove, 1957.

———. *The Literature of the Spanish People.* Cambridge: Cambridge University Press, 1951.

———. *The Spanish Labyrinth.* Cambridge: Cambridge University Press, 1943.

Brian, Denis. *The True Gen.* New York: Grove, 1988.

Bruccoli, Matthew J., ed. *Conversations with Ernest Hemingway.* Jackson: University Press of Mississippi, 1986.

Donaldson, Scott. *By Force of Will: The Life and Art of Ernest Hemingway.* New York: Viking, 1977.

Eastman, Max. *Love and Revolution.* New York: Random House, 1964.

———. "Bull in the Afternoon." *New Republic* (June 7, 1933), pp. 94–97.

Fuentes, Norberto. *Hemingway in Cuba.* Secausus, NJ: Lyle Stuart, 1984.

Goytisolo, Juan. *Realms of Strife: The Memoirs of Juan Goytisolo.* Translated by Peter Bush. San Francisco: North Point Press, 1990.

———. *The Young Assassins.* New York: Knopf, 1959.

Griffin, Peter. *Along With Youth: Hemingway, The Early Years.* Foreword by Jack Hemingway. New York: Oxford University Press, 1985.

Hanneman, Audre. *Ernest Hemingway: A Comprehensive Bibliography.* Princeton: Princeton University Press, 1967; supplement issued in 1975.

Hemingway, Ernest. *The Sun Also Rises.* New York: Scribner's, 1926. Republished as *Fiesta,* London: Cape, 1927.

———. *Men Without Women.* New York: Scribner's, 1927.

———. *A Farewell to Arms.* New York: Scribner's, 1929.

———. *Death in the Afternoon.* New York: Scribner's, 1932.

———. *Green Hills of Africa.* New York: Scribner's, 1935.

———. *To Have and Have Not.* New York: Scribner's, 1937.

———. *The Spanish Earth.* Cleveland: Savage, 1938.

———. *For Whom the Bell Tolls.* New York: Scribner's, 1940.

———. *Across the River and Into the Trees.* New York: Scribner's, 1950.

———. *The Old Man and the Sea.* New York: Scribner's, 1952.

———. *A Moveable Feast.* New York: Scribner's, 1964.

———. *Islands in the Stream.* New York: Scribner's, 1970.

———. *The Dangerous Summer.* New York: Scribner's, 1985.

———. *The Garden of Eden.* New York: Scribner's, 1986.

———. *True at First Light.* Edited by Patrick Hemingway. New York: Scribner's, 1999.

———. *Hemingway on War.* Edited and with an introduction by Seán Hemingway. New York: Scribner's, 2003.

———. "The Art of Fiction XXI." Interview by George Plimpton. *The Paris Review* 18 (1958), pp. 61–89.

Hemingway, Gregory. *Papa: A Personal Memoir.* Preface by Norman Mailer. Boston: Houghton Mifflin, 1976.

Hemingway, Jack. *Misadventures of a Fly Fisherman: My Life With and Without Papa.* Dallas: Taylor, 1986.

Hemingway, Leicester. *My Brother, Ernest Hemingway.* Cleveland: World, 1962.

Hemingway, Mary. *How It Was.* New York: Knopf, 1976.

Hemingway, Valerie. "*The Garden of Eden* Revisited: With Hemingway in Provence in the Summer of '59," *The Hemingway Review* 18, 2 (1999), pp. 102–13.

———. "A Tribute to Gregory H. Hemingway." *The Hemingway Review* 22, 2 (2003), pp. 45–50.

———. "Lady Luck: Take Her or Leave Her" [story]. *North Dakota Quarterly* 68, 2–3 (2001), pp. 28–35.

———. "The Author as Character: Notes on the Life of Ernest Hemingway as Reflected in His Papers." *The World and I,* April 2000, pp. 296–309.

Hotchner, A. E. *Papa Hemingway.* New York: Random House, 1966.

Kert, Bernice. *The Hemingway Women.* New York: Norton, 1983.

Mellow, James R. *Hemingway: A Life Without Consequences.* Boston: Houghton Mifflin, 1992.

Meyers, Jeffrey. *Hemingway: A Biography.* New York: Harper and Row, 1984.

Miller, Madelaine Hemingway. *Ernie: Hemingway's Sister "Sunny" Remembers.* New York: Crown, 1975.

Montgomery, Constance. *Hemingway in Michigan.* New York: Fleet, 1966.

O'Connor, Ulick. *Brendan Behan.* London: Hamish Hamilton, 1970.

Plath, James, and Frank Simons. *Remembering Ernest Hemingway.* Foreword by Lorian Hemingway. Key West: Ketch and Yawl Press, 1999.

Plimpton, George. *Out of My League.* New York: Harper, 1961.

Reynolds, Michael. *Hemingway: The American Homecoming.* Cambridge, Mass.: Blackwell, 1992.

———. *Hemingway: The Final Years.* New York: Norton, 1999.

———. *Hemingway: The 1930s.* New York: Norton, 1997.

———. *Hemingway: The Paris Years.* Cambridge, Mass.: Blackwell, 1992.

———. *The Young Hemingway.* New York: Blackwell, 1986.

Ross, Lillian. *Portrait of Hemingway.* New York: Simon and Schuster, 1961.

Sanford, Marcelline Hemingway. *At the Hemingways: A Family Portrait.* Boston: Little, Brown, 1962. Enlarged as *At the Hemingways: With Fifty Years of Correspondence Between Ernest and Marcelline Hemingway.* Edited by John E. Sanford. Moscow: University of Idaho Press, 1999.

Viertel, Peter. *Dangerous Friends.* New York: Doubleday, 1992.

Woodham-Smith, Cecil. *The Reason Why.* New York: McGraw-Hill, 1954.

INDEX

Running *with the* Bulls

Valerie Hemingway

A Reader's Guide

A Conversation with Valerie Hemingway

*Jennifer Morgan Gray is a writer and editor
who lives outside of Washington, D.C.*

Jennifer Morgan Gray: Your memoir teems with vibrant, colorful detail. Did you keep a journal throughout your life and refer to it while you were writing *Running with the Bulls*? How long did the book take you to write?

Valerie Hemingway: I have never kept a journal as such, but I have always written down descriptions or incidents that I find interesting and want to remember. I also came from a generation of avid letter writers. I often kept copies of my own letters—using Hemingway's method of placing a piece of carbon paper between the pages—and always the letters of others. I referred to these materials when writing my memoir. I spent about a year writing the first draft. With that draft, I composed an outline and shaped two chapters for my agent to show to publishers. When I sold the book to Ballantine in May 2003, I had a deadline of December 1, 2003, to hand in the final manuscript. I kept that deadline.

JMG: Why did you begin the book with Ernest Hemingway's funeral, then frame part of the book as a flashback to what came before. In what way was his death and burial a pivotal moment in your life?

VH: Initially I wrote my book starting at the beginning. My agent said he was anxious to get to the part where I first met Ernest Hemingway. I felt that my childhood in Ireland was an integral part of the story, and I did not want to underplay it. The agent's comment gave me the idea that the impatient reader could be placated with a glimpse into the adventures that lay ahead.

Certainly the two funerals, first Ernest's, then Mary's twenty-four years later, were pivotal moments in my life. A parenthesis in a way: the beginning and the end of something.

JMG: Along the same lines, do you ever consider what might have happened had you not interviewed Ernest Hemingway on that fateful assignment in Spain? What path do you think your life might have taken had you not crossed paths with the Hemingways?

VH: If I had not interviewed Hemingway, I would probably have returned to Ireland at the end of the year, found myself a job as a journalist, and lived happily ever after. (Possibly unhappily ever after, but since I'm inventing here, it might as well be happily.)

JMG: The book boasts an extensive bibliography. Are there any books that you relied on in particular, either as a frame of reference or as creative inspiration? Did you read or reread Hemingway's novels—those published while he was alive or posthumously—while you were writing?

VH: I listed many titles in the bibliography because I am familiar with the biographies and their authors. They could be helpful to people reading about Hemingway for the first time. Also, I listed any books I had mentioned in the text. I have never read any of the Hemingway biographies through because I knew him well for two years and worked on his papers for another four years—meaning that, in all likelihood, I know more about Hemingway and his work than any of the biographers. I read extensively and always like to probe new subjects, not revisit old ones. Every few years I reread Hemingway's works. I do this for certain other favorite authors, for instance, James Joyce and Evelyn Waugh. I most recently reread *A Moveable Feast, The Sun Also Rises, For Whom the Bell Tolls, Byline Ernest Heming-*

way, and *The Garden of Eden.* I frequently read one or another of Hemingway's short stories.

JMG: I find it amazing that after your initial meeting with Ernest Hemingway, you forgot your promise to go to Pamplona with him! To what do you attribute your casual attitude toward a writer around whom most people were awestruck? Why do you think both of you got on so well? Were you surprised when he first hired you to be his summer secretary?

VH: First of all, in 1959 I was living from hand to mouth as a freelance journalist and giving a few lessons in English: I was not at all sure that I could afford a weeklong trip to Pamplona. I had no idea that Hemingway intended to pay my expenses—except for the train fare. Hemingway was almost completely unknown to me. He was not famous in Ireland, and I had no idea he was such a revered literary figure. In Pamplona I began to observe how famous he was, not just among the Americans but also with Spaniards and foreigners.

I think it was precisely because I was unaware of his exalted position that we got on so well. He could tell that I was not interested in him because he was famous. He also liked the fact that I was Irish. I was flabbergasted when he asked me to be his secretary. I thought it was his idea of a joke. He liked to play practical jokes on people.

JMG: Your time with the Hemingways enabled you to travel the world. Was there one place with which you particularly fell in love?

VH: I had been to France and Spain as a sixteen-year-old. Cuba was new territory for me, and it was there that I became close to both Mary and Ernest. It was my first trip to the tropics, and I thought it was a magical place. Cuba was an island and small—just as my native Ireland was. It was warm and welcoming and filled with music and friendly faces.

JMG: You formed a friendship with Mary that lasted through the years. When you initially met her, what was your impression of her? How did your time in Cuba after Ernest Hemingway's death solidify your relationship? After you married Greg, how did your friendship with Mary change—for the better or for the worse?

JMG: I liked Mary from the very beginning. She was petite, pretty, with fair hair and blue eyes. She spoke her mind in a way I was not used to in a woman. She was funny, original in her ideas, could curse like a trouper, and had no haughtiness or pretense about her.

When the two of us spent five weeks in Cuba after Ernest's death, we were drawn together by the memories of our last months there with him. Mary tried to understand why he killed himself, and I was one of the few people she felt she could confide in and completely trust.

Marrying Greg changed my relationship with Mary. She was always a little wary and distrustful of me after that. Greg really disliked her and made no effort to hide it—except when he thought he might be able to borrow some money from her to fund one of his harebrained schemes, such as buying the Irish mansion. As the years passed, I saw Mary more and more on my own, and we reestablished a close connection.

JMG: "As sure as anything, in due course Hemingway's affection for you will wane," a friend tells you (page 83). Did you feel that this prediction ultimately came to pass? To what do you attribute Hemingway's strong affection for you during this point in his life? What was Mary's attitude toward you during that time?

VH: Hemingway's affection for me did not wane, probably because he died before it had run its course. Hemingway told me that he had fallen in love roughly every decade of his life, and each time he had written a novel. Ten years before he met me he had fallen in love with the nineteen-year-old Italian girl, Adriana Ivancich. He wrote *Across the River and into the Trees* and then *The Old Man and the Sea* as a result of his passion. I think when I walked into the Suecia Hotel in Madrid to interview him, or sometime shortly thereafter, he imagined that a new and wonderful novel was in the making.

At first Mary dismissed me as another hanger-on. When I arrived in Cuba she was quite distant, but she gradually included me in her activities. I'm sure she recalled Adriana's visit to the *finca*. Mary was smart enough to realize I did not pose a threat to her marriage, so she decided to make the most of the female companionship.

JMG: You depict Hemingway's faltering eyesight as an absolutely devastating loss to him. How did it irrevocably change his persona? How did it strike at the heart of what he could always rely upon—his writing?

VH: Hemingway read approximately three books a week, as well as many magazines and newspapers. He fished and hunted, both of which required keen eyesight. The fear of losing that capacity was devastating to him. Concern about his condition interfered with his ability to write and contributed to the deep depression that led to his decline and suicide.

JMG: You say that Hemingway had "strange standards regarding young women" (page 131). Were you ever the recipient of this attitude?

VH: Hemingway was married four times, and I suspect had many affairs with women. I can speak only of the short time I knew him, which was in the final two years of his life. He idealized young women and expected them to be pure. His attitude was paternal rather than that of a suitor. For me he was a chaperone or father figure, not a lover.

JMG: What was your initial impression of Fidel Castro, whom you met during the early years of his power? Why do you think he helped you and Mary Hemingway? Do you think the Cuba that you knew when you first visited is gone forever?

VH: I was rather enchanted by Castro, a very earnest young man with a mission. He was an idealist, a thinker, a reader, devoted to making a better country for his people. He had charm and yet was shy. He clearly admired and respected Hemingway and was greatly honored to meet the American writer. Remember, I lived in Cuba before I spent any time in the United States.

I think Castro helped Mary and me out of respect for Ernest's memory and because he had the power to do so.

The Cuba I enjoyed in 1960 does not exist anymore. Indeed, few places remain the same two generations later. The Ireland I grew up in is no longer recognizable. We can preserve such places only in literature and art.

JMG: You discuss the power and the burden of bearing the Hemingway surname. How did you teach your children to handle this? How have they reacted to this book?

VH: My children first learned of their Hemingway connection when they attended school. What is important in life is who you are, not to whom you are related. I taught my children independence of mind and spirit. I gave them an excellent education. The rest was up to them. I would venture to say my strategy worked.

My children have told me they are very proud of me. One son set up a website for the book as a Christmas gift, another accompanied me on my east-coast tour. My daughter and her husband arranged a reading and signing in their hometown and gave a superb party afterward to introduce me to their friends. When she first read the book, my daughter wrote to me, "This is the first time I have felt proud to be a Hemingway."

JMG: The last thing Hemingway said to you was: "No matter what, no matter where we are or whatever happens, I will always be with you. You can count on that" (page 148). How have you carried those words with you in your life? How have they guided you?

VH: For many years I avoided the subject of Hemingway as much as I could. I didn't grant interviews. I didn't write about my encounter with Hemingway or about working with him and later his papers. Always, in the back of my mind, I have felt that I should never do anything to betray Hemingway's trust in me. If someone is with you, it requires you to adhere to that person's standards, and for the most part that is what I have tried to do.

JMG: What about Greg first attracted you to him? How did your whirlwind courtship compare to the realities of being his wife? Did your years with him influence your view of Ernest (especially in light of their troubled father-son relationship) or of Mary?

VH: Greg was an enchanting person. We spent a good part of four days together at the funeral. He was funny and clever. He was a startlingly good athlete and amazingly articulate. I knew nothing about him except that he had "gone bad," and that had no bearing on the person I met at his father's funeral. The courtship was intense and a lot of fun. He was living in Boston then and I was in New York. It took several years of marriage before I realized how disturbed he was, and yet I still hoped. My years with Greg did not influence my view of Ernest because we simply did not discuss his father. Greg harbored great anger toward both his parents. The man I knew and the father he knew were two different entities. Just as Greg was not mentioned at the *finca*, Ernest was not discussed in our home.

I would say that my view of Mary did not change because of my marriage to Greg. I have always judged people on personal experience. Greg resented Mary. Therefore anything he had to tell me about her was biased. I was not influenced by his opinion.

JMG: After your many struggles with Greg, including his transvestitism, what was the ultimate last straw that led to your divorce? Was the postscript that deals with Greg in the initial draft of *Running with the Bulls,* or did you add it later?

VH: Greg filed for divorce, not I. I realized he was sick and in need of medical help. If he could have received that help, he stood a chance of achieving something in life. When he realized what I was trying to do, he filed for divorce.

The postscript was not in the initial draft. Since Greg's death was a matter of public record, I was advised to mention it and record my reaction. The final three pages of the book are a condensed version of a eulogy I gave for Greg at the Hemingway Society International conference in Stresa, Italy, in 2002.

JMG: You have held a variety of positions in journalism and publishing. How was tackling a memoir of your own life different from working with the words of others? Was there a single aspect of this book that you found the most challenging? The most exhilarating?

VH: Working with one's own words is both harder and easier than working with the words of others. Harder because you have to sit and create, to impose discipline and adhere to a schedule whether the muse is willing or not. Easier because there are no restraints, no misunderstandings. There is freedom and pride in accomplishment.

What I found most challenging was trying to sort out and condense a vast amount of material—the highlights of almost sixty years—to produce a coherent and flowing story. I know exactly how exciting or harrowing parts of my life have been. Would I be able to convey those emotions to the reader with only words?

The most exhilarating aspect of writing was reliving those wonderful early years and realizing for the first time how exceptionally lucky I was to have lived such a life.

JMG: At the conclusion of the book, you say, "This is my time to speak" (page 291). What made you decide that the moment had come to share your story? Did you find it difficult to break your silence?

VH: Over the years I had refused to be interviewed on the subject of Hemingway or the Hemingways. Gradually, biographers invented a persona for me. When Picasso painted Gertrude Stein's portrait, she said to him, "That doesn't resemble me." He replied, "It will." Such also is the power of the written word. I came to the conclusion that if I wanted to correct my image before it was cemented, I would have to tell the story in my own words. When news of Greg's tragic death was splashed in the tabloids and regular press, I was deluged with requests for interviews. I felt that, rather than continue to hide, I should speak out. I intended to end the book with our divorce.

It was not easy for me to write about personal matters. I would rather report someone else's tale. Now I am glad I have done it. I have been amazed at the positive response. I receive letters daily from people who have been touched by some aspect of my story.

READING GROUP QUESTIONS AND TOPICS FOR DISCUSSION

1. Would you separate Valerie's life into two distinct periods—before Hemingway and after Hemingway? Why or why not? What would be the dominant characteristics of each of these eras?

2. What about Valerie's personality enabled her easy assimilation into Hemingway's madcap life? How does she view being with him as an adventure? In what way does she yearn for freedom?

3. Do you feel that Ernest was a Henry Higgins to Valerie's Eliza Doolittle—that is, did he attempt to shape and mold her? What does she seek to learn from her mentor?

4. Have you had a mentor relationship? How was your relationship similar to or different from Valerie's relationship with Ernest?

5. Did you know much about Ernest Hemingway before reading this book? Have you read other biographies of Hemingway? Is the picture of him that emerges from *Running with the Bulls* similar to or different from your preconceptions of Ernest Hemingway?

6. How are Valerie and Ernest both scholars of writers and good writing? How does Hemingway's advice to Valerie about writing shape her career path? Based on this memoir, what similarities and differences in writing style might Valerie share with Ernest?

7. Why do you think that Hemingway adopted first a paternal and then a more romantic interest in his young secretary? Why does he ultimately view her as "indispensable" to his life and work?

8. What do you think Ernest Hemingway's inner circle might say about Valerie Hemingway and her influence on his life?

9. "Only with his absence could I appreciate the intensity of his presence," Valerie writes on page 88. What about Ernest Hemingway is larger than life? How does he become more frail, fragile, and human in the course of this memoir? Ultimately, why do you think he takes his own life?

10. Cuba is a strong presence in this book. How does the prerevolutionary island compare with the place that Mary returns to after Ernest's death? In your opinion, why did it seem like such a magical place to the Hemingways? Why do you think Cubans still revere Ernest Hemingway, both his books and his memory?

11. Both Ernest Hemingway and his son Gregory grapple with their own internal demons. How does each man struggle in different ways? How do they present their problems to those around them? How would each have benefited from the psychological advances present today?

12. How does Valerie's interlude with Brendan Behan change her life? What is her attitude about their night together?

13. How does Mary seek to be a maternal figure? In what ways is she non-maternal? Does her mind-set about motherhood echo Valerie's attitudes in any way?

14. The importance of leaving a legacy is a theme that courses throughout the book. In your opinion, what is Ernest Hemingway's most enduring legacy? How does Mary ultimately control her husband's legacy? What do

you hope that the legacy of your own life might be, and who would you most want to shape it?

15. "I came to know a great deal about Ernest, more than I have ever gleaned about another human being," writes Valerie on page 210. How does this understanding of Ernest Hemingway shine through in this book? How do you think it might have contributed—for better or for worse—to her marriage with Greg? Is there a person who you think might know *you* better than anyone else in the world?

16. How does loyalty and money figure into the Hemingways' inner circle? How does Mary see Greg as a traitor, and vice versa?

17. What about Valerie is so fascinating to the men in her life, from Ernest to Brendan to Greg? How does each seek to guide her? In turn, what attracts her to each of them?

18. What are the clues that Valerie gives early in the book about what was wrong with her marriage? Were you surprised to learn that Greg was bipolar and a transvestite? How do Valerie and Greg's family help him until the end of his life?

19. Why do you think that Valerie Hemingway chose this moment to write her memoir? How is her viewpoint into Ernest Hemingway's life a unique one? What questions would you like to ask the author about her life?

A native of Ireland, VALERIE HEMINGWAY moved to
Spain when she was eighteen. In 1959, while working as a
journalist in Madrid, she interviewed Ernest Hemingway.
Two months later Hemingway hired her as his secretary, a
job which took her all over Spain, to France, and to Cuba.
She was a researcher at *Newsweek* in New York at the time of
Hemingway's death. Mary Hemingway invited Valerie to return to Cuba to help sort out her late husband's papers and
bring them back to the United States. For the next three
years, Valerie arranged and cataloged the Hemingway papers
for eventual presentation to the John F. Kennedy Library in
Boston.

She also worked in publishing in New York from 1963 to
1967. In 1966, while she was publicity director of New
Directions, Valerie married Dr. Gregory H. Hemingway,
Ernest's youngest son. They lived in Florida for two years
while he pursued a medical residency and she read fiction
for *Publishers Weekly*. Upon returning to New York in 1969,
Valerie wrote a quarterly newsletter for the Guinness-Harp
Corporation. In 1980 the couple moved with their family to
Bozeman, Montana, where she continues to reside, enjoying
a career as a freelance writer and editor.

ABOUT THE TYPE

This book was set in Bulmer, a typeface designed in the late eighteenth century by the London type-cuttter William Martin. The typeface was created especially for the Shakespeare Press, directed by William Bulmer; hence, the font's name. Bulmer is considered to be a transitional typeface, containing characteristics of old-style and modern designs. It is recognized for its elegantly proportioned letters, with long ascenders and descenders.